THE
BOOT ROOM
BOYS

THE BOOT ROOM BOYS

Inside the
Anfield Boot Room

Stephen F. Kelly

CollinsWillow
An Imprint of HarperCollinsPublishers

First published in 1999
by CollinsWillow
an imprint of HarperCollins*Publishers*
London

© Stephen F. Kelly 1999

1 3 5 7 9 8 6 4 2

A CIP catalogue record for this book is available
from the British Library

ISBN 0 00 218907 0

Set in PostScript Sabon by
Rowland Phototypesetting Ltd,
Bury St Edmunds, Suffolk

Printed and bound in Great Britain by
Clays Ltd, St Ives plc

The HarperCollins website address is
www.fireandwater.com

Photographic acknowledgements
Allsport 2tr, 6t, 7t; Empics 3c; Liverpool Echo 4t, 4b; Steve Hale 1t, 1c, 1b, 2tl, 2b,
3t, 3b, 4tc, 4bc, 5t, 5c, 5b, 6c, 6b, 7c, 7b, 8t, 8c, 8b

Extracts on pp 192–4 from *Dalglish – The Autobiography* by Kenny Dalglish
reproduced by permission of Hodder and Stoughton Limited

Contents

Acknowledgements

In writing this book I have received the assistance and good wishes of many people, all of which has helped ease the burden of compiling this collection. Only a handful of people refused to be interviewed. But I would especially like to place on record the help given me by Liverpool Football Club, and especially by vice chairman Peter Robinson, whose assistance at an early stage helped pave the way for many interviews.

But equally I should also like to mention all the following people who at some stage have provided me with help either in arranging interviews, giving interviews, or simply supplying information. These include, though in no special order, the following:

The directors, players and staff of Liverpool Football Club both at Anfield and in particular at Melwood, Peter Robinson, Rick Parry, Tom Saunders, Gerard Houllier, Phil Thompson, Ronnie Moran, Sammy Lee, Roy Evans, Brian Hall, Miriam Griffiths, Phil Neal, Alec Lindsay, Ian Rush, Emlyn Hughes, Ian St John, Alan Hansen, Mark Lawrenson, Ian Callaghan, Ian Cotton, Steve Hale, Ivan Ponting, Gordon Burns, Bob Greaves, Ian Ross, Ian Hargreaves, Phil Chisnall, Barrie Holmes, Jim Gardiner, Phil Taylor, Alan Brown, Tommy Lawrence, John Bennison, the Football League Managers' Association, the staff and proprietors of the Amblehurst Hotel in Sale, Ray Spiller and the Association of Football Statisticians, Geoff Twentyman junior, Brian Souter, Alan Brown, Alan Kennedy, Jane Kennedy, David Fairclough, the *Liverpool Daily Post and Echo,* Roger Hunt, the staff and proprietors of the Four Seasons Hotel in Hale, Willie Miller and the Liverpool Former Players' Association, the staff and proprietors of the Moat House Hotel in Liverpool, Mike Berry, Joey Jones, Wrexham Football Club, John Aldridge, Tranmere Rovers Football Club, Don Jones, Stan Boardman, the West Lancashire Golf Club, Jan Molby, Jessie Paisley, Willie

Stevenson, Steve Morgan and the Redrow Group, the Carden Park Hotel, John Bennett, Linda Bennett, staff of the Thistle Hotel at Haydock, Jim Beglin, Chris Lawler, Arthur Hopcraft, Daphne Hughes and Mark Owen.

I would also like to pay tribute to my mother, Mary Kelly, whose encouragement and love over the years have been of such importance and should never go unacknowledged. Thanks also to my parents-in-law, Anthony and Marjorie Rowe Jones, for their regular bouts of child minding, copies of newspapers, and ongoing interest.

I should also like to place on record a vote of appreciation to my colleagues in the Media division at the University of Hudders-field and to the division's Oral History Unit. Their encourage-ment and interest has always been of enormous support. An acknowledgment must also go to my publishers, CollinsWillow and especially to my editors Michael Doggart and Tom Whiting, whose idea this was initially, and to my agent John Pawsey whose continuing advice and guidance has been so beneficial over the years.

But of course my deepest thanks, as ever, go to my wife Judith and to my children Nicholas (now a season ticket holder at Anfield) and Emma. Over the years their love and support has provided me with so much encouragement, and in particular their cheerfulness and understanding during the often painful months of compiling this book, has helped ease the burden, to say nothing of the many hours spent by my wife transcribing lengthy interviews.

My thanks to all these people.

STEPHEN F. KELLY
Liverpool, June 1999

A Note on the Research and Editing of Interviews

The interviews contained within this book were recorded on a Sony Minidisc player. Each interview was then transcribed and broken into sections to be included in the relevant chapters. As little editing of interviews as possible has taken place. Where editing has occurred, it has been carried out in order to make the interview as coherent and readable as possible. Hopefully the meaning has not been destroyed. Slang and dialect words have been retained so that the reader can feel the character of the interviewee. The interviews, however, have not been included in full. Some repetitions and irrelevancies have been dropped. The occasional correction has also been made (dates, games, players, etc) in order to save any embarrassment to the interviewee and to avoid any confusion for the reader. People's memories are not always as accurate as they imagine!

A few extracts from newspapers, magazines and books have also been included.

The Great Soccer Mystery

In a way this book is a detective story. It is an attempt to unravel one of the enduring puzzles of modern football. It might just as easily have been called *The Mystery of Liverpool Football Club and Its Phenomenal Success*. And like any good mystery story there are trails and leads that take you into many dead ends. The question is simple. Why were Liverpool Football Club so triumphant over a period of a quarter of a century, an era which brought four European Cups, two UEFA cups, 13 league titles, five FA Cups, five League Cups and a few other finals? The answer is so much more complex. People have tried to explain it all before. But never with any degree of certainty. The mystery remains, and possibly always will.

What is offered in the accompanying pages is a forensic analysis in a series of statements offered by those who witnessed the astonishing success of a football club over 25 years. Take these together, mull them over, and somewhere you may begin to find the answer to the question.

But really our story begins and ends with the boot room, one of Anfield's most celebrated institutions, for it is here that the reader is most likely to find the solution to the puzzle. For more than 30 years the boot room was at the heart of Liverpool Football Club, not only witnessing but being a vital component in the club's success.

Everyone has their own impression, their own picture of this little room down the corridor by the dressing rooms under the Main Stand at Anfield. But of course, not everybody was privileged to even peep around the door of the boot room, let alone ever go in. Certainly no one, but no one, ever entered without permission. Even the players had to wait for an invitation. It was a no-go area for players. Club captain and legend Ron Yeats claims he was only ever invited in once.

It's been called many things in its time. Tommy Smith conjures up the image of a 'shed' at the bottom of the garden where the lads could go and have a natter and a cup of tea while Peter Robinson describes it more formally as the 'officers' mess'. Phil Neal paints a picture of a cosy little kitchen that ought to have had a fireplace in the corner with Bob Paisley's slippers warming on the hearth. Someone else describes it as a tardis, a magical, small room where so much seemed to happen. Others such as Gordon Burns think of it as the 'war room' where battles for trophies and honours were planned and formulated.

When Roy Evans finally turned his back on the boot room in November 1998, he talked of 'too many ghosts on the wall'. You knew exactly what he meant. The boot room for all its history and tradition could also be a prison for anyone under-achieving. One too many reminders of what had gone before. Graeme Souness had similarly found himself trapped back in the early nineties, only to be forced out when he tried to change things. Souness, being Souness, astonishingly even agreed to the boot room being torn down. For many that was sacrilege and spelled the end of his brief reign.

The more you think about it, the more convinced you become that maybe there was something strangely magical about the boot room. There was certainly a superstition about the place. The boot room had to be left as it was; interfere with anything in there and the club's fortunes might change. You couldn't even move the furniture around – as Tommy Smith once discovered when he had the temerity to take an old carpet out for a bit of a sweep. He was promptly told to put it straight back.

It was as if some old gypsy had cast a spell on it that would only work if things were left unchanged. Maybe one night in those frustrating early years at Anfield Shankly secretly smuggled a passing gypsy into the bowels of Anfield and asked him to apply some magic to the place, in the desperate hope that it might get them out of the second division. If he did he would not have been the first manager to look for inspiration from such a source. These days they're more likely to be into *feng shui* but that surely would never have been part of the Shankly culture.

It was always known as the boot room, even before Shanks arrived. It was just down the corridor from the dressing room and measured no more than eight feet by eight feet and was the place where they stored the boots, cleaned them and repaired them. But then shortly into Shankly's reign at Anfield, Joe Fagan and Bob Paisley took up residence. They didn't have anywhere else to go. Shanks had his own office and obviously needed its privacy while the dressing room offered no respite or privacy for Bob and Joe. They needed somewhere to go where they could escape the noise and banter of the dressing room and have a bit of peace and quiet after training and all their chores were done; somewhere where they could have a cup of tea and a sit down. It was also a hidey-hole where they could occasionally imbibe of something a little stronger than tea. Both Paisley and Fagan liked a drink whereas the teetotaller Shankly never indulged, not that he would have objected to them having a drink but best maybe that it was done away from the manager and players. They could lock the door, keep quiet if someone came knocking and put their feet up for ten minutes. It was their escape. It was as simple as that. And that was how the legend began.

Although Shankly is often revered as the man who founded the boot room, the truth is far different. Shankly in fact had little to do with it, spending only limited time within its four walls. He had his own office and although he was never an 'office man', he left his coaching staff to their own quarters. From time to time he'd drop in, usually after training and maybe talk things over – how was so and so's injury, what did they think of such and such a player in training, or even what did they reckon to the possibility of signing a someone or other? It was always informal. But generally Shankly left his coaching staff to simply get on with it.

The boot room began to take on legendary proportions in later years as success began to overwhelm the club, and in particular when the coaching staff began to invite their 'oppos' in for a drink after the game. And it wasn't just for a cup of tea. Joe Fagan, through his connections, had managed to get hold of

some Guinness export. It was unusual in those days to play host
to the coaching and training staff. No other club did it. Visiting
managers would nip upstairs after the game to see their directors
and have a drink while the players would adjourn to the players'
lounge, leaving the coaching staff behind in the dressing room
to clear up the mess and pack everything away for the journey
home. But the kindly Paisley and Fagan took it upon themselves
to invite them into their cubby hole for a drink. It all began so
informally but in time it was the one thing so many managers
and coaches looked forward to eagerly. After all, they didn't
look forward to the game too much as usually they ended up
on the losing side. And so they'd sit in there on an upturned
crate or two supping a drink pulled out of a cupboard.

What always surprised most visitors was the genuine warmth
and friendliness. There may have been fire, spit and controversy
on the pitch an hour earlier but once inside the boot room it
was all forgotten, as if it had never happened. Eventually their
manager would come searching for them and he too would end
up being invited in and offered a drink. In time visiting managers
would not even bother going upstairs, they'd make straight for
the boot room with their staff in tow. There they'd sit and natter,
about the old days when they were players, characters they knew,
the chit-chat of the game, players they rated, and so on. And as
they imbibed, so the Anfield coaching staff would take advantage
by giving them the third degree on any player that might interest
them. Others from the Anfield coaching staff would join them
as well, and in later years a celebrity or two. They rarely talked
about the game they had just been involved in. Shankly, Paisley
or whoever the Liverpool manager was at the time would pop
his head around the door and have a quick word, but once the
visitors had gone they would wander back for a more lengthy
chat with the coaching staff. Then they'd talk more seriously
about the afternoon's events – what had gone wrong, what had
worked, injuries, and the rest. They might even be there until
seven at night, depending on how much they needed to talk.

Sundays also became an important day. It was a tradition for
injured players to report into Anfield on a Sunday morning.
Rather than wait until the Monday, Paisley thought it important

to get to work on the injury as soon as possible. So, again, after everyone had been treated and the place had been tidied up, they'd retire to the boot room for a Sunday lunchtime drink. If the manager was present for any of these chats then inevitably they would focus on tactics, transfer possibilities, forthcoming games, and so on.

And of course during the week and on a Sunday they would fill in those volumes, detailing the training, weather, injuries, anything that might be of importance. In future years they would look back and compare so that vital decisions could be made for the future. What price those volumes now.

This book then is an attempt to paint a picture of life at Anfield behind the boot room door. What was it like in there, how did it all begin, who went in there, and what went on inside its four walls. The picture will help to unravel the mystery of how much the boot room contributed to Liverpool's unrivalled success over the years. Managers and coaches came from all over the world to spy on the Liverpool system; all left scratching their heads convinced that they had missed a clue or that something had been deliberately left out of the daily itinerary.

Of course there will never be a simple answer. It was probably many things; from the down-to-earth experience of the boot room staff, to the quality of the players, to the stability and continuity of the club, and maybe even the fanaticism of the flag-waving Kop. In the end, I leave you, the reader, to make of the detailed evidence what you will. And, most importantly, for you to unravel the part played in this success by the boot room, one of Anfield's most celebrated institutions. You must be your own Sherlock Holmes and make your own judgement on why Liverpool were so successful over a quarter of a century and more. Hopefully you will find enough clues here to solve the mystery.

CHAPTER ONE

The Shankly Years

It was there long before Bill Shankly ever arrived at Anfield and was, as the name suggests, simply a boot room, a room where they stored the players' boots. Just like every club up and down the land. And, in truth, it was no different. It was certainly no bigger than an average store room. It measured perhaps eight feet by eight feet. The walls were dominated by racks on which hung the boots of the club's many players. There was also steel shelving, the sort you can buy in any DIY store and make up yourself. There wasn't much else, a girlie calendar and maybe an old photograph pinned on the wall. There wasn't even much in the way of seating, just a couple of old upturned wicker baskets, the sort that would once have been used for carrying the kit. And there were usually also a couple of upturned iron beer crates, again used for seating. There might also be a fixture list pinned up somewhere and always bits of kit lying around, along with the expected paraphernalia of a boot room: studs, screwdrivers, socks, an old shirt, a towel and so on. It was never the tidiest of places.

And on one of the shelves, or more usually, hidden away from public view in a cupboard, there was the odd bottle of scotch. You could also usually spot a bottle or two of beer in one of the crates. The drink was not just for the general consumption of those who inhabited the boot room, but for visiting managers and coaches after a game. Shankly never drank but the others liked a tipple or two. Over the years it was to become a tradition to invite the visiting manager and trainers in for a drink after their side had been given a good hiding out on the pitch. Bottles would be opened and everyone would join in the gossip.

Of course the boot room was about much more than that. But let us not chase ahead of ourselves. Suffice it to say that during the fifties and even before then, the boot room was no more than what its name suggested. All that was about to change and a legend was set to be born.

When Bill Shankly strode into Anfield in December 1959 he found a club desperate for success. Not since 1947 had Liverpool won anything. That was the last time they had lifted the league trophy. Prior to that they had been a highly successful club, winning the league title for the first time in 1901, then again in 1906 before winning it back to back in 1922 and 1923. They had appeared in the FA Cup Finals of 1915 and 1950 but had been unsuccessful on both occasions. Then in 1954 they had crashed out of the first division, bottom with just 28 points. They had conceded 97 goals. Six teams put five or more goals past them that season, including a run that saw them let in 15 goals over three consecutive games in December.

The pundits guessed that it would be a short stay in the lower division. After all, this *was* Liverpool, one of the biggest, and most successful, clubs in the land. But no matter how they tried Liverpool did not seem to be able to escape the vicious clutches of the second division. Year after year they failed narrowly, often leading the table until Easter when they would unwittingly throw all the efforts of the previous months away. They were third on two occasions and fourth twice before Shankly arrived. It seemed they were cursed, never to escape the division.

The manager at the time was Phil Taylor, a gentle sort of character, and former wing-half with the club, who had won a championship and FA Cup runners-up medal in the postwar years, usually partnering Bob Paisley in what is now called the midfield. But try as he might, Taylor could not conjure up the right mix to bring success. He even boasted a handful of inter-nationals, principally Billy Liddell, the glorious Scottish winger, and the bonny-faced Tommy Younger, Scotland's number one goalkeeper. There was also Alan A'Court, who played on the wing for England during the 1958 World Cup finals, and Johnny Wheeler who had won a couple of England B Caps and played in the 1953 Matthews Cup Final when he was with Bolton.

Admittedly his best days were behind him but there was also Ronnie Moran, later to become a key figure in the boot room story, who had played for the Football League. At the back end of his managerial reign, Taylor also snapped up the popular and effervescent Dave Hickson, from local rivals Everton.

But none of it worked and as the pressures increased Taylor wisely opted to resign. Taylor was living on borrowed time; the previous season they had lost 2–1 to non-league Worcester City in the third round of the FA Cup. It was the biggest cup shock in the club's entire history and must still rank as one of the most spectacular in the entire history of the competition. Taylor probably would have been pushed anyhow and there is plenty of evidence to suggest that the board were already looking around for his replacement long before he had officially resigned. Maybe Taylor had already indicated that he wanted to go and he was certainly in his own words 'tired' at the time. It came as no surprise when he officially quit in November 1959. By then his successor had been lined up.

Bill Shankly had been manager of Huddersfield Town for just three years. During that time he had created a stir without really generating much in the way of results. Town were in the second division, even lower than Liverpool, but it was the bunch of youngsters at the club who were attracting the attention. And above all it was a scrawny waif of a kid called Denis Law who was creating the headlines. Shankly might not have been the person to sign Law but he had certainly brought him on during his reign. And there were others, including full-back Ray Wilson and winger Kevin McHale. The Huddersfield youngsters were creating a buzz around the division and Shankly was more than happy to take the credit for their emergence. It had certainly not gone unnoticed at Anfield.

The problem at Huddersfield was that there was no money. Shankly had even tried to sign a couple of young Scottish players he had spotted, Ron Yeats and Ian St John, but the board at Leeds Road would not put their hands in their pockets. It irritated Shankly, as indeed it would continue to do so even at Anfield, when the directors refused to back his instincts by coughing up the cash.

On Saturday 17 October 1959 Huddersfield, fourth in the table, played Cardiff City at Leeds Road. They lost 1–0, albeit to a side in second spot. Shankly was dispirited, it was Town's fourth defeat already that season. As he left the ground two figures approached him across the car park out of the encroaching gloom. It was Tom Williams, the chairman of Liverpool and his fellow director, Harry Latham. They had come on a mission to recruit Shankly as their new manager. They introduced themselves and after a few courteous words asked Shankly if he would be interested in joining the best club in the land. Legend has it that Shankly promptly asked them if Matt Busby had quit United. Liverpool supporters today would squirm at that suggestion! But to cut a long story short Shankly indicated that 'yes', he would be interested in joining Liverpool. He knew Liverpool was a big club. He had played against them enough times when he was a wing-half with Preston North End. They had been league champions five times and had one of the most devoted followings. The rest, as they say, is history.

Shankly joined up, not due to start until 1 January 1960. But such was his enthusiasm that he walked out on Huddersfield early and was ensconced at Anfield by Christmas. He even went to watch Liverpool reserves playing on the Saturday before he officially took over two days later. It was typical of the man.

Shankly's first task was to introduce himself to the backroom staff. There were a number of them. Bob Paisley had been a Liverpool player since before the War, having previously won an FA amateur cup-winners medal with the famous north-east cup fighters Bishop Auckland. During the war he had been in the army, serving in the Western desert campaign and later as part of the liberating force that swept through Italy. Paisley had returned to Anfield in 1946 to play as a half-back in the side that went on to win the league championship. It was the only professional honour he was to win as a player. In 1950, having scored in the FA Cup semi-final against Everton to set up a Wembley final, he was then dropped for the big occasion. He had retired from playing in 1954 and had taken up a post as trainer.

Alongside Paisley was Joe Fagan, a dour-looking, Lancashire lad who had enjoyed a fairly undistinguished footballing career

with Manchester City, Bradford, Altrincham and Nelson before
having a spell as trainer of Rochdale. In fact, Shankly had tried
to sign him when he was managing Grimsby Town. There was
also Reuben Bennett, a man reputed to be as hard as nails, who
took most of the training. Shankly already knew Bennett through
his brother Bob. Bennett, a tall slightly balding Scot, was generally regarded as something of a ruthless trainer but nevertheless
was as popular as any man who has ever inhabited the boot
room. Finally there was Albert Shelley who looked after the
dressing rooms, making sure that they were tidy and that everything needed was provided. Shelley had officially retired as first
team trainer shortly before Shankly arrived but they couldn't get
rid of him quite so easily, so Albert simply shuffled around the
dressing rooms doing anything that was needed. Bob Paisley had
taken over his old job as first team trainer.

The secretary of the club was Jimmy McInnes, a half-back
who had made just over 50 appearances for the club before the
war. McInnes, another Scot, was stationed further down the
corridor from Shankly. Tom Bush, another pre-war old-timer,
was usually about the place as well, doing whatever he could to
help while Arthur Riley, the groundsman, had been around since
the mid-1920s and had kept goal for Liverpool more than 300
times. Riley, a tall commanding figure, had subsequently become
the club's groundsman and would give an astonishing 54 years'
service to the club.

Shankly called all his back room staff into his office and told
them straight away that their jobs were safe, as long as, he added
threateningly, they remained loyal to the club and players. He
didn't want to hear any stories, any tittle-tattle. 'I want everyone
to be loyal to each other,' he told them. It was a concept that
was to remain vital to the philosophy of the club throughout the
years. And so the great adventure began.

Shankly may have shown considerable loyalty to his staff but
the same could not be said of the players. They were below par.
Within a year or so the vast majority of them had been moved
on, either to other clubs or simply forced out of the game. They
were not good enough as far as Shankly was concerned. Others
had been pensioned off, reckoned too old for the rigours ahead.

But again all this would take time. It was said that when Shankly visited the training ground at Melwood he had a near fit. He couldn't believe the state of it. There was even a tree growing on the pitch. It soon came down. The whole place needed a good lick of paint. A new training routine was also inaugurated, aimed at developing stamina as well as skill.

There was never going to be any overnight miracle. Even Shankly knew it would take a couple of seasons. At the end of that first season Liverpool had finished in third position, yet again missing promotion by a whisker. Since his arrival they had lost only four league matches and two of those were his first couple of games in charge. It was a positive start but it would need to be improved upon the following season. But, still playing with too many of the old guard, Liverpool were to miss out on promotion again. Although Shankly was getting rid of many players, and he had been largely unable to sign new players, his hands tied by a board of directors reluctant to spend more than a few thousand on any player. He finally persuaded them to dig deep and the arrival of Ron Yeats and Ian St John was to mark a definite turning point in the fortunes of the club. It would be money well spent with their signings providing the catalyst for future success.

Within the year Liverpool were champions of the second division. Ian St John scored 18 league goals while Roger Hunt struck a phenomenal 41 league goals in 41 games, a record which still stands today. The Kop celebrated in a fashion that was soon to be echoed in football arenas across the world.

Back in the top flight after an absence of eight years, Shankly set about consolidating. A new goalkeeper was called for, and Tommy Lawrence was promoted part way through the campaign from the reserves while a teenage Tommy Smith appeared towards the end of the season. Half-back Tommy Leishman was moved on, not quite up to the part, with the sleek-looking Willie Stevenson, a cheap import from Glasgow Rangers, taking over his number six shirt. They ended the season in eighth place, a creditable performance for a newly-promoted side.

The next season there was a little more tinkering. The biggest coup was the signing of £35,000 winger Peter Thompson from

Preston North End. Thompson was another part of the jigsaw, a flying winger who could supply the crosses for Hunt and St John. Shankly was now set for an assault on the league title although you would hardly have guessed it from the way they started; three defeats before mid-September and all at home. The title was won in the spring with seven successive wins, culminating in the 5-0 thrashing of Arsenal at Anfield. Liverpool were champions. It was to be the beginning of a glorious 25 years when Liverpool would go on to dominate the domestic game and sweep across the continent to become one of the most famous names in European football.

The following season Shankly's side accomplished something no other side had managed in 70-odd years, bringing the FA Cup back to Anfield. It came on a rain-soaked Saturday in May as Ian St John dived to head the ball into the Leeds United net. Astonishingly, as Phil Chisnall testifies in these pages, Shankly missed the supreme moment, more concerned at the whitewash on his trousers! Another myth destroyed. And when the cup came home, a million turned out to greet their conquering heroes.

A few days later 54,000 of them crammed into Anfield to see Liverpool take on the European and world champions Inter Milan in the semi-final of the European Cup. It was to be one of the most momentous occasions in the history of Anfield as Liverpool were inspired by a Shankly masterstroke when he ordered the FA Cup to be paraded around the pitch as the two teams took the field. The noise was deafening, frightening even, as the Kop greeted the appearance of the trophy. The Italians watched on, bemused by it all. Within four minutes Liverpool were ahead. They eventually won 3-1 although it should have been more, a perfectly good goal from Chris Lawler being disallowed. Shankly described it as the greatest game he had ever seen. Sadly the return leg was a disaster as a series of bizarre decisions from a highly questionable referee left Liverpool 3-0 losers.

But the club was on a roll. The following season they won the league title again and reached the final of the European Cup-Winners' Cup. But there would be no more trophies for seven long seasons. The side of Yeats, St John and Hunt had grown old, replacements were needed and the boot room worked overtime,

debating, watching and deciding on their new line-up. By the
early 1970s the new formation had been installed. Emlyn Hughes
had arrived from Blackpool while Alec Lindsay, Ray Clemence
and Kevin Keegan had been plucked from the bargain basement
of the Football League. Local boy Steve Heighway had been
brought in from non-league Skelmersdale and Brian Hall had
been signed as an amateur. John Toshack was a club record
signing from Cardiff City. Chief Scout Geoff Twentyman had
done his job well.

The beginnings of a boot room had also emerged. Although
Shankly was not a fully signed-up member, his influence
undoubtedly pervaded everything at Anfield. Shankly set the
trend, the others followed. Bob Paisley, Joe Fagan, Reuben
Bennett and Ronnie Moran had all worked painstakingly at
implementing the footballing philosophy which Shankly encap-
sulated.

In 1973 they were champions again but then a year later came
the defining moment for Shankly with the 1974 FA Cup Final.
Despite Newcastle striker Malcolm Macdonald's boasts of what
he was going to do to Liverpool, Shankly's team romped home,
finding little trouble with Macdonald and his team-mates, though
two of them were later deemed good enough to join Liverpool.
In truth it was one of the most one-sided finals in years. After
the presentation and lap of honour, Shankly returned to the
dressing room and slumped into a corner with a cup of tea. He
was tired, his wife Nessie had been ill that year though she was
now well on the road to recovery, and he himself felt that the
time had come to pack it all in. He'd thought about it at the end
of the previous season but the time didn't seem right. He'd lost
his edge. Victory no longer had the same sweet smell as it had
in earlier years. He'd won the league championship three times,
the FA Cup twice and the UEFA Cup. He'd also had a few tiffs
with the establishment at Anfield although in truth they were not
particularly serious. Certainly there was no ill feeling. Perhaps, as
some have suggested, he simply felt that he was not appreciated
by the board. Anyhow, whatever the reason, and even today
there is still conjecture, it seemed to Bill Shankly that this was
as good a time as any to call it quits.

At a surprise press conference a few days later Shankly intro-duced his latest signing, the Arsenal striker Ray Kennedy, and then announced to a perplexed world that he was quitting the club and retiring. For a moment there was a stunned silence. Journalists looked agog at one another. There had been no hint of it whatsoever. It seemed inconceivable that Shankly could quit Liverpool and go into retirement. The two were inseparable. When the word spread, the city of Liverpool was flabbergasted. People raced out of their offices to buy the early editions of the *Liverpool Echo* and normally busy workplaces downed their tools; there was just one topic of conversation. Why was Shankly going and who would be taking over? A new era was about to begin.

MIKE BERRY
The Messiah

As with most people in Liverpool you're born a red or a blue. I was born in the south end of Liverpool and I was born a red because my dad was a red. He used to take me to matches, sit me on his shoulders, standing in the Kop. Then I progressed to the boys' pen and started to watch them on a regular basis throughout the sixties, the seventies and then the eighties, the so-called glory years. I watched them develop under Shankly as a real force in British and European football. Shankly was the Messiah and to be in his presence as I was once as a young boy, you felt as though you were in the presence of God. You were privileged. I listened to two conversations and both stuck with me for the rest of my life. He was the dominant influence, a great passionate man.

STEVE MORGAN

A Perfect Time

I was born and bred in the Garston area of Liverpool, a pretty tough working-class area, typical two up, two down. My parents (my father was in the RAF) lived with my grandfather who was a big Everton supporter and it was at the time when Everton were close to the top of the first division and certainly in contention for championships. Liverpool were in the second division but even as a three or four year old I began to realise that there was another club besides Everton and it was called Liverpool. I preferred red as a colour and the fact that my uncle and everybody were supporting Everton made me go the other way and support the underdog of the time, second division Liverpool. I was about seven years old when I went to my first match which I think was against Leyton Orient and it grew from there.

My first memories have always been of Bill Shankly as the manager and the start of what was to become the great sixties side. It was just the perfect time as a kid to become a Liverpool fan. I can remember vaguely them winning the second division when I was about eight or nine years old. I remember the excitement of coming into the first division and playing teams which I had always looked up to. I used to go in the boys' pen in the top corner of the Kop and watch these teams. In those days I probably went to half of the home games with a few mates. When we won the league in 1964, it was just unbelievable. When we won the cup the following year, I couldn't get to the cup final because nobody would take me and we couldn't get tickets so we were watching it on television. Afterwards I remember getting on my bike and riding up and down the road with a big flag and scarf and bobble hat and just going absolutely berserk, singing 'We've won the cup.' It was the first time ever that Liverpool had won the cup. I remember all the press cuttings of the people in the town centre round St George's Hall, it was wall to wall people.

As a kid Shankly was just God; whatever the man said, you hung on every breath. Of course there wasn't the television coverage in those days so you tended to read the papers more to find out what he had said. He could have said the sky is green and the grass blue but whatever he said, he was just God. Everybody held him in the highest esteem.

We all went to the Ajax game thinking we were going to do it. If noise could have lifted the roof of the Kop off, it would have been sent over the other side of the Mersey. I think Shankly could convince people that you could walk on water or fly through the air, he just had that magic and that aura about him.

But for all his talents Bill Shankly made his errors. I don't think he recognised quickly enough that he had to make changes. He showed a lot of loyalty to the old guard, to Tommy Lawrence and Ron Yeats, and Ian St John and Roger Hunt and Billy Stevenson and Gordon Milne. I think it was obvious to the fans. I can remember around the 1967/68 season thinking, these are our heroes but they're just that half a pace too slow. In the end he made the sweeping changes but I think if you could criticise him at all you'd say that should have been done a little sooner. But you are talking about a man who put charisma back into Liverpool Football Club. You're talking about a man who brought us from oblivion back up to being one of the top teams in Europe. We didn't win anything in Europe under Bill Shankly except the UEFA Cup, but we became the team of the sixties from what he inherited, a bit of a rag-bag second division club. More importantly, he instilled a passion and a pride and an aura into Liverpool Football Club that exists today. That Shankly spirit lived right throughout the club. You still talk about the Shankly spirit and there are very few people in history that you talk about in that way. You can still talk about the Churchillian spirit but there are few people who have affected so many people's lives in the way Bill Shankly did for the people of Liverpool. Whether you are a football fan or not, he had a huge impact on the city.

Nobody expected Bill Shankly to go. For any Liverpool fan it just wasn't something that you thought about, you just thought he was going to be there for ever. It was such a shock. People remember where they were when President Kennedy was assassinated, they can remember where they were when they heard about Princess Di's death; well, I can remember when I heard about Bill Shankly. I thought, 'It can't be right, it just can't be true.' I'd never considered there could be life after Shankly.

ALAN BROWN
The Calendars

I used to pop in the boot room with Roy Evans. He was a youth then, a young first team player. Shanks was there. We had been to the Open Golf with Geoff Strong, Roger Hunt and Cally when we first heard that Shanks had packed it in. We were all so surprised. We were sitting there having a drink when we heard, no one thought it possible. No one had any inclination whatsoever. Bob took over and made Roy coach and that was when it all started. I started going into the boot room with Roy most weekends. We used to go to the reserves, watch them and then go in afterwards. After every game Bob, Tom Saunders, Ronnie Moran, Roy and then the managers would come in.

We used to have calendars of naked women on the walls. That's something I don't think the Frenchman [Houllier] would have. Then we started serving drinks and the other managers would come in. Everybody used to look forward to it every time. It was a good thing. It was so cheerful. No one was on money in them days, even Bob wouldn't earn much. Not many had cars. It was all atmosphere, they'd come in and enjoy a few drinks, a few beers and then they brought out a bottle of Scotch.

Joe Fagan used to train up here with Guinness Export in Aughton on their football pitch. He used to get Guinness given to him, a couple of crates in return for training them. So we had Guinness and cans of lager, there was that big harp on the can. Players weren't allowed in. They used to pop their head round the door but they weren't allowed in. We used to sit on boxes, not seats, the boots would be hanging up in rows and we used to sit on these containers, baskets, skips, that they used to take with them everywhere they played. Now they've got these brilliant cases but back then they were all baskets. It was cheerful and enjoyable. Bob Paisley always drank Scotch, Shanks didn't drink of course while Ronnie Moran always drank a beer.

The visiting coaches would come in. They didn't have an entourage then, there'd be only two or three at most. They didn't all go away. Smithy also used to come in when he was looking after the youth team, and then Phil Thompson and Chris Lawler, John Bennison, Hughie McAuley. By the time Hugh came, it was fading.

ALEC LINDSAY

'You Can Talk, You Know'

When I first went to Anfield, I tell you, it was some experience. I came from Bury and I used to watch them on television in Europe and all that, but actually going and sitting in the same dressing room it was a bit, to say the least, frightening. It took me a long time to get used to it. I didn't say half a dozen words in about twelve months, I don't think. Ian St John once said to me, 'You can talk, you know.' I was overawed but I kept on going.

They kept trying me in different positions and then finally at full-back. I think that was Bob Paisley's idea actually. When I came I was a defensive wing half but he wanted to play me attacking, so I had a spell upfront. I played in the reserves, scored a couple of goals and they tried me upfront but I was a bit slow. Eventually they tried me at full-back, I think that was a last-chance saloon job. Any rate, I did all right.

In the boot room then there was Bill Shankly, Bob Paisley, Joe Fagan, Ronnie Moran, Reuben Bennett. Roy Evans was playing at the time but then started coaching. At first that was a bit strange, Roy training us when a few weeks before he had been training *with* us. But he took to it well. He was a good lad. I think he had a bit of a raw deal at Liverpool to be quite honest.

I didn't really go in the boot room. I'd see them going in and out of it and Shanks used to go in occasionally. Shanks was so funny, so many jokes. He was one of the most dedicated men

I've met in my life. The stories you hear about him, about life
and death being more important, it was true for him. There were
a lot of characters. They just wanted to win. Bob Paisley was
quieter but he was always there. He knew football, he knew
what he was talking about. He was always in the background
because Shanks came over so well talking. He was a natural
whereas Bob wasn't, but Bob knew football through and
through. Joe Fagan, Ronnie Moran, they were Liverpool through
and through.

I went there in 1969/70, at the end of the Tommy Lawrence,
Ian St John era. There was Kevin Keegan, Ray Clemence, Larry
Lloyd, myself, Stevie Heighway, Cally was still playing, and
Emlyn Hughes. That was the team of the seventies. We got into
the cup final against Arsenal but we were a young side then.
They were a bit too experienced for us and I think it showed on
the day because we went back in 1974 and we'd had that two
or three years' experience. Newcastle were a young side and it
showed with them.

We had a good team, a good team spirit. There were no little
cliques, everybody was in it together. We were frightened of
nobody. Shanks was the instigator of that, he thought we could
beat anybody. The team hardly changed. We were frightened of
getting injured and not getting back in. A lot played on with
injuries, never told anybody. I don't suppose it's doing them any
good now. Sometimes you see the team today and they don't
look as if they are enjoying themselves, their confidence is low.
But we just wanted to play.

Reuben Bennett was a nice fellow, an old Scotsman. He used
to be there every morning. We used to have a bit of a warm-up,
a nice leisurely jog around the field, loosening up, a laugh and
a joke, relaxing. Reuben always used to take us. He was a fit
old bugger. Nobody knew how old he was. He was a good man
to have in your squad. We'd be talking as we jogged, mainly
about what was on telly the night before. Then after we'd done
that we'd start the serious training. I say serious but it was mainly
five-a-sides. Before the season we used to train hard but we were
playing two games a week, so didn't need to train as hard during
the season. But there was no messing about with the five-a-side.

When Shanks left, it was a huge mystery. I haven't a clue why he left. And a lot of people still don't know. Even the lads I've seen since still wonder why. I certainly don't know. It came as a shock. We'd just won the cup. We had one more game, a testimonial game for Billy McNeill at Celtic and that was his last game. I still don't know to this day why he went. Bob Paisley and Joe Fagan were first and reserve team trainers. We fully expected Bob to move up. They seemed like a close-knit group of people. They each knew what they were doing. Whoever took over would have brought in new ideas, so they'd be upsetting everybody. This way nobody was upset. Everybody was gobsmacked because Shanks was so dedicated, not just about football but about everything. It wasn't as though he was bad with his health. I don't even think Bob knew he was going to do it.

After he quit, Shanks used to come down to the training ground. He was a bit lost. Football had been his life. Before he'd come down in the morning, then go to the club in the afternoon. If there was a game on he'd go and watch it, all day every day. That's why when he suddenly jacked it in nobody could understand.

BARRIE HOLMES
The Fans' Faith

There was a great deal of faith on both sides. The club, the boot room, etc, had faith in the fans, and vice-versa. I remember a game where Liverpool played Ajax and lost the first leg 5–1. Before the second leg Shankly came on the radio and told everyone that we'll not only beat them in the second leg but we'll beat them by seven clear goals. The beauty of this was that you went to the match believing that they would and even when they didn't, it ended up 2–2, you didn't feel any bitterness, or betrayal.

BARRIE HOLMES
Europe

I first started going to the games in 1963. Although I had been born in Liverpool my dad had been in the army and I had been all over the place. I came back to Liverpool in 1963 and have been a regular ever since. Like many people I started on the Kop and then progressed up to the Anfield Road End and now I'm in the Paddock. The first game I saw was a defeat at home to West Ham in the 1963/64 season; we lost 2–1. I only went to one other game that season, Sheffield United at home which we won 6–1. We won the league that season but it was the following season that I started going regularly and I've missed few home games since.

I remember the very first European game against Reykjavik; I think the difference between that and the league games was the atmosphere. Because we'd won the away leg quite convincingly it was very much a party atmosphere. At one stage the whole Kop was willing Reykjavik to score, it was a different atmosphere altogether. The game I remember after that was the Cologne game, particularly because in the end it finished up 0–0 and the tie was decided on the toss of a coin. That brought the excitement of European nights home to you. Then we played Anderlecht; that was one which brought home the value of Shankly and the rest of the boot room. Belgium had played England a week or so before and there had been quite a few Anderlecht players in the Belgian side who had done very well against England. Shankly had been saying how good they were and how Liverpool didn't have much chance. But we won that game 3–0 at home. That was probably the first time that I realised the expertise of Shankly in motivating players and perhaps conning the opposition as well.

That whole season in Europe was a tremendous experience and culminated in the Inter Milan match. Of all the other European games I've been to, that one had the best atmosphere I have ever experienced. Inter Milan were renowned as the top European club and in the home leg we just tore them apart. That was sensational, especially with the FA Cup being paraded around the ground before the game kicked off. I think that was a Shankly boot room decision. Although the crowd were well hyped up for the game, I think that took them to a higher level altogether and I think that rubbed off on our players. More effectively it had this impact on the Italians who looked scared to death, like they didn't want to be there. I think we learnt a valuable lesson in the return leg which is now infamous for the referee. Certainly Shankly and the boot room learnt an invaluable lesson about how it is over two legs and that you cannot take anything for granted.

I don't think people knew about the boot room at this stage. In those days it was very much Bill Shankly who was the focal point of everything. He was the man who did the talking, the man who the fans had faith in. I think it was only afterwards that people came to realise the importance of Bob Paisley and Joe Fagan. In those days Ronnie Moran and Roy Evans were still playing and had not joined the training staff. There was not much of an idea about the boot room then. It only came as Liverpool's success built up. Prior to that it was just Shankly.

BILL SHANKLY
The Simple Things

From the day I started at Anfield, the training was planned. We knew exactly what we were going to do each morning before we went to Melwood. Everything was tabulated on sheets of paper. This was the basis and everything stemmed from it. Bob Paisley, Joe Fagan, Reuben Bennett or myself would do something and one of the others would say, 'I think we could do without that,' or 'I think we could add this,' so the branches of our system sprouted out just like a tree.

'Everything we do here is for a purpose,' I said. 'It has been tried and tested and is so simple that anybody can understand it. But if you think that it is so simple that it is not worth doing, then you are wrong. The simple things are the ones that count.'

An extract from *Shankly* by Bill Shankly (Arthur Barker).

BOB GREAVES
A Warm Club

I've probably seen, as a journalist, hundreds of games at Anfield. It has to be hundreds, spanning the mid-sixties onwards till about six or seven years ago. So, like many others I've seen the development of the old rickety stadium to what it is today. It has always had that feel about it of a very special place, partly because it is the city of Liverpool and Liverpudlians, scousers, call them what you like, have all got the sharpness, that wit, almost acerbic side to them sometimes, but always very funny, and also they can be very warm. It was always a warm club to go to and it was always run, I got the impression, very well.

As a journalist, if you wanted to go and watch the players training or do interviews with them, you had to go through a system of phone calls, committees almost. You couldn't just wander in as you can with some other clubs, you couldn't just turn up willy-nilly. They all seemed to know what jobs they were doing, they always seemed to know at what level their job finished and somebody else took over. If you wanted to talk to a particular player, it was all done in a very efficient and very friendly way. It was always, and has been, a very efficiently run football club, organisation or business as it now is.

I remember meetings with Bill Shankly and Joe Fagan, and there was always Tom Saunders around in an avuncular and almost authoritative style, always these same faces. The faces didn't change a lot. There might have been changes in personnel on the playing field, the odd change in the management, but basically the club was run by the same faces. The faces didn't get much older either. The people got older but the faces never seemed to change a lot. I've known Peter Robinson for donkey's years but has he really changed? He's gone up through the ranks there. He's *El Supremo* now but whenever I see him he always looks the same.

I remember sending a Granada researcher to interview Shankly once. The researcher's name was Ian White and he was new to television. He'd never interviewed anybody of Bill Shankly's stature before. It was a quick interview we needed about somebody being injured and whether they would be available to play that Saturday. I said, 'Ian, there's nobody else around, you won't be appearing in vision, take a camera crew and go and talk to Bill Shankly.' His name was White and his face went white. He said, 'I don't think I can go and interview Shankly, he won't know me from Adam.' I said, 'He's very friendly, and he won't be bothered who you are, just go over there. Get the camera behind your head and keep it on Shankly.' I remember also saying, 'Ian, here's a tip, whichever shoulder the camera is over, keep your head the other way because Shankly is inclined to get excitable as you know. And when he's excited he's inclined to spit, there's a spray, but if you duck your head down you'll be okay. So, off went Ian with my advice and tips for this fairly meaningless interview. When he came back, I asked 'How did it go?'

'Oh,' he says, 'fine, it was as if he had known me for ten, fifteen years.'

'Yes,' I said, 'that's Shankly, that is Liverpool, nobody's foreign, nobody's new, you're part of the Granada family, so you're part of Liverpool. But how did the interview go?'

'Oh, okay,' he says, 'but something funny happened,' he adds. 'You were right about the spittle so I kept my head down.'

'So what happened ?'

'Well, he said to me just before we started, "Ian, I just need to make a phone call before we start the interview. Do you mind if I just take two minutes?"'

I said, 'No, no problem, Mr Shankly.'

So he made the phone call and was apparently ringing Ron Yeats because the phone call went, almost literally, . . . ring . . . ring . . . "Is that you Big Man, how ya feelin' Big Man . . . I know you've got a cold, Big Man . . . D'yae need the club doctor, Big Man? . . . D'yae need any tablets, Big Man? . . . Will yae be awright for Saturday, Big Man? . . . Yae don't need any tablets, Big Man . . . All right, Big Man." The phone goes down and then he turns to me and says "Ian, that was the Big Man!"

Anybody who watched *Granada Reports* over the years will remember some of these names in this anecdote. This is the post-Shankly era at Anfield. After Shankly had stopped and quit, I started seeing him at football matches all over the north-west. I saw him two or three times at various games, twice in particular at Maine Road. I used to watch him if I spotted him at a game and he would always leave his seat in the directors' box or the guest spot in the stand, about four minutes before the end of the game. I didn't give much thought to this, just thinking that he was driving back to Liverpool. But no, I then got to realise that he was deliberately leaving early in order to find an elevated position when the crowd of directors, pressmen and honoured guests came out so that they would always find Bill at the top of some chairs. He would just stand there like the Pope, and many people on Merseyside did consider him to be a Pope-like person. He would stand there with his arm outstretched to shake a few hands. He would then have the stage to deliver.

I left the Maine Road press box after one game, and there he was on the stairs shaking hands when he spotted me. He then launched into a detailed character rundown of everybody who was then working with me on the Granada nightly programme. He delivered for about four minutes by which time there was a crowd of 200 to 300 people. He gave this superb performance which went roughly like this: 'Bob, you're a man of the people, you might be an ordinary looking man but you are a man of the people, you say it how it is. Then there's Trevor Hyett. People look upon him as a bit of a buffoon because he has a gap in his teeth but he's an educated man. He's a musician, been to university. Then there's David Jones, that big, tall gangling man, looks like a policeman, walks like a policeman, but no, a wizard of the art of journalism. There's Anna Ford, serene, beautiful, clever. There's Tony Wilson, he hates Liverpool but not all Liverpudlians hate Tony Wilson.' He went on and on through about ten others, absolutely detailed character pen pictures of these people who he must have watched hundreds of times. He could detail them as much as I could who had worked with them all for years. It was quite amazing. Like all his other performances, it was very deliberate. It sounded ad hoc. They looked off the cuff. But most of them weren't. A very clever man.

BOB PAISLEY
The Same Goal

In the August of 1959 I moved up to be the first team trainer after Albert Shelley retired. Bill came to take over as manager in the December of that year. I never feared for the sack, although you know there's always a possibility when a new manager takes over.

Bill called us all together and made no bones about it, he was the boss. He said he would sort the team out. He would get you into conversation and you could sway him, but he was sorting it out. In the end he stated there was a lot wrong at Liverpool, but the staff were all right, and he was keeping it.

There was no way you could not work for him. You get to know people and how they tick. I knew I could work with him and sometimes went out of my way to help. It was my job to do so. You can sense when people have a bit of respect for you, and you could feel that Bill had respect for us, and we for him and it paid off all along the line. We were all working towards the same goal.

He detested it if you couldn't be definite about a player's fitness. I was the physiotherapist and I had to give a verdict before he would pick the team. He didn't like you to sit on the fence, he liked you to make a decision. He was an impatient man, but we never had a row about any of my decisions on fitness. In fact in the 15 years I worked with him we never had a row at all.

An extract from *Bob Paisley, An Autobiography* (Arthur Barker).

BRIAN HALL

A University Lad

I first came to the club in 1965 as a university student and played for three years as an amateur whilst at university. That'll never happen again. I would go training on a Tuesday night with the other amateurs, Ted MacDougall, Dougie Livermore, Phil Boersma. My only contact with the club would be when I was playing in the reserves. I'd be shown into a dressing room to meet some guys I'd never met before, certainly in the early days. In those days the reserve team played on a Saturday afternoon so Bill Shankly was not there. As I played more games for the reserves, I'd see more of Bill Shankly, Bob Paisley and Joe Fagan who was the second team trainer. Ronnie Moran took the A team. I think it was 1966/67 when Ronnie Moran won the Lancashire League with the A team. My actual contact with the club didn't therefore really happen until the 1967/68 season when they offered me a full-time contract.

Albert Shelley was the old stager in the long white coat or brown coat shuffling around sweeping up after everybody. He could always handle the dressing room banter from all these young lads. He was old enough to be their grandfather but he could handle them, always had a good answer. He was a lovely man, though I never knew him that well.

I never had any thoughts of being a professional footballer whatsoever, my life was geared to doing 'O' and 'A' levels. For a young lad off a council estate in Preston to go to university was like manna from heaven, a much smaller percentage of the population went to university back then. I turned down opportunities at Preston North End, Bolton and so on. The only reason I chose Liverpool was because of the Beatles and the music scene. I thought this must be a wonderful place to go to. A friend of mine wrote to Liverpool Football Club to get a trial for me and he showed me Tom Bush's reply. He'd written back saying, 'When he starts at university, send him down on a Tuesday or

Thursday night.' So I started at university doing maths and the pal of mine who was also doing maths with me, said, 'You're going to go for that trial, aren't you? I'll come down on the bus with you." So, I said, 'Okay, I'll give it a try.' I walked in with this letter and Tom Bush told me to come on in. I got changed and went out. Reuben Bennett took the training. I hadn't done any training because I had been working as a bus conductor, I'd done nothing. I was shattered. Then at the end of this we went into a game. At the end of the game, full eleven-a-side, after half an hour the whistle goes and I start trudging off, and I hear 'Where dyae think yer going, son?' This was Reuben. 'I'm going to get a bath.' 'Half-time,' he said. That was my first experience of Reuben.

They signed me on there and then. I was in the A team the following Saturday against Everton. Reuben had boys going to teacher training college, and university. Being a Scotsman he realised the importance of education and fulfilling your potential. I'd mentioned to Reuben, I think in the final year at university, about maybe becoming a professional. It was almost a throwaway line. I hadn't decided what I wanted to do when I finished. Reuben jumped on me, turned round and said, 'Don't you give up your studies, you mustn't.' My first thought was that they were obviously not interested in me as a pro. But in retrospect it was a terrific piece of advice, and very unusual. It wasn't so much what he said but the power and force with which he said it. My father of course had watched me playing since a little boy from the touchlines. He'd never say a word, you didn't in those days. Then he watched me playing for Liverpool with Reuben bellowing and swearing from the touchlines. He said to me, 'Who on earth is that man?' It was a culture shock. The first difference I noticed was the number of kicks I got on the legs. This was for real.

Tom Bush was a nice man. He had children at college so there was an understanding. I was perceived as something different to the rest of the boys coming through the system, but even though Reuben was an enormous taskmaster they at least understood my position and were good to me. I had one run-in with him but there was never any grudge. The next day he would be as friendly as ever. Any criticism was immediate, that was the way things were. If things didn't go right, you got told in a very aggressive way. It was done, and it was finished.

I remember playing in the reserves with Geoff Strong. He was a bit special, a hell of a player. He played a ball up to me, then he carried on and I should have given it back. I didn't, I hung on to the ball and lost it. So he blitzed me. I was beginning to learn by this time; the only way to deal with it was to turn round and tell him to sod off. I just stormed straight back, my next thought was, 'What have I done?' At the end of the game however, Strongy came up to me, put his arm around me and said, 'Well done, son'. I thought yeah, it's not university out there, debating things for hours, it was instant, immediate and very aggressive and unless you met aggression with aggression you wouldn't survive.

I think in those days Tom and the others were multifunctional. There were only six or seven staff in all. He administered the amateur players, looked after their registration. He did all that and sorted out travel expenses on a Saturday. The coaching was done by Reuben and Ronnie. When he came back up to Anfield Tom would do things about the office, so I think his role was multifunctional. But he had no input into the football, it was just administrative.

I can only pass on to you an amalgam of bits of stories that I've been told. I don't know how true they all are. You've probably heard the story that the room where the boots were stored had to be locked and so it became a refuge for Albert, Bob, Joe, and so on. After the game some of them would go for a wee dram so that the boss didn't see them because Shanks didn't drink. In time it grew. I think it was also a place where visiting managers could go after a game, lock the door and have a wee dram. Inevitably, when you've got a group of people who are all football people they talk about football. There was good banter as well because the adrenalin was flowing after the game. Over the years they would also start going in there after training and it just evolved within that simple framework.

There was never anything fancy, complicated or intellectual about what we did at Liverpool. Everything was simple and that's what made it work. That was the key to it. I don't know who first got hold of this myth about the boot room. Anyhow, inevitably the numbers who wanted to go and see it grew. It was the place where you could get a drink and talk to the likes of Bob and Joe. Their friends also started to go in. As a player you never went in, you might see them in there having a chat as you passed by. It was only after I had finished playing when the myth was well and truly established that I went in. I remember calling during the week, it was a bit special for me to be invited. If I came to a game in the early eighties, I would always go there. They'd invite me in, saying, 'Come and have a beer.' It was a wonderful experience for me to be invited into the inner sanctum. It was fascinating to enjoy once again that real football banter, the stories that would pop up, that little group of friends. There is in any very close community an in-house sense of humour. There are little phrases and so on that they understood but which outsiders didn't. It was great for me to listen to that again. I used to think that the boot room was a legend but it was also the tattiest, dirtiest, scruffiest little place you were ever likely to come across because really it was the place where the kept the kit. That's my memory of it. You'd lean against the wall, sit on a skip. You'd always get up out of your chair for the more senior members of the staff. Tom was getting a bit old then, so you'd offer him your chair. It was hierarchical in that sense.

IAN HARGREAVES

Primitive Days

In some ways it was not all that different before Shankly came. Bob Paisley I found very, very interesting. Bob was coming to the end of his career as a player and was very worried that he was going to be laid off at the end of the season. He was in his thirties, had been in the army and had not won a cap or anything. He told me he was getting prepared to go back to his old job, his trade as a bricklayer. When he first came on the staff in 1939 he'd helped to build the old Anfield bench in his spare time as a brickie – that's the old bench they used to sit on. During 1955/56 Paisley was not playing so much and he was offered the job of reserve team trainer by the old chairman, T.V. Williams. Bob accepted because he wanted to stay in football and he said to me that in those days if you were reserve training you were really down to the lowest of the low. The thing is, he said, at Liverpool there are two factors. One, he said, it was really the stiffs. It was providing a game for anyone who was recovering from injury or just giving some youngsters a game. He said that after a week or two he went to the manager, Don Welch, and said, 'Look Don, would you mind if I made the reserves competitive?' He said, 'What do you mean?' So, Bob said, 'Well, I don't want to be in charge of a team that don't really want to win'. Don said, 'Well, if you want to, you have a go.' So Bob put a note on the board which said that from now on he wanted a reserve team that was going out to win every match and if anyone just wanted a run-out, then they could forget it, they wouldn't get picked.

Bob told me that they'd never won games, nobody even kept the score. But they started winning and started playing. Within a year or two, he said, players were standing down from the first team because they wanted to play for a team which won.

If you look at the Central League championship, he made a great success of it, and Houllier would be advised to look at it too. They won the Central League championship about 11 times under three or four different coaches. But it was always the same, you go out on the pitch, you're in the squad and there's only one way to play, you go out to win. We don't mind who we're playing, we go out to win. Bob said it completely changed the attitude. And he always insisted on this as he moved up.

The other thing he said was that you wouldn't believe how primitive it was. We didn't have any subs. If anyone was injured, went down with a knock or whatever, it was a cold sponge down the back of the neck and that was a great reviver. You didn't take a player off if he could stand up because you would lose the game. He thought this was not a very good idea and he asked permission of the club, and eventually got it from John Moores, to get permission from the Liverpool hospitals to go to the Royal and sit in on the accident department and watch the treatment.

He did this for a year or two and began to learn what you did for basic injuries, sprains, tears, pulls and so on. And he took a correspondence course as well. When he finished he said he was the only trainer in the Football League medically qualified. He actually had medical qualifications. Bob said to me, 'I'll tell you how bad it was. One game in the old days when Liverpool were playing, Billy Liddell was knocked unconscious. He collided with someone, went down. The then trainer was Albert Shelley, he ran him up and down the terraces and eventually pushed him back on again. This was just before half-time. Liddell went out in the second half and ran around like a man in a dream, and I said to him afterwards, "How are you feeling, Bill?" And he said, "What do you mean?" "What do you remember?" He said, "I don't remember anything about the game at all." He played half unconscious the whole game.

Later, Paisley could spot an injury off the television set. The guy would go on playing and they'd say, 'You've got it wrong this time, Bob.' Then the guy would finally limp off. Bob never got it wrong.

Albert Shelley was there before Bob Paisley. I don't really know much about him but he was one of the long-serving people. Just before Shankly came, Reuben Bennett arrived. He was the chief coach. It's well known that when Shankly came in he kept the whole lot on. Bennett was very very popular. He was an exceptionally tough man. He didn't have time for people who would not walk through the pain barrier. He was a Scot. I don't know how much he had to do with the actual tactics. It always struck me that under Shankly they almost worked out their tactics on the pitch because players were expected to have some *nous* about them. If you were the left winger you were expected to know how you were going to play. Bennett liked the odd game of golf. He was very popular. I went to his funeral and it was unbelievable. There were a hundred people or more, it was an awful wet day and there were a dozen relatives and neighbours and about four Liverpool squads going right back, hardly anybody missing at all. People who had not seen each other for years had all come back for Bennett's funeral. Emlyn Hughes arrived with his wife and it was, 'Oh hello, Emlyn.' Nobody was in the least bit interested in him. I can't help feeling that Emlyn must regret not being part of the Anfield legend. I'm sure he must believe that he is, but in his heart of hearts he must know that he is not. But for the man who brought the European Cup home, it must be a bit shattering.

IAN HARGREAVES
Press Conferences

Shankly arrived in December 1959. He'd been at Huddersfield. I was in the press box when he turned up for his first game which I think Liverpool lost. He was sitting there with a scarf around his neck and I thought, this is the man they've brought in who says he's going to do wonders. He sat there looking grim. He was not the easiest person to understand at press conferences. He set a pattern that so many Liverpool managers followed. When you're giving a press conference, particularly after a match, how often does someone put their foot in it by making a daft remark, then wished they hadn't? Shankly used to get away with it by coming out with the most incomprehensible rubbish you've ever heard in your life. We all know those famous phrases. At Ajax, he asked, 'What do you do against a team that play defensive football on their own ground?' This is against Ajax who were five up at half-time!

Against Borussia Dortmund in the Cup Winners' Cup Final, he said that we were beaten by a team of frightened men. Everybody was so busy laughing that they didn't think about it. And of course in the end he never said anything about his own team. He always gave himself two or three days to think about things before talking to the press again. Then he'd say, well, we did this wrong and whatever and everyone would agree. So often managers come out with something in the heat of the moment and they then regret it because we see videos and so on. Now Bob Paisley was almost incomprehensible anyway. Hardly anyone understood him because he never finished a sentence. You'd think, 'What the hell's he talking about?'

IAN HARGREAVES

The Electrical Machine

I was always aware of the Anfield boot room. I'm sure it was always there. Shankly just moved into it. In those days there wasn't a huge stadium. If you look at pictures of it, it was simply a basic ground with the old stand and not much else. Nobody dreamt of having a press room or anything like that.

Nobody ever went into the boot room without an invitation. There'd be Paisley, Reuben Bennett, Fagan, Ronnie Moran and in later years Roy Evans, and visiting managers and coaches, even they would be invited in. After the game nobody else would be in. After they'd seen the team was okay, they'd return to the boot room and put their feet up. They had a crate of ale in there, they'd pull out some beers, just relax and talk over the game. What they did in the week was similar. They'd train at Melwood and come back afterwards, bring the boots back, put them away, then sit and chat. It was a bit like a school common room, I suppose. Shankly was not an office man at all. He didn't believe in sitting around or behind a desk. He was even talked into having a secretary. At one time he had an old typewriter and typed out his own letters, which took him ages.

One of the funniest stories Bob Paisley told me was that when he was trainer they got this electrical machine, I don't know what it was. He discovered that this worked miracles, it was some kind of physio machine. The papers called it a magical machine. Bob Paisley was the person who operated it. Bill got so excited. Bill saw him doing things on people and he used to go out on the street and drag people in to try it. He found a couple of pensioners one day and came back with them, one was limping and the other had backache and he insisted that Bob treat them. The final straw was when he brought in this old man with a whippet and they decided to try it out on the whippet. Bob told him to bugger off as he was not going to try it out on the bloody whippet.

The youth coaches also went in the boot room from time to time. And there was Tom Saunders. He did every job although he was technically in charge of youth development. He used to go and watch teams for them as well. And there was John Bennison and Hugh McAuley. And I imagine if the groundsman wanted to, he could. Arthur Riley was there for over 50 years. And if he wanted to, although I imagine he didn't, he could just go and knock on the door. I'm sure there would have been a time when someone would have said, 'Hey Arthur, how are you doing, come on in, have a beer, how's the pitch' or whatever.

They very much leave people to their own jobs at Anfield. They tend to look for somebody very carefully and then leave them to get on with it and just keep an eye on them. Arthur Riley was there for 50 years and I think his father had been there before him.

And there was Geoff Twentyman as well. Geoff used to give you the impression that he had spotted half the finest talent in England. I have no idea at all whether that is correct or not but they had a very high percentage of successful players. Who found them I do not know. I wouldn't wish to knock Geoff Twentyman but my own guess is that to give him too much credit is a little misleading. I would think however that he should take some credit. Chris Lawler was also there as reserve team coach for a while.

It is significant that since Liverpool have stopped winning things their reserve side has stopped winning as well. They almost got relegated the other year. Now that has got to have some significance. They used to bring players through, Ray Kennedy is the obvious example and Geoff Strong to an extent. They would drop out of the first team then come back three months later playing in a different position and become tremendous players. Alec Lindsay was another one, returning as a left-back having signed as a midfielder-cum-striker.

IAN HARGREAVES

Playing For The Fans

I was in the ground long before kick-off for the Liverpool-Inter Milan game but you could hear the singing way back in the centre of Liverpool. I've been to some games but never anything like that. The crowd were going on wanting to see the FA cup and Gordon Milne and Gerry Byrne came out with the trophy just before kick-off and the crowd went absolutely berserk. Who actually suggested it I don't know, but I heard later it was Shankly.

Shankly was the man who changed everything. Well, he didn't change things in one sense because he took what he had there and developed it. He always claimed that he could have done the same thing at Huddersfield, given the support, because he had good players but the management wouldn't buy the players he wanted. He'd wanted to buy Yeats and St John when he was there. And he had Ray Wilson and Denis Law. His motto was keep it simple. He wouldn't have claimed there was any magic. But I think he contributed to the spirit of the club, that you play here and we are going to be the best, we are 100 per cent together. He once told a player he was transferring to another club, 'Look son, you might be the third choice here but you'll be the best player where you are going.' That was his attitude. He was all for elitism, you are part of the best team there is. But to be part of it you have to prove it all the time. He had total rapport with the crowd. The Liverpool crowd were something special then. They're not now, they've been spoilt.

IAN ROSS

The University of Football

My career started in Glasgow. My first trial was with Barnsley.
I was very fortunate with the YMCA where I played in Glasgow.
Kenny Dalglish played there as well. The chap who ran the team
then, Bobby Dinnie, is still involved in it now. He said, 'You're
not going to Barnsley, you're just going on a trial for experience.'
After that I went to Chelsea when Tommy Docherty was manager, I was only 16 then and London was a big place, a bit big
for me. After that I went to Arsenal for a trial. I could have gone
to any of them because they all wanted me. At that time I wasn't
sure that I wanted to be a professional footballer. When I went
to London I was staying in a hotel and for a young lad
from Glasgow who hasn't travelled too far, it wasn't the right
thing.

Then I was on holiday in Fife and I was invited to Liverpool.
I travelled down and had a week there. I wasn't in a hotel, I was
in digs. Fortunately the digs were in Kemlyn Road which was
very handy and there was a lad in the digs who was my age who
I still keep in touch with. There was something about Liverpool
which I felt at ease with. But of course the biggest factor was
the manager of Liverpool at the time, Bill Shankly. When I went
back to Glasgow on the train, Bobby Dinnie met me and asked
me how I liked it. I said I quite liked it and he said, 'Oh, that's
good because Shankly has already been on the phone and wants
you to go back and sign.' That was the 1964/65 season, they
had just won the cup.

The boot room was always the main focus of everything. First
thing in the morning you'd go in and pick your boots up. It was
always a good place to be, cleaning the boots, there was always
a hub of activity around the boot room. I never had to clean the
boots because I had signed as a professional straight away. It
was just the young apprentices who had to clean the boots. It
was just a small tiny room and you couldn't see anything else

but boots and skips. First thing in the morning, all you would see would be the kids cleaning the boots and maybe Reuben Bennett popping his head in to make sure they were doing it properly.

Reuben travelled everywhere with the boss. I'm sure they kicked ideas around. Reuben always took the warm-ups at training. There was something special about him. He knew when to kick you up the backside. He'd ask, 'Have you got a problem, son?' He was just always nice to see around.

Ronnie was a great help to me. I only played in the third team once and then it was always the reserves. Ronnie had just finished his first team career and he played at the back in the reserves. It was so good to have someone of his experience around you. Funnily enough Roy Evans and I played centre-backs and neither of us is very tall. But we never used to lose matches. I've got more Central League trophies than anyone I know.

Bob was more of the tactician. He was like everybody's father. He had forgotten more about football than any of these modern coaches will ever learn. I sat alongside him on the bench and just listened to the comments, he could see things happening long before they did, in some instances earlier than Bill. He'd change things and then argue with the boss afterwards. Bill was the charismatic character and Bob was the tactician. I had a good insight into all that. They never argued. They would disagree but never argued. In fact there were never any arguments at Liverpool, certainly not that the players could see.

Discipline was a word that was never mentioned, honestly. People ask me how it was instilled. It was just there, the code of conduct. No one was ever late for training. I remember playing in Ferencvaros. I was sitting with Ian St John and Big Ron and I felt afraid. Ian said, 'Don't be afraid, just don't let the boss down.' Nobody would let the boss down. If you did, you weren't involved. Of course we made mistakes but we didn't let the boss down. A huge contrast to what happens today. Shanks made us believe we were special and we were. I was very lucky. Shanks would go into the boot room after the first team game. They'd discuss it, and always invite the opposition in and nine times out of ten congratulate them on putting up a good show. Shanks would always tell them they had a great team and had been a bit unlucky. It was only special people who were invited in. We kids couldn't get near it.

After they entertained the opposition, the real post-match inquiry would take place, after all the opposition had gone. 'Well, what did you really think about that? How good were we?' They'd be there until they felt they had talked enough about it. But it's a different ball game today. I often wonder how the boss would have managed today. Agents! There was only one agent as far as the boss was concerned and that was 007. I remember him saying that. He wouldn't deal with agents. But it was a special place then. Everybody would talk about the boot room but it was just another place where all they talked about was football, nothing else. You talked about anything else and they would shut you up. They were real deep-thinking football people.

I was involved in the game against Celtic. I was fortunate to go with them and we lost 1–0. Then there was the return game at Anfield when all the bottles came on to the pitch and with four minutes to go the referee decided enough was enough. I was in the Main Stand for that, still learning my trade. I played against Bayern Munich. Funnily enough in the first game I played left-back. We won 3–0, Alun Evans scored a hat-trick. I remember when we travelled to Munich, the boss pulled me aside and I thought, 'Ah no, I'm not playing,' but he says, 'Ian son, they've only got one player, this big Beckenbauer. So, you're not playing left-back tonight.' I'd heard of Beckenbauer, so he made me play against him. 'When we lose the ball, just make sure he doesn't get it,' he said. We played a sweeper then. So I didn't let him have it. I played tight on him and made sure he was never free to get it. Funnily enough I scored that night. There was only 20 minutes to go. I'd already missed one chance. They got a corner and I remember Beckenbauer coming up for it and I obviously marked him. Big Ron cleared the corner and it went to Peter Thompson. The instruction was when we've got the ball, leave Beckenbauer. I think he had thrown the towel in by then. They were three down and I was first out of the box and I thought, I'll go and support Peter, that's what we did in those days and Peter rolled one 25 yards across, and it went straight into my path and I belted it in. I thought, 'I've done a great day's work, haven't I, not only stopped Beckenbauer, but scored one myself.' Anyhow a few minutes later Gerd Muller put one in and it ended up 4–1 on aggregate. I thought, I'll get the wink off the boss tonight, that's all we lived for, that wink off him. Anyhow, he looks at me and says, 'You little bugger, you should have scored two!' I'll never forget it, *you should have scored two*. Not, you've just played one of the best players in the world out of the game! But that was Shanks. You'd do anything for one of those winks. He was one of those fellows. If he said go jump in the canal, you'd do it, then you'd come out and ask why. You wouldn't question him beforehand. The rest of the lads will tell you the same.

It was the university of football. For the first day's training I was next to Ron Yeats and my shoulders stop where his legs start. There were people like Ian Callaghan, so professional, Roger Hunt, Gerry Byrne, Gordon Milne, great players, great men, full of character. The first four seasons we were there, they used about 14 players. And we are talking about 65–70 games a season. You've heard it before: 'What's the team, Bill?' 'The same as last year.' And that's a fact. Now they use 15 players in a match.

The season I left, I think I played 36 games out of 37. Then the boss left me out. I wasn't happy, nobody would be. I said maybe it's time to go and he said, 'Would you like to speak to Villa, for the last six months they've been on the phone every week wanting to buy you?' I said, 'Yes, I'd like to speak to them.'

I met with Villa. Bill had said, 'Don't do anything until you've spoken to me again.' I said, 'Of course not.' Well, Villa wanted me to sign there and then that night. I said no and the wife and I travelled back to meet Shanks. For four hours he tried to talk me out of going. But Phil Thompson was on his way up then. I was never a great player. I could have been there maybe like Roy Evans. But I don't regret things. Shanks wanted me to stay and I could have done, maybe ended up in the reserves, mind you, and that's what made me decide. I was never quick. I used my head. If I had been quick I would have ended up an international. The poor man's Bobby Moore, I was called!

IAN ST JOHN
New Red Kit

The one thing I always remember about the Kop was that I had to run up and down it. On wet days when we didn't go out to Melwood for any training, Reuben Bennett, our trainer, used to take us on to the Kop and make us run up and down it countless times. I don't know how many steps there are but I do know that they have been covered many times in my sweat. In my days the Kop was very inspirational. We were always aware of the heaving mass of people. The gates would be shut at 1pm and they'd be there all afternoon swaying one way and then the other. I thought the Kop roared in our days.

Those early days in the second division were memorable. We had some great games then. It was the start of a surge. We led the second division from start to finish and I particularly remember that final game against Southampton at Anfield. I had been sent off in a previous match and I was suspended so I didn't play. But I was watching. The crowd were fantastic. At the end of the game we came back to the dressing room and Shanks made us go back out on to the pitch. We all ran around the pitch and then went up the Kop end. I had a nice white mac on and it got splattered in mud. We had a great rapport going with the Kop. There were lots of new lads in the side: myself, Ron Yeats, Gerry Byrne, Gordon Milne. The Kop really took to us. We were running up good scores as well. We needed them to lift us and they needed us. It was a relationship.

Those early European games were memorable. That night against Inter Milan, the Kop was inspirational as they were in the earlier game against Anderlecht. I suppose that was the first really big European night at Anfield. We'd played Reykjavik in the first round but they were a small unknown club and they didn't really matter. Then we faced the Belgian champions in the next round. They had a great team that formed almost the entire Belgian national side. Not long before we played them Belgium had taken England apart. Shankly was very impressed by them. They were all wonderful players.

That night was the first time Liverpool played in all red. Shanks had decided that we should wear red shorts as well as red jerseys. We tried them on and we all liked them. Then Ron Yeats and I said, 'Why don't we have red socks as well?' So Shanks says, 'Okay, let's see what they look like.' He found a pair of red socks and put them on Ron and he looked like a giant, very fearsome. So that was it. Shanks said, 'All right, we're in all red from now on.' I think the Kop was a bit shocked when we appeared in this new rig-out. But it seemed to make them roar us on even more. And after that we had to stay in red.

It was also the night Tommy Smith made his debut. Shanks was a bit worried about playing him because it was such an important game and he was so young. So he had a word with Ron and I on the quiet. 'Don't worry,' we told him, 'he won't let you down.' Smith was a man when he was eight. So Smithy made his debut and he didn't let anyone down either. We won 3–0. I scored the first goal after just nine minutes, much against the run of play. Then just before half-time I managed to get the ball off one of their defenders and passed it to Roger Hunt. That was 2–0. Then Ron Yeats headed a third minutes after the interval. Before the game Shanks had been telling us that Anderlecht were no good and we'd easily beat them, but after the game it was a different story. He was going around telling the press that Anderlecht were one of the finest sides he had ever seen. Anyhow, the Kop loved that night and it gave them a taste for European football.

JOHN BENNETT

Bringing The Cup Home

I was there until 1966 and I went through some of the glory years. We went down to Wembley for the Cup Final. The final against Leeds was an unbelievable game. Gerry Byrne was just fantastic in that game; to play like that with a broken collarbone was superb. Liverpool that day were superb because Leeds were a fine side. I don't think there's been a more titanic game than that. We travelled through the streets of Liverpool on the coach, what an experience seeing those crowds, thousands of them. It was something else that, it was staggering to see so many people, absolutely unbelievable. The roads were jammed and the noise, it sent shivers down your spine, it was awesome.

JOHN BENNETT
An Apprentice's Lot

I joined Liverpool straight from school. I had been in the Liverpool schoolboys side. In those days you used to get the scouts coming around. I had a Mr Cooke from Everton come as well, wanting me to sign for them but I was always a Liverpool fan and it was always my dream to play for them. This is 1961/62, Shanks was already manager. I was on £7.50 a week.

On a Monday we came in the morning and cleaned the ground. We didn't have Monday off like the pros. We had to brush the Kop, the whole Kop. What annoyed me was that the lads who had gone to Everton didn't have to do that because the council used to clean Goodison. They used to get a team in to clean it but at Anfield we lads had to do it. It took us a while, it was a few hours' work. There were a good few of us, could have been as many as ten or fourteen apprentices. We swept it all up and put it in bins. Occasionally we'd find things like money but I don't think anybody found anything worth shouting about. We did the Kemlyn Road stand as well. In those days it had bench seats and wasn't the easiest thing in the world to clean.

Then later in the morning, about 11 or half past, we'd have a five-a-side game against Shanks and the others. We'd play them in the car park at Anfield at the back of what is now the Main Stand. It was just tarmac. It was all the young lads against the staff. You daren't kick them. When they went into the tackle with me they were hard. With there being only four of them they would have at least one of the apprentices on their side, not an enviable position to be in for a young lad as you'd end up doing a lot of their running. I've only ever been exhausted twice in my life, totally out on my feet. It was a pre-season and we'd trained quite hard in the morning and in the afternoon we did ball skills. Then we finished off with a five-a-side. I was chosen to go with the coaching staff and playing against lads like myself who can run. I was doing a lot of running for my own side, and I was absolutely knackered. I was so exhausted, I was seeing double. On my side would be Joe Fagan and Bob Paisley. Bob had a cartilage problem. He eventually got it seen to. He got by with it and he wouldn't let it bother him. At their age they couldn't do an awful lot of running so you had to do the running for them. Nobody liked being on their side. Bill Shankly would play as well. Everything you've heard is absolutely right. He hated getting beat. I've seen it when he wouldn't let the game end until he'd won. He was a winner, totally competitive, they all were, Joe, Bob, Reuben. When you've played against Joe Fagan you knew it. He was the hardest person to get past. I can't ever remember getting past him, he was so good. He had long legs and seemed to get them everywhere.

One stare from Bob and it made you go cold. He was quite frightening at times. He wasn't somebody you would want to upset, I think even more than Reuben. Joe wasn't quite so dour as the others. But Bob I would not like to upset. I was in awe of him but I had the utmost respect. I knew that he was only trying to teach me the way the game should be played. Bill was hard as well but to be fair he didn't take the training. He only came in for various things like shooting. He was one of those people who when he kicked the ball, he had a style about him. He wouldn't just go at it, it was done with style, total body movement. He had obviously been a great player in his time and you could see that even at the age he was then. We got a bit of rough treatment in these games, they'd knock you about. The way I saw it was that they wanted to harden you up. Bob was the main one for doing this. I don't mean that they kicked you but they would give you a good nudge and send you flying. And remember, we were playing on tarmac. But that didn't bother us. I know he only did this to harden you up. And yes, it was done very deliberately. There was no such thing as a foul. You asked for a foul and they'd just ignore you. They set the rules as well, so the game ended when they said and at the score they wanted. But it was all done as part of building you up as a professional, with a winner's attitude.

On a Tuesday we'd be in, change, and then get the coach to Melwood with the others. Then we'd train there. There was always plenty of banter on the coach but the young lads like me didn't associate with the first team. It was a bit of a class system: the apprentices went around with one another and the first teamers stuck together. We didn't socialise with any of the first team. It was an awful big squad as well with 40-odd pros. I can remember the A team being full of professionals and there were an awful lot of amateurs who didn't get a game.

At Melwood we'd start with a jog around the pitch. The thing about Liverpool to me was that they had a good training system. They never pushed you too hard really, except at the right time. So we'd start off with a jog, a couple of laps then we'd do stretching exercises with Reuben, then we'd do sprints, ball skills, shooting practice and, of course, work on the boards. We did a lot of that. Then after a couple of hours we'd end up with a five-a-side. We always finished with a five-a-side, the young apprentices against the staff. Then it was back to Anfield for lunch.

We apprentices would have to clean the dressing rooms and the passageways. There was always a lot of work to do. We wouldn't leave until 3 or 4 o'clock. That would be the pattern every day although we tended to leave early on a Friday, maybe have the afternoon off.

One of the many chores we had to do was cleaning the boots. I remember the boot room as a dingy little place. When I first went there the guy who looked after it was Albert Shelley. As you know, he was an old player. Albert was a bit of a character. He was a nice guy, I liked him but he didn't suffer fools gladly, he was quite caustic with some of his remarks. He wasn't averse to saying so-and-so's a bit of a this, that and other. He was like that even to the first team players. He was a good guy, a bit of fun. He just looked after the boot room. I don't think he did much else, just maybe re-studding the boots and so on. I'd go in there and clean the boots, polish them. It was just one small room then. We all had our own jobs. I was fairly well organised and the lads used to call me the 'General'. I used to try and get them sorted. Some of them would sit around doing nothing so I'd say, 'Come on, let's get done, so that we can get on home!'

I was in the youth team and was involved in the FA Youth Cup. They were the Under-18s, and included players from the A team and the reserves. I started off in the B team, then moved up into the A team then finally the reserves in the Central League. It took me three years to get into the reserves. They had a big staff, you'd have 20-year-old lads in the A team. That's the way it was then, they could afford to have bigger staffs. Shanks came up to me at the end of that season and said, 'You've had a good season.' But the next season I was still in the B team, I didn't go up. There was no place to move up, it was difficult to break through. Tommy Smith was exceptional, he was a man when he was a boy, he moved up quickly but he was one of the few who did. Chris Lawler made it through pretty quickly as well. He was a nice lad although again I didn't socialise with him, he was older. Quiet lad, very likeable, I always had a lot of time for him. He was a good player, one of the first attacking full-backs, scored a lot of goals.

JOHN BENNETT
Hard Men

I had the utmost respect for Shanks. He knew football inside out but he wasn't someone you could go and talk to about everyday things. If you had been having trouble with your girl-friend, he wasn't the sort of person to go to, not that you'd go to any of the others either. I would feel that I was wasting his time with something like that. You were in awe of him. I think these days there are people you can go to at clubs but there weren't in those days. They were hard men and they expected you to be the same. When I met him years later at Everton's training ground at Belfield he was much more relaxed. This was after he had left Liverpool. He was a different person. You could have a joke with him; he was not the guy I knew as my manager.

JOHN BENNETT

An Escape

The back room staff never met in the boot room when I was there in the early sixties. I never noticed them getting together in there although thinking about it, there was nowhere else to go, only the dressing rooms and the treatment room, that was it. So the boot room could be the only place they could get together. It wasn't really developed then, it became more of an institution after I left. They could escape there, lock the door and talk about the game.

JOHN BENNISON

Reuben Bennett, The Hard Man

Reuben Bennett was a dour Scot, as honest as the day is long. He didn't stand fools gladly. He tended to exaggerate things. He took the longest goal-kick in the history of the game. He was playing at Crewe and he took a goal-kick and the wind was blowing. It blew the ball on to a passing train and it finished up in Southampton. He was supposed to be a very hard man. He'd gone down injured on his knee once and taken the skin off. It was full of matter, so he said, 'Just give us that wire brush,' and he just scrubbed it clean. Another tale was that when he was in the army he was taking bayonet training and they were coming right at him with their guns and bayonets. He'd knock each bayonet to one side and then say, 'Next,' and so on. Anyway one time he was not quick enough and the bayonet's gone right through his arm. So, he just pulls the bayonet out and shouts, 'Next!'

When I first came here Reuben was on his way out because Shanks had just left. He would come in and make the tea. He'd trot around, but he wasn't with any group of players. What he did do in those days was to go and assess the opposition. He'd always play in the games, the five-a-side. He'd always play upfront. I'd say, 'What's the most you've scored in a game, Reuben?' He'd say '27, John, 13 on the volley and the other 14 on the half-volley.' We were playing one game between the boards, and there was hardly ever a break. I said, 'What's the score Reuben, is it 15–3?' He replied, 'No, it's 16–3 John. Give 'em nothing.' I thought, what does it matter, 15 or 16! I realised one week why. One Friday morning, we were having a five-a-side game. Now these games were fiercely fought. My mate Tom Saunders was on the other side. I picked my side and I picked all the little ball players. Now the other guys were bigger. The ball goes out and Tom shouts, 'Our ball.' I said, 'No it's not, it's ours.' But then I said, 'It doesn't bother me, if you want it, have it.' From that throw-in they promptly scored and the next minute instead of it being 5–3 it's suddenly 5–5. And I'm thinking of Reuben, give 'em nothing! That's how quickly a game can change.

A greatly liked man was Reuben, very honest. A dour man who didn't laugh a lot. But when he spoke you took notice, he spoke with authority. If you were going over the top anywhere, you'd want Reuben with you, a man of integrity.

PETER ROBINSON

Guinness Export

The formation of the boot room, from my understanding, was down to Joe Fagan because Joe at that stage had a connection with the Guinness football team that played in Runcorn. They were a Merseyside team and because of that they started to send cases of Guinness and beer across to Joe. As a result, Joe started to entertain the visiting coaches and managers on a Saturday afternoon. So it was mainly Joe, Bob and Reuben Bennett in the boot room. It developed further as the years went on with Roy and others but I would have said that the founding members of the boot room were those three. Not Bill Shankly, other than to go to take Reuben away after games; Bill certainly was not a boot room man.

I think that the fact that they were sitting there having a glass of beer was probably quite foreign to Bill's culture. Bill wasn't a drinking person. The only time I can ever remember Bill having a glass of alcohol was on flights abroad. He wouldn't admit it but I don't think Bill was the best flyer. He would occasionally have the odd sweet liqueur but apart from that I never saw Bill have a drink.

Joe, Bob and Reuben would meet after the game and then they started to invite the visiting manager and trainers in. In those days of course there weren't the number that travel today. There would only be the manager I think, very few had an assistant manager initially and probably a coach and someone, whoever it might be, who ran on with the magic sponge.

It started to develop from there because they used to meet in the boot room during the week after training just for a chat. Why they met in there I don't know, but they used to sit on the skips that were in there. It was not the most comfortable place but it started then to develop further than being just a matchday room.

It really developed more under Bob than it did with Bill. It developed with the entertaining, especially when they gained access to the beer. They used to come up and see me and I used to give them a bottle of whisky as well. I say I did, the club used to give them a bottle of whisky, they had to entertain these visiting managers, etc.

The only office that anyone had on the managerial side in those days was Bill's so they would probably sit in there during the week with something on their knee and write up some sort of records on fitness or whatever. I don't remember Bill being in the boot room other than to pop in to take Reuben away or just to pop in to say to Joe or to Bob, 'We're in tomorrow to see so-and-so, or something' but Bill was not a member of what I would look upon as the boot room clan.

That's maybe destroying something of a myth but that is how I understood it. It was in existence before I arrived, of course. I came in 1965 and it was functioning before then but others that joined it were people like Tom Saunders. Albert Shelley was here as well. The one story about Albert Shelley and Bob that always intrigued me was that in those days the trainer wore a white coat during the week. He always had this white coat on. After Albert retired on the following Monday morning not a word was said, but Bob appeared in the white coat. He assumed the duties. I always remember seeing Bob in the white coat for the first time. I don't remember too much about Albert. But he was very respected and I could tell you that nobody ventured on what was his territory. The main people then were Bill and Reuben. Reuben was brought here by Bill. Reuben had been a former goalkeeper. He was an exceedingly strong man and took the majority of the physical training work, the running of the players, etc. And then there was Bob, and Joe running the reserve team.

Bill tended to see people in his office. He was a great psychologist, Bill. On match days he would operate in the corridors. Some of the things that happened were quite amusing. I remember him standing just inside the home team dressing room which is across, if you know Anfield, from the visitors' dressing room and we were playing Chelsea. They arrived and I remember, because I was in the area at the time, Bill apparently talking to someone else in the dressing room. But he was actually talking to himself because there was nobody there other than me. He was saying how the Chelsea players were so pale and white and were terrified of coming to Anfield. They were hearing all this when they arrived and I think it absolutely destroyed them. It was a wonderful sight. That was typical Bill.

PHIL CHISNALL

Busby and Shankly

I was born in Davyhulme in Manchester. I went to school at English Martyrs in Urmston, and played for Stretford Boys, just down the road from United, Lancashire boys and then England Boys. This was just before the Munich disaster. There were half a dozen clubs I could have gone to but it was always on the cards that I would go to United. I left school at Easter 1958, just after the crash, and signed for United immediately. They even took me down to the Cup Final when we lost to Bolton. Being a 15-and-a-half year old, I was never really aware of the mood after the disaster. I played about 50 games for United in the league.

I was at United until I was 22. I played in the Youth team and later made my debut for United at Everton when I was 19. Then in 1964 I went to Liverpool. They had just won the league and had some really great players. I played in Liverpool's first ever game in Europe, in Reykjavik. Mind you, I'd been around playing in Europe with United. When I went to Liverpool I was playing in the England Under-23s and I did hear from someone in the press that I would be going with the full squad to South America. It also came out that Shankly had made a bid for me. I didn't have to leave United, they didn't want me to go but at the time they had Nobby Stiles, Denis Law, David Herd and Bobby Charlton and I was not getting games at that level. Even players like Giles and Stiles were not getting games every week, so it was difficult. I think it was the journalist Derek Potter who told me that Shanks wanted me. Shanks had said that he fancied me as a player because I could do unusual things with the ball. So he came in and made a bid for me. I don't look upon it as a bad move. Things were different in those days. After a match, playing in front of 60,000 Ian Muir and I used to get a bus home. The queue would be up to White City and we'd be in the queue and everyone would be talking to us about the game. We were part of the community but now it's different.

It was the first time I had met Shankly. He came to Old Trafford to talk it over with me. He was a very enthusiastic Scotsman.
When he was in the company of Busby, you could tell that he
respected him. He treated him a bit like a god. Shanks always
looked up to him, down-to-earth blokes from the Scottish coal-
fields they were. Shanks was very funny in his own way and he
could get things out of people that others couldn't. Busby was
more of a father figure, Shanks was more about psychology. He
used to come up to Old Trafford regularly to see Busby.

It was the end of the season, I was getting married. The England full team was going to South America and I had been playing
for the Under-23s. The Under-23s were going to Israel. I was
either going to go with the Under-23s or the full team. Well,
when the Under-23s team was announced I wasn't part of it,
then I signed for Liverpool. I went to America with Liverpool
on a tour. I had been told I was going on the full England trip
but I didn't. I don't know what happened.

What I can remember about the boot room was after training.
It was unusual to have so many people involved in the training.
At United it was just Jack Crompton but at Liverpool there was
Shanks, Paisley, Fagan and Reuben Bennett. They all had their
kit on and were involved in the training. Reuben would do a
good warm up and then do the intensive training with the four
or five others who were there. They'd be pushing you all the
time, especially on the boards; it was hell. They'd be throwing
the ball at you from different angles on the boards. You'd do
that for two minutes and then they'd give you a minute's rest
and off you went again. They did lots of that but always with
four or five trainers involved. It was a lot harder than United.
Busby always said that if you were at United you had something
to offer so you played more off the cuff. When I went to Liverpool
I realised that theirs was more of a team game and that they
were fitter than any team in the league. It showed as they used
to steamroller the opposition. Busby might have been involved
in training at United but there were more at Anfield who were
involved every day.

After all the training we'd have a five-a-side. The juniors would play and then the reserves and finally the first team. Shankly of course had his own side with Paisley, Fagan, Ronnie Moran and Reuben Bennett. Now I think, and this is only my opinion, they used to get a lot of young lads coming down, particularly from Scotland on a week's trial or from Wales, or the south and what they used to do was pick five of them out and have a five-a-side against them. I always had the opinion that they used to test them out, elbowing and booting them.

Shankly always had to win, they'd be playing all day and they always ended up getting a very dubious penalty and Shanks would slip it in. Then it was, 'Right lads, that'll do.' End of game and he'd be looking to see their reactions. It was all very clever. See how they react to getting beat or elbowed. After that was over we went back on the coach to Anfield still with all the gear on. The trainers would then go into the boot room for a cup of tea and would discuss the morning's events.

PHIL CHISNALL
Shanks' Psychology

Shanks was brilliant on football. He used a lot of psychology and was very funny. I think he was a bit naive in worldly things. We were playing Fulham one day, I think we won 5–0 and it could have been ten. We overran them and after the match someone asks Shanks, 'What do you think of Fulham then?' He says, 'They're the best side we've played all year!' Now that's what he was like. In other words, it meant, what's the rest like? You were lucky to get in that Liverpool side. If he thought it was right to drop you, he would.

He was clever. I don't think he was ruthless and he would not think of himself as ruthless but he would do what he thought was right. I don't think players lived in fear of him. He was very funny. He was James Cagney. He loved *The Untouchables*, he loved people who were against the norm. He wouldn't stand for agents and so on, he wouldn't be able to handle them. He would dismiss them as nothing. On a Friday night we would go to

Lymm to stay in a hotel and someone would say, 'What time are we leaving, boss?' He would say, 'Well, what time is *The Untouchables* on?' That would decide when we left.

He was a terrible driver. You could hear him revving the car up and the gearbox would last about three months. He was in Liverpool one day going down a road with double yellow lines and traffic lights when he just stopped and went into a shop. A policeman comes up and starts taking details. 'What's going to happen now?' asks Shanks. 'Oh, you'll probably be fined,' says the policeman. 'Oh no,' says Shanks, 'you can have the car,' and he just walks off. It wasn't his, it was the club's, so he just wanders off and leaves it. It didn't worry him. He went against convention.

PHIL CHISNALL
Team Talks

Bob Paisley was a quiet man from a mining area, from adversity. He was a down-to-earth working-class bloke. Shanks would always refer to him. 'Isn't that so, Bob?' he'd say. They worked well together. One extrovert, one introvert; same as Busby and Murphy. You couldn't help but like Bill. Paisley would put that little bit in at the end, the tactical thought. He didn't say a lot but when he did it was worth listening to, no shouting or bawling.

Reuben Bennett was a hard man. He must have been 50-odd then. He didn't seem to eat a lot but he was so fit. He did all the training. I think Shanks described him at one time as the hardest man in the world. We were in America one time and something happened on the field. Reuben was giving it all, someone had tackled him and I always remember Shanks saying that he was tackling the strongest man in the world. He used to smoke like a trooper but he was very fit for his age. He just did the running and training, the warm-ups and exercises.

Some of Shankly's team talks you wouldn't believe. He came into the dressing room once and said, 'The Red Sea, amazing how it opened up.' We all looked at him and he went on about it for half an hour or so and then it was, 'Right lads, that's it.' And he didn't say anything about the match. He was charismatic, but he was also in awe of things. He didn't like cheats or anyone like that. He thought football was a religion. I remember him saying to the players once, 'This is your religion.' If you lost a match he would go quiet. He didn't like anyone having a laugh. He would be pacing up and down and he would be saying to Bob, 'Someone in there's having a laugh, Bob.' He didn't like that.

He wouldn't keep us in the dressing room on the day giving us a lambasting. There weren't many occasions anyhow when we were overrun. We were so fit, that's why we dominated for so long. We were fitter than anyone. As you know when you are tired you give the ball away, but we didn't because we were so comfortable on the ball. If you are blowing a bit and the ball comes to you, you're more likely to make a mistake. I think that's why we dominated so much. I think now everyone has come up to that fitness. Now it's all about skill. United have probably got as much fitness as anyone and with their added skill they are that much better. I was a lot fitter at Liverpool than I was at United. We used to lose half a stone in the morning at training, especially pre-season because we would then have to go out again in the afternoon.

We beat Leeds United in the Cup Final. We didn't have subs in those days. Gordon Milne had been injured so they took 12 of us down. And it was either Geoff Strong or myself who was going to play. I was playing in midfield then, I didn't play that many games. I was on the bench with Shanks for the Cup Final. It was raining and we were sat in that section under the royal box, in a kind of tunnel where there was all this whitewash on the walls. There were a load of coppers there also sheltering because it was really throwing it down. It was all a bit crushed and we were squeezed up against the wall. We had these grey suits on, just for the day out. We all had the same. Shanks was leaning on the wall and he got all this whitewash over his pants. I was watching the game, Cally went down the right wing, crossed and Saint knocked it into the net. But all that Shanks was interested in was this bloody whitewash which he'd got over his pants. 'Who scored that?' he asked, as he brushed his pants furiously. It was amazing, bloody amazing. He hadn't even seen the goal. 'Oh, St John,' I said. 'This bloody whitewash,' he went on. He wasn't interested. He didn't think they'd get beat, he thought they were invincible. He didn't say, 'Have Leeds scored?' He took it for granted that it was Liverpool.

Liverpool was the place to be in the sixties. Liverpool were a good side and so were Everton. They'd already won the league and they won the cup and then there was the music, the Beatles, Freddie and the Dreamers, and so on. Even the anthem they've got from Gerry Marsden. It was boom time, a vibrant place. Liverpool were winning things, the crowd was singing.

I remember when we played Inter Milan in the semi-finals of the European Cup. We were in this hotel in Italy. We were sat there having our dinner and he was listening. He said, 'What's them bells?' Anyway, it was a monastery up on the hill and every quarter of an hour the bells used to go. So he went up to see the monks and asked them to muffle the bells because he didn't want the players kept awake at night by the noise. They'd probably been ringing them for about a thousand years but he wanted them stopped. He even told Bob Paisley to get up there with some bandages and muffle the bells. Paisley apparently walked off and would have nothing to do with it.

EMLYN HUGHES

No Secret

The boot room was the very heart of Liverpool. It was where it all happened. Outside you had the Kop, but down there under the stands you had the boot room. That's where the manager and his coaching staff would be, before a match, after a match and during the week. That's where they hatched out their plans, plans that made Liverpool Football Club the greatest club in Europe. You'd see them in there and we used to wonder what they were up to, who they were talking about, who might be about to get the chop, and so on. I rarely went in there and you certainly didn't go in there unless you were invited. On reflection, I think it was more the coaching staff who hung out in the boot room. I don't remember seeing so much of Shanks down there. It was mainly Bob, Ronnie, Joe Fagan of course, Tom Saunders and a few others. And when Bob became manager it became even more important but he really was one of the boot room and he would still spend a lot of time down there.

It was just across the corridor from the dressing room, and as the name says it was just an old boot room, But of course it was more than that. Bob and the lads made it their home, their office. That's where they would go. They didn't have an office of their own, so I suppose they had to hang their coats somewhere and that place was the boot room. It became their base. Once training was over and we'd all had our baths, they'd tidy up and then retire to the boot room for a well-earned cup of tea and a natter. They'd chat about the things that had happened in training that day. 'So-and-so had done well, such-and-such a player looked tired, or so-and-so's injury needs a bit more treatment.'

They had a book as well and one of them would write everything down in the big book so that they would know for future reference what treatment had been given, what the weather was like, what they had done in training and so on. That was so important. Yes, if I have to say what was most important about Liverpool in my time there, it would be the boot room and the Kop. That's what really made the club tick.

I don't think there was any particular secret. There was no magic man down there. It was the people. They were so committed to Liverpool. They ate, drank and slept Liverpool, day in, day out. But more than that, they understood their football. They knew it inside out. Bob had been around since before the war and I don't think there was a better judge of a player than him. They had the knack of choosing good players. Of course, they got the pick of the bunch because everyone wanted to come to Liverpool but it's still easy to make mistakes and the thing about Liverpool was that they rarely made a mistake in the transfer market. Almost everyone who came turned out to be a good player and in many cases an even better player once they got to

Anfield and in the team. I can think of only a few players in my time there who did not make the grade.

It was good fun as well. I don't think I ever heard any arguments. They'd shout at us from time to time but you never heard them shouting among themselves. They each knew their jobs and they got on with it. There was a terrific atmosphere. Every morning they'd be having a go at one of us, taking the mickey, all the time taking the mickey. They never let you get too big-headed. That was the Liverpool way, keep their feet on the ground, even if they're an international. There were no superstars at Liverpool, they treated everyone the same, from the young apprentice to the England captain.

PHIL THOMPSON

Calendars and Boots

When I first came to Liverpool in 1969 as a 15-year-old, everything about the club impressed me. The boot room then did not have the great character, the great mystique, that it went on to have. In those early days Bill Shankly didn't spend too much time in the boot room, that wasn't his domain, it was more Joe Fagan, Ronnie Moran and Bob Paisley's place.

The amazing thing was that it was one of the few places in football where visiting coaches were invited in. People forget that our boot room was unique. It didn't happen at other places. Our coaches went to other clubs and just left after matches. Liverpool was one of the few places where you were invited to have a drink with the training staff, and discuss what had happened. Any problems that had occurred were forgotten about. That was the great thing about it. It was part of a learning process for a young man growing up as a young player and a young professional. Seeing the friction on the touchline and then forgetting about it when the game was finished. Liverpool were the only ones who invited people in for a cup of tea or a drop of Scotch as it was in those days. It was wonderful. It was a lovely way to do things. It was something other clubs began to do as they copied other things which Liverpool did on the field.

It was strange in those days when they started it because it was probably the most ill-equipped room at Anfield. There wasn't much in there, there was nothing to it, everything was quite easy and laid back at Liverpool. We had the kit room but it was quite orderly. In the boot room the only thing which looked organised were the boots which would be on the players' numbered pegs. There were old boots lying about on the floor, old skips, wicker basket ones and plastic ones. There were probably only two seats in the room. There were also metal shelves which would be full of rubbish. That took up an awful lot of room. Then there were the cupboards in the side which housed the most legendary books in football. They had entries for every day, every bit of treatment which a player had, the weather from day one, the state of the ground, warm-ups. Everything went in those books. Ronnie, Bob and Joe kept them. Everything was documented, but it was quite rough and ready. I think Ronnie and Joe would still have theirs. I did the same when I was a coach here and I still have those books in my house. And coming back here again this time, I still keep the books going, just to remind us. It would help us over injuries, how they got injuries, how they were treated, how they responded. At the start of each season they would look back and plan. The thing about the boot room was that they never stood still, they would move on, things would be changed. It was never a case of time stood still, it always moved on but gently. That way you never noticed. The best changes in business are those that go unnoticed, especially in successful business. The old cupboards which must have been painted 50 times in a beige paint also housed the lager.

One of the most important things that everybody looked forward to, especially the visiting coaches, was to come to the boot room. That had its own privileges. The big thing which everyone liked to come and see were the topless calendars. It was absolutely incredible. They'd come in, and they'd have a good look at these before the chit-chat began. Around November/December time they'd start arriving because people knew that the new calendars would go on the wall. Very popular with the apprentices who would sneak in for a look. They were behind the door and if you ever see any photos of the boot room you never see the calendars because no one was ever allowed to take a photo from that angle, it was always from one angle, always to the left. I have never seen a photo of the wall that had the calendars. In fact there are very few photos of the boot room at all.

A lot of discussions did go on in there, much of them spontaneous. It was never planned, ideas would just come about while the coaching staff were sitting in there. As a player you were not allowed in. I'm not saying we didn't go in. Sometimes you would get called upon by the coaching staff. You thought, 'Uh, uh, I must have done something wrong.' And usually you had. Or else you might not have been playing, so they would ask you in and ask your opinion, then you'd have a chat about it. Those were the only times you went in. Don't forget that there were a lot of personal things in there, scouting things. Things about players, match reports, things not for players' eyes. Now and then you might go in with another pair of boots. But you always knew that it was out of bounds.

ROGER HUNT

Shankly and Ramsey

Alf Ramsey was a great manager but in a different way to Shankly. He would do more tactically than Shanks. He'd talk about the game a lot more. Shanks was enthusiastic and talked a lot whereas Alf was quieter and would come and have a quiet word individually with you. He was a deep thinker. When I look back, and it didn't hit me until much later, but when you look through the England team that won the World Cup you've got a team there that were all 100 per cent men. They might not have been the best players in the world, and it was the same with Liverpool, but wherever you were, Uruguay, Scotland, Sweden, they would give everything. Character-wise, you knew they would not let you down. So in that way Ramsey and Shankly were similar, they liked players with character who were committed. They wanted people to put it in at 0–0, not when you were winning 3–0. None of them wanted players who would disappear in a game.

ROGER HUNT

Training Was Fascinating

Before Bill Shankly the training was okay but there was more running and longer stuff. When Bill Shankly came, nearly everything was done with the ball, even stamina training. Then they introduced the famous boards at Melwood. I don't know whose idea it was. They're just like a goal boarded up. You can do marvellous routines on them. For me as a goalscorer it was a dream. I could practise shooting with people laying balls into you at all angles, turning or you could have it for exercises for three players and it was also good for goalkeepers. At the end of all that you could use it for three-a-side or five-a-side games, which was very popular. We played a lot of these little games rather than the big practice matches. You could always tell that if they had us doing full-scale practice matches, we weren't doing very well. Everything was done with the ball. I once remember scoring a goal against Derby in a cup tie and Shanks afterwards saying that was because of the boards and the work we had put in there. He could see that. It was technique. The training was interesting, very interesting.

Reuben Bennett was what we called the warm-up man. He'd take the training to start off with, some gentle runs and exercises. All the time there was a bit of banter going and Reuben used to be having a bit of fun, giving it back. Bill Shankly, Bob Paisley and Joe Fagan would be wandering around in and among the lads but Reuben was in charge of that session. We'd have 20–25 minutes and then break up into groups and do different variations of exercises. But we didn't do much weights which they do a lot more of these days. We did quite a bit on set pieces although we were never the best at these.

ROGER HUNT
Discipline

There wasn't a lot of discipline problems. I don't remember anybody being fined for misconduct. I'm not saying there wasn't any misconduct but it only needed a word here and there. If another player wasn't pulling his weight the players themselves would have a word. If a new player came in and he wasn't doing things the Liverpool way, the other players, never mind the staff, would have a word. There was this kind of spirit in the club. Now every one of those players, and you can go through all of them, wanted to win things. They were all dedicated. The older professionals would go to the younger lads and say 'You don't do things that way here, lad.' But the youngsters never grew up that way anyhow because they had already been sorted out. Ronnie Moran was another hard task master who never gave you much praise. It was always a case of, 'Okay, you did all right there but don't rest back on your laurels, we've got another game next week.' That was the way the club went about it.

ROGER HUNT
Bob and Joe

When I first went to Liverpool my first few games as an amateur were in the A team and reserves. When I got into the first team Bob Paisley was the first team trainer. He was very helpful to me. He was a canny Geordie. He knew the game inside out. He wasn't the best communicator but he was brilliant. He could see things in matches and in players and he was particularly good on the injury side and treatment. Tactically he was very aware as well and I think tactically he put a lot of ideas into Shanks' mind. He'd been at Liverpool right from before the war. He spent all his career there and he was a real Liverpool type, loyal, down to earth. I always remember him giving me encouragement after I had finished my first game, telling me where I could do better and how to improve. He was very, very helpful.

The same can be said of Joe Fagan. He was in charge of the reserves when I first played. Bob and Joe were hard task masters but if you were doing your stuff they were terrific. But if someone was not pulling their weight or not giving 100 per cent they were down like a ton of bricks. They worked well together getting players ready for the first team. I think this is why the club was so successful. There was nobody trying to get somebody's job, nobody felt threatened. Shankly ruled it but the other three were utterly loyal to him. It ran throughout the club. The players had a will to win, they all wanted to do well.

ROGER HUNT
Anfield Characters

I signed amateur forms in 1958. I was still in the army then so it wasn't until I came out in 1959 that I signed full professional forms, in July. Phil Taylor was still the manager then, he was there until December. I got into the team while he was still the manager. The boot room, as we came to know it in later years, didn't really exist then although obviously some of the characters like Bob Paisley were around. He was then first team trainer and Joe Fagan was reserve team trainer while Reuben Bennett was the coach. There was also a character knocking about the boot room and the treatment room called Albert Shelley. He was quite a character. He was, I think, an ex-Southampton player. He'd been at Liverpool for years. He didn't rate the modern-day player and was always telling us how useless we all were. He was not connected with any specific team in Anfield. He was just a sort of dog'sbody, helping out wherever he could. There was also the groundsman, Arthur Riley. I think his father had been there before him. Then there was Eli and Sammy down at Melwood. In Phil Taylor's day this crowd would go into the boot room but there weren't the same kind of meetings going on after games. That didn't happen until some years later.

Everything changed when Bill Shankly came. We had new training methods, he got us new kit as well. All the training kit used to have holes in it. He started spending money on players. He obviously had a tremendous influence on the club itself but he didn't change any of the staff. Modern-day managers tend to bring their own staff in but Bill Shankly kept the same characters, he stuck with them and they were very loyal to him. He was very much about loyalty, particularly to his players. It was quite unusual that he didn't bring anybody else in.

I don't think Bill Shankly bothered with the boot room much. He also didn't like going in the treatment room. The treatment room was next door to the boot room. He didn't appreciate players being injured. If you were injured at Liverpool, you were forgotten. We had all the best equipment in the treatment room but he would not go if the players were in there. He just did not like to see injured players on the treatment table, they were no good to him.

I used to go into the boot room to pick up my boots. A lot of the apprentices would be knocking about there. It was part of their job to clean the boots and polish them up.

Reuben Bennett was very, very popular. I think he was an Aberdonian. He was a real hard man. He'd been brought down from Scotland. He was more of a fitness man than a coach, he concentrated on getting the players fit and the routines. That was his role. He became Bill Shankly's right-hand man. They would go away together watching matches; he would be a sounding board for Shanks. He was another man who was loyal and dedicated. He was very popular with the players. He used to tell us all these stories from when he was in Scotland, all grossly exaggerated!

In the afternoons you'd see him standing outside Anfield in shirt sleeves when it was ten degrees below. He used to say he didn't feel it. We went away to Majorca once or twice on end of season tours and Reuben, who liked a drink, used to say that he liked nothing better than to take the top off a bottle of Scotch and drink it until it was empty. He was always first up

when we were away and he'd say he'd cither been for a five-mile
run or a five-mile swim. He was a bit of a tall story man. I don't
think they were completely true although he might have believed
them himself. The one thing about Reuben however was that he
would not take any decisions; he liked to leave that to others.
A pal of mine, Mike Ellis the reporter, went to interview him
one day at Reuben's house and of course the whisky started and
all these anecdotes came out. There's Mike thinking he's getting
a great piece. Then when Reuben's finished he says to Mike, 'I
don't want any of this in the paper, you know.' But that was
Reuben.

RONNIE MORAN

Boot Room Apprenticeship

I joined the club in 1949 from school, as an amateur. We only
trained on Tuesday and Thursday evenings at Anfield. I was not
really a football follower then. It was not long after the war. I
couldn't get to games because of transport and during the war
there had been no real games. Football only started again in the
autumn of 1946. But we still didn't go to games because we
were playing football in the morning and afternoons. Sundays
were the same. I never knew I would be involved in football, I
just enjoyed playing it. I was playing for Bootle Schoolboys and
a scout came along and I finished up signing amateur forms for
Liverpool. A week later I was playing my last game for Bootle
Schoolboys when I was pulled aside and it was a scout from
Everton asking me to sign. I said, 'If you'd been here a week
earlier I would have signed for you.' So I had no allegiance in
those days, Everton or Liverpool. It's different these days.

I got to know Albert Shelley. He was first team trainer, but
he was a down-to-earth man. The training in those days was
vastly different. Then, when I started playing in the C team, then
the B and A team when I was 17, Don Welsh was the manager.
I was serving my time as an electrician with the Mersey Docks
and Harbour Board and Don offered me part-time terms in Janu-

ary 1952. You only had two weeks' holiday in those days and I would save my two weeks and come training at Melwood for the two weeks because they had just got Melwood in 1950.

When I first joined, Jimmy Seddon was trainer with the reserves. Now he was the old Bolton player who had played in the 1923 Cup Final for Bolton. I think he had three Cup winner's medals. The trainers hardly ever got changed in those days. They had their ordinary clothes on and they would either wear a brown coat or a white coat. They would walk around the track at Anfield, watching the training. One of the first things I learnt off Jimmy was 'look after your feet'. He had bad feet. Anytime he bought any shoes, he had to cut the sides out because of the bunions. So I did look after my feet. Jimmy took the reserves, Albert the first team. There was no boot room in those days.

I was club captain when Bill joined in 1959. Joe Fagan had come in 1958, Reuben Bennett in 1959 as chief coach, just before Bill came. Bob Paisley was coach then and Phil Taylor was acting manager. Don Welsh had finished in 1956. Phil had been on the coaching staff and he was promoted to acting manager. I don't think he was ever full manager, just acting manager. Bill arrived in December 1959. Bill must have known the strengths of Bob, Joe and Reuben because they were all kept on, not like happens now when a new manager comes in with his own staff. I was still playing when all these people started.

I would say that the boot room legend was created by Bob Paisley and Joe Fagan. All it was was a small room at the top of the passageway in the old stand where all the kit was kept where Joe and Bob packed all their skips, Joe with the reserves, Bob with the first team. After treatment had been finished in the afternoon they would have a natter and a cup of tea. It spread from there and after matches they would invite the opposition in. No matter whether they had won or lost they would invite the opposition in. There was no players' lounge in those days. It was a matter of finish the game, maybe a little talk, and then on to the bus and they'd be away by 5.30pm. They'd go in the boot room for a quick natter and maybe one of Joe's famous Export Guinnesses.

Then, when the new stand was built, the new boot room was

built. The boot room then moved down to the centre. There was a double door which was the drying room; all the kit was hung up in there. The small door adjacent to this led to the boot room. At first it was just one big room. On the left was a bench where the kids cleaned all the match boots. We had hooks put up at the end and boots would be put on them after the kids had cleaned them. After a while we had the room halved so that it would be a bit more private for us. The kids could clean the boots and that, and we could be in the main boot room. People coming in would have to knock on the door; players wouldn't just walk in, they always had to knock. No one was allowed in it, they could knock and come in if invited but they couldn't just walk in, even when I was a player.

I would describe Bill Shankly as a boot room person but he was not an originator. It was Bob Paisley and Joe Fagan who created it. Bill would not stay long after games. He would have his press conference after the game. He never got changed for the game, he was always smartly dressed. He'd meet the press outside, then they'd be away and Bill himself would be away by quarter to six, off home to his wife and kids. He wouldn't stay. He very rarely came into the boot room, even to say cheerio. I started on the coaching side in 1966 when Bill offered me a job but the boot room was going well before then. I'm not saying he wouldn't come into the boot room, we'd have meetings in there, but any top meetings would be held in his office.

A lot of clubs started getting boot rooms going. They saw ours, and I think we were the first, and they set their own up. Even Brian Clough used to come into our boot room after a game.

It didn't matter who we played or what the result was, even Central League games, we'd invite the opposition in. It wasn't just football people. Sometimes I've known 40 people in there, not too often, but maybe after a European game. We wouldn't talk about the actual game on that day, other things would be discussed, the old days, stories and so on. We were always generous, even though none of us like losing. Even if we'd lost at home, we'd say well done. The game's over, there's nothing you can do about it. The first thing was shake hands, then ask them to come and have a drink. If we'd won, we'd tell them they were unlucky. It was a case of us not getting big-headed. And this was the way we also treated the players.

We would listen to things. I was always taught here, not to try and take everything in. You have to be careful, some things are good, some not so good, you have to latch on to what is good. I think in the game nowadays the players get told too many things, do it this way, do it that way, you're not controlling the ball properly or whatever. I learnt from the likes of Shanks, Bob Paisley and Joe Fagan. We all thought on the same wavelength. We never had arguments or real differences of opinion. The man who had to make the final decision was the manager and I worked with all three of them as manager. When it was decided which way to do something, we did it. And if it didn't work we didn't turn round and say, 'Well, I told you it wouldn't work.' Once a decision was made you stood by it. He was the manager and you'd had your tuppence halfpennyworth and you stuck with it. We didn't mix socially. Shankly would go straight home after games or to the occasional game and certain functions. I never saw him drink. And the rest of us didn't mix socially either. We'd have a drink in the boot room but that was it.

One of the other things at Liverpool is that players had freedom on the pitch. If it was the wrong way you'd be into them, but if it was the right way it was fine. You like to see players thinking on the pitch. The good players would do things on their own. At other clubs they'd be saying, 'Oh, he shouldn't be doing that.' We had success because we had players who could do things off their own bat and didn't have to wait or be told to do this or that.

I think the bond with Bill Shankly, Bob Paisley and Joe Fagan was crucial. We'd all have our say in meetings and sometimes if you threw something in it was taken up. It wasn't a case of 'he's got no experience'. It was good because we were all of a kind. I remember when Bill first came here players were getting transferred right, left and centre. I used to room with Alan A'Court and we used to say to each other, 'I wonder when it's our turn?' What I learnt then was that I didn't need Bill Shankly to tell me to go out and enjoy my training. When I came on the coaching side it came home to me why I was kept on. We worked the way Bill wanted us to work: train hard, play hard. He didn't like players who didn't want to do the training. Some players don't give 100 per cent at training but there weren't many here. We didn't do anything out of the ordinary.

I'd train anywhere, I always enjoyed it. It was getting us fitter, making us better players and you only become better players by working hard and picking things up. Some players don't pick things up, they make the same mistakes week in, week out. It's the same on the coaching side. You can be drumming it into a player without being too dogmatic. It still goes on. Bill always said, play it simple. When we played two-a-side, three-a-side, five-a-side, he always stressed, play it simple, give it to the nearest player in your shirt or if a better pass is on, play it longer. It's no good playing it to the nearest player if he's got three players surrounding him. Certain people can't pick that up. The good players know what you're on about.

When Bill offered me the job he called me into his office. It was the end of the season and I thought, maybe a third or fourth division club might offer me something and I'd go there. But he asked if I would like a job on the coaching side. I'd never had any experience in coaching. What could I do? Well, he said, there's the kids. He said you can sign on as player coach. In those 18 months Joe Fagan kept playing me in the reserves, in midfield. Me in midfield! But what a great experience that was. As time went on I realised Joe Fagan knew what effort I put in on the pitch. I was a shouter and could transmit things to players on the pitch. Joe and me spoke the same language. We learnt things from one another.

RONNIE MORAN

Shanks at Lilleshall

We used to go to Lilleshall for a week. Shanks only went once. It was the managers/coaches' course. I'll always remember the first year we all went. There was Bill, Bob, Joe, Reuben and myself. We went down in the car and you had to report Saturday afternoon by 5pm. You had a general meeting with everybody. Walter Winterbottom was in charge and he had his staff coaches. Then we were split into four groups. You had a group leader and he'd have a natter for half an hour or so. You didn't do anything else then on a Saturday. It was really just a get-together with other managers and coaches; it wasn't a course where you had to pass an exam. But Bill only went the once. 'I'm staying here,' he said. The five of us were stopping at a nearby hotel we used to stay at for games at Wolves. The food at Lilleshall was all right but you'd be on 'jankers' as we called it. They had a rota where you had to take turns in washing up. Joe and I didn't mind it but Bill did. We started Sunday morning and we weren't in the same group. Bill was in another group. We broke off for lunch and because we weren't staying there we had to go in the café for our lunch and weren't with the main group. We'd have a sandwich. The course lasted from the Sunday morning until after lunch Friday. Sunday night and we're in the hotel: 'We're going home in the morning, Bob,' said Bill. We'd only been there a day. 'We can't go home now,' says Bob. 'Oh, I don't know,' says Bill, 'I'm fed up.' Any rate we stayed but Monday lunchtime he comes over and says, 'We're going this afternoon.' 'Oh no,' says Bob, 'we have to stay.' Anyhow to cut a long story short we went home on the Tuesday. We had to go together because we were all in the one car. We couldn't say no, so after lunch on the Tuesday, we got changed and buzzed off home. But Joe and I went back the next year. We enjoyed it, even though we did have to do the washing up and so on. We went for five or six years.

STEVE HALE
Mr Shankly

I first started covering Liverpool in a professional capacity as a photographer in 1970. I didn't come into much contact with Shankly early on but I was told that he knew everyone in the local media. He always put you through your own little apprenticeship. He played you on a long line for a while to see what you were made of, how you reacted to things. For example, he was always very, very good with appointments. If he said he would see you at 2pm, woe betide you if it was one minute past two when you got there. He would maybe keep you waiting to see how you reacted to him being late. I found all this out later from more senior colleagues in the business.

It was a long time before I dared to call him Bill. All the old timers called him Bill and I was in awe with them being able to get away with it. To me it was 'Mr Shankly'. I called him that for quite a few years. I was even taking that famous photo on the steps of St George's Hall and all the other photographers were calling, 'Bill, Bill, Bill' and I bellowed out, 'Mr Shankly, this way,' and I think that's why he turned: 'Who the hell is calling me Mr Shankly?'

I went to Melwood with an old reporter from Charlie Buchan's monthly football magazine. Shankly had come up from London and I introduced my reporter colleague to him. I said, 'This is Bill,' and I suddenly bit my lip and got worried but it was okay. I'd put my time in by then and after that I continued to call him Bill. He gave a lot of respect to people no matter what level of life they were and he expected the same back. He was from the old school. What fascinated me were his wonderfully polished shoes, it was his old army background. He had these steel toe caps and heels and you could hear him walking down the corridors. He was also always talking and you could hear him around the corridors or wherever.

I got my first glimpses of the boot room at this time. In those days the corridors were long, it was a bit of a rabbit warren. If your face was known you were given a lot of freedom. If you went to Anfield after training the players used to go back there to shower, change and have a bit of lunch. It was nothing to find the local media standing waiting in the corridors. It was very free, easy and happy. Insofar as I know nobody ever took liberties. It was nothing to walk past the old boiler room and see Joe Fagan or whoever sitting with a cup of tea talking to one or two of the reporters. Or you might see someone from the local radio station doing an interview. Now it's very different, it's all controlled and done in such a way that you know what you are going to get before you go in. There's not even any off-the-record stuff now.

The boot room was a small room, like an averaged sized bathroom in a semi. To one side there was some old steel shelving, like you would put together yourself. The seating was one or two proper chairs but mostly it was skips. There was a perspex board pinned to the wall on which the coaching staff used to write things on. Ronnie Moran told me once that after one good training session he went in there and wrote on the board 'just like Real Madrid' so that others coming in and out would see how good they were.

It was a very unassuming room. It's the stuff of legends now. In thirty years I only ever stood in it three times, when I was invited in. I didn't take it upon myself to walk in. Two were when they'd won the championship and the last was in the late eighties when Ian Rush came back to Liverpool from Juventus and he wanted some picture taken in there with some of the players.

TOMMY LAWRENCE

Hard Times

I joined Liverpool in 1955. There was a boot room then. It was where they used to do the commentaries after the match for the 5 o'clock *Sports Report*. I don't know why but they actually set up the old microphones in there. It was a genuine boot room even then with the boots set out on the walls.

Albert Shelley was from the old school. As soon as he saw you he would say, 'You'll never make it!' He was one of those kind of people. When I first started Albert used to have a ball and he used to paint it white every week. In those days there were no floodlights so when it was going a little bit dark in the second half they used to throw this white ball on. If it had gone over the stands I don't know what they would have done because it was the only white ball and Albert used to paint it every week. This was what it was like in those days. He'd sit there and he used to have a cigarette and paint this ball white. At twenty past four they'd throw it on the field. They used to say, but I don't know if it was true, that at the end of the season that ball would be about size seven because it was painted every week. It became so heavy by the end of the season because it had been painted so often. You wouldn't think it now, but they only had one ball.

The kit in those days was also unbelievable. We got the hand-me-downs in the fourth team. There were holes in the socks and so on. Albert also used to wear a white overall. He'd sit in the box and if a player went down injured he wouldn't get out. He'd shout at them, 'Gerrup!' He wouldn't bother at all. His favourite thing was that if he saw you in any different kind of clothes – and in the fifties, we used to wear winkle-pickers – he'd say 'You'll never make it son, you'll never make it!' I don't think he had a good word to say about anybody, he really was a grouchy old man.

TOMMY LAWRENCE

Injuries

Bob Paisley, lovely man Bob, I liked him a lot. He was very quiet. He wasn't good at expressing himself but he did know players, he really did. He was a good foil for Shanks. He got on so well with Joe and Reuben. For three men of that age they all got on really well. He was a funny fella, Shanks. He wouldn't let anybody else criticise you but he would. After a game if you'd had a nightmare he'd come in and he'd railroad you, really hammer you, then he'd walk out and tell everyone that lad had a great game. He would never ever criticise his players and that's why we liked him so much. No matter how bad you'd played he'd never criticise you in public. We did think he was a little bit mad but for us he was brilliant. If you were injured he wouldn't speak to you at all. If you got injured on the Saturday he would see you on the Monday and he'd say 'How is it?' and you'd say, 'Not so good.' That was it, he wouldn't speak to you again. He'd come in Thursday and say 'is it any better?' and if you said 'a bit better,' he wanted to know if you'd be all right to play. Then Friday would come and he'd walk in and he'd ask you, he'd never ask Bob, always you, and if you said 'No, I can't make it,' he'd say 'You don't want to play, do you?' and he'd just walk out. Then the next week when you were fit he'd say 'Aye, you did right there not to play.'

I only missed about two games in eight years. I got injured at, I think, Chelsea. I pulled a muscle when we had a game against West Ham and Jim Furnell came in for me. I couldn't play. And every day Shanks came in and wanted to know, was it any better than it had been the day before. What can you say? On the Friday morning he came in and Bob said, 'You've got to run round the pitch.' Well, you can't run with a pulled muscle. He was looking at me running round and round Anfield. He went inside then the next time I came round, Bob called me over. 'Come here,' he said. 'When you come round next time, just say you're fit. Then he's got to make the decision.' Bob knew I wasn't fit and deep down so did Shanks. So I ran around again and Shanks appeared and called me over. 'Come 'ere son, come 'ere, how are you?' 'I'm all right,' I said, 'I'm fit.' 'You're a f***ing cripple, you couldn't play for your life.' So the decision was made and he was quite happy then. Then the next week when I was fit again, he said I did right not to play.

If you'd had a bad game he said, 'Hey, Tommy son, a goal-keeper would have saved that,' and just kept walking. Then when he came back he said, 'Hey, Tommy son, you're allowed to use your hands, you know.' And he'd just carry on walking. Then when he was outside he'd say, 'Tommy Lawrence, aye had a great game.' Fantastic fellow.

I've never known a team that got on so well with each other. Everybody liked each other. Even now if we have a do, everyone turns up. I think in 1981 Liverpool were invited to Germany for some reunion and the England team was as well. I think eight of the England World Cup-winning side turned up but there were 18 of us. There was some team spirit.

We had a back four of Ronnie Yeats, Tommy Smith, Chris Lawler, and Gerry Byrne. They could all play but none of them were fast. They decided it didn't work the first game but they decided nobody would sell themselves in the tackle. I would play further out. I was frightened to death. We tried it at Melwood. 'Right, Tommy, you're not playing on the six-yard line. When the ball's on the halfway line, you've got to be on the eighteen-yard line. If the ball shoots through you've got to be out and kick it, a sort of stopper.' Well, I'm standing there and the Kop is giving me some stick: 'Get back on your line!' they're shouting. No goalkeeper did that in those days. I thought, oh my God. They worked out that no front man would be allowed to get by them, you had to get in front of them, jockey them as they all do today. Who actually decided this, I don't know. We did it at Melwood a few times, nobody was to sell themselves. If they got past you the next man was to come out and take him. There was always somebody behind you. There were very few people who beat us. I'd come out and kick the ball like keepers do today. The only time we struggled was when we were square and they'd shove the balls diagonally and I'd still have to go for them.

There were only about two players who could beat us and that was Jimmy Greaves and a little fellow called Tony Field who played for Blackburn and Sheffield United. They used to run across and then dart through. You didn't get sent off then either, so I could hit them. I used to bring them down. It was only a free-kick, you didn't even get a yellow card. You were saving goals 30 yards outside the box. If they pushed it past me I'd just hit them. Nobody bothered or took your name. These days I'd be sent off. But it worked. The reserves played that way as well. That's why they won the Central League about ten years on the trot. All teams played the same way. If I was too late and they scored I'd get all hell from the Kop for being off my goal line.

The training was the one thing they did change. On the first day back at training you had to run from Anfield to Melwood, train and run all the way back. You didn't have shoes like you have now, you just had pumps, running on hard roads. After two days of that you couldn't walk. We'd do that for the first two or three weeks. It really was hard. Then when Shanks came he said, 'You play on grass, so you train on grass.' He stopped all the running on roads right away. So with Shanks at Melwood we then started doing quick training. We'd just do lapping around the track, little shuttle runs. I don't know where they went, him and Bob and Joe, but he came back with all these new ideas. We seemed to be the only club doing that then. He didn't like Lilleshall, he didn't like boards with diagrams on them or somebody posh talking about football, that wasn't Bill.

I remember America in 1964. We were there for ten weeks and Shanks lasted about ten days. We were in this hotel room this night, it must have been early because we were going out. You could hear Bill because you could hear him everywhere. He was on the phone to Nessie. He was saying, 'Nessie, Nessie, I'm coming home. These Americans know nothing, know nothing about football. You know, they've never heard of Tom Finney!' And he went home the next day.

His favourite TV programme was *The Roaring Twenties*. He always thought he was James Cagney with his hat and that. He used to walk like Jimmy Cagney used to walk. We came back from America and it must have been the start of the season and he said, 'I want to see you all in my office, everyone who's been to America.' So we thought, 'Oh hell, what's happened here?' He had all the old photographs of these old gangsters, Bugsy Malone and so on, all around the wall. He'd collected them in America.

He loved Matt Busby. He thought Matt was fabulous, he really did love him. We were away somewhere and Roger Hunt and I were out and Matt was there and he didn't know Bill had been ill. I didn't know him from Adam but he knew us, he was like that, Matt. Anyhow, he bought us a drink, and said, 'How's

Bill?' And then he said, 'He's got to get another outlet than football, you know. It's all building up inside him.' And it was.

I remember one year he didn't come back. He was a lot younger then. He didn't turn up for pre-season training for a fortnight. Nobody ever knew what was wrong. He never turned up, we never saw him at all.

TOMMY SMITH

An Old Cardigan

To me the boot room was like an old cardigan or a worn out pair of slippers. It was something you felt comfortable in. We all wear an old jumper from time to time, or stick with a battered old hat. People might say, 'What in the name of God is that you're wearing?' But so what? There are men all over the country who hide away in the shed at the bottom of the garden. The boot room was the shed in the heart of Anfield, a place to get out of the way from the pressures of the day, have a beer and a chat and generally relax. It became a national institution, but this was to do with the aura of success that surrounded Liverpool rather than this room in which you couldn't swing a cat. It was actually two rooms, accessed off the corridor leading to the dressing rooms. The small outer room was the place where the kids cleaned the boots. At the back was the tiny inner room which had all the boots hanging on the wall. It contained one or two lockers for the staff, being a safe place where you could leave your things. Like at any factory or office you need somewhere to get away from the job. The boot room became a very private place, and even the most senior of players were not allowed in. You'd knock on the door to ask one of the staff a question and be told to go away in no uncertain terms. They would actually lock the outer door so there was no way in.

This was the place where the senior coaches could sit together and have some time without being disturbed. Some people might try and tell you that it was like some military bunker in which the great battles were plotted. You get this image of maps on the walls, pinpointing ships and aeroplanes. I can assure you it was nothing like that at all. There would be times when players were discussed, both ours and possible signings. But this was not the main function of the boot room. It was more of a place to take it easy and wind down.

When I was club captain I was always very nervous about going and knocking on that door. I just kept away because I knew that was what the staff wanted. Even Bill Shankly did not go in there too often although he was the man who encouraged it and first started to talk about the boot room boys and their importance to Liverpool. I felt it was a privilege when I was first invited in, but by then I was much older and on the back room staff myself.

WILLIE MILLER
Paisley, The Knowledge

When I'm doing the dinners with the likes of Tommy Smith or anybody, they always say that Bob Paisley was the most knowledgeable man they had ever known on football. For example, if a player took a knock and went down injured, Bob Paisley sitting from the dugout could look across and say, cartilage, six weeks. And that's before the trainer got on there with the bucket and sponge. His whole life revolved around football and he just seemed to be totally aware of what was going on although he couldn't convey that into words. Apparently his team talks were a riot. But he knew exactly what was going on. I think that was part of the success. I don't think he's ever had the credit he deserves. For example, Shankly was the motivator and everything else but I think a lot of it came down to Bob Paisley's knowledge. This is stuff I've learnt from the players, I know. At the time nobody knew because Liverpool kept everything very much to themselves. For example, the signing of players. You never knew they were in for a player. It just seemed to happen overnight. Not like now where they are linked all the time with this player and that player.

WILLIE STEVENSON

Reuben the Hard Man

I joined Liverpool in 1962 from Glasgow Rangers. I found the experience a little bit odd because Rangers had a very rigid structure. You couldn't just go and say, 'I want to see the manager'. You didn't see him around the stadium very often. You had to make an appointment with the secretary downstairs to see Scot Symon who was then manager. At Liverpool Shankly was there the whole time. He was up and down the corridor, he'd be in the dressing room, in the boot room, you always had access to him unless you had a personal problem when you would speak to him privately.

The boot room was like a sanctuary to Bob Paisley, Joe Fagan, Reuben Bennett and some of the players because it was the one place Bill Shankly didn't go in particularly often. It was a sanctuary to Bob Paisley in particular. I don't know whether he did this on purpose but Shankly did seem to avoid it. Of course Joe Fagan, Bob Paisley and Reuben could go there and have their little chat. If it had been anywhere else Bill Shankly would have been straight in. It was their sanctuary where they could escape. They would discuss things about players, who they'd like to get and so on, amongst themselves.

We used to go in there, especially after a midweek game if we had done particularly well, and have a few beers and a laugh. You wouldn't find the whole team going in but there would be one or two of us. We had a players' room but that was only about ten foot by ten foot and the sandwiches had been made the day before. The tea was bloody cold as well, nothing like they have nowadays. So we used to sneak into the boot room. 'Is it okay?' 'Yeah, come on in,' and we'd sneak a bottle of beer or two. This was Joe Fagan's export Guinness. It was fairly well stocked with beer. Of course on a Saturday all the players had their wives and friends and you couldn't invite them into the boot room so we would go into the players' lounge.

After I had left Liverpool I went back a couple of times. I can remember Bob Paisley being in there once and I asked him direct, 'Bob, why did you let me go from Liverpool? What was the reason?' And all Bob would say was, 'You'd lost your sparkle.' I knew that he was right but it took me a long time to take that in. He was right, I had lost it. I was not the same at Stoke as I was at Liverpool.

Bob Paisley was there and Reuben Bennett as well. Reuben was as hard as nails. He didn't tolerate wimps too much. He considered any feeling of pain or hurt was soft. One time we were in Blackpool. It was really, really cold. I think it was the 1965 winter when all those games were off. We were on the beach playing in snow and the water was iced out to about 30 or 40 feet. Anyhow one of us kicked the ball into the water and Reuben says, go and get it. We told him to bugger off. So he called us a load of wimps and promptly proceeded to run into the sea, swim out, get the ball, and come back and carry on playing. He only had shorts and a T-shirt on. We all had balaclavas, hats, gloves, pullovers. He called us a load of wimps, that was Reuben. Very strong man, strong willed, and he imparted that sometimes more than Shankly did. He was close to Shanks, both being of course Scotsmen.

The magic of the boot room was the characters in it and the amount of verbal stick that went on between them; you had to be quick. Sometimes they could be insulting with a nice smile on their face. The repartee was good. Sometimes Bob and Shanks would say things that they didn't realise were funny. But they were and you had to be careful not to snigger too much. I enjoyed it on the occasions when I went in although I probably went in on more occasions after I left Liverpool. It was an honour to be invited in because invited you had to be, you couldn't just walk in. Managers and the trainers would come in and see Bob, discuss what had happened, what they were doing. They were all quite friendly. All this nonsense about clubs hating each other is just not true.

On the occasions that I went Bob would always be in the boot room. He'd be there with Joe and all the staff. I think Bob enjoyed it in there. He probably felt more at home there than in the office.

CHAPTER TWO

The Paisley Years

In hindsight it was obvious who should succeed Bill Shankly as the next Liverpool manager. There was really no other candidate other than Shankly's number two, the avuncular Bob Paisley. But at the time it was not quite so cut and dry. As Peter Robinson admits, the board did puzzle over a successor; the appointment of Paisley was never a foregone conclusion. There was a view that the club ought to be looking to an experienced manager. Indeed Paisley's name did not even crop up initially. In the papers a variety of names were bandied about including Gordon Milne and Malcolm Allison. Even Shankly was never sure. It was said that when chairman John Smith spoke with him about a successor, Paisley was never suggested until a good half hour into the conversation when Smith raised his name. 'Aye,' replied Shankly, 'that's a good thought.' The appointment of Paisley as his successor had never occurred to him. The fans were also anticipating the arrival of an outsider; it had never occurred to them either that Paisley should step up. They didn't know much about him except that he was the man who raced on the pitch with the magic sponge when someone went down hurt.

Fortunately good sense prevailed and within weeks Paisley was installed as the new Liverpool manager, his first major task to lead Liverpool out at Wembley in the Charity Shield. It's said that on his first day in the job, he called all the players together and told them in that rich north-east accent of his, 'Ah neva wanted the job, but you've got me and that's it.' A new regime was to begin with the boot room about to become the focal point of the club.

Bob Paisley had been born in the small mining village of Hetton le Hole in Durham in January 1919 where, as he was fond of telling people, coal was king and football was a religion. The mines provided the employment, football the fun. But the football was also an escape route from the mines, their continual danger, pitiful wages and the inevitable pneumoconiosis. By the age of 14 Paisley had signed schoolboy terms with Wolverhampton Wanderers but as they hesitated over offering anything better, Paisley left school and followed his father into the mines. It was to be an experience he would never forget. Three months later his father was stretchered out of the pit and could not work for another five years.

Ironically, the Hetton pit was closed within a matter of months and young Paisley promptly found himself on the dole but by chance he soon found work as an apprentice bricklayer, a trade which was to come in handy years later at Anfield when he helped build the dugout. It wasn't long either before Bishop Auckland, the most famous north-east amateur side of all, signed him up. He was to spend two years with them, even winning an FA Amateur Cup medal before Liverpool jumped in with an offer in May 1939. Paisley had little hesitation in travelling south to sign up but by the time he arrived at Anfield, Britain was on the verge of war, and he would soon be signing up for a new employer.

The new season lasted only three games before Prime Minister Neville Chamberlain addressed the nation that fateful Sunday morning to tell them that 'As from midnight Britain was at war with Germany.' Within 24 hours football had been cancelled and within weeks Paisley had enlisted in the army ready to play his part. He served in the war, mainly in the Middle East, as a gunner, but also in South Africa and finally as part of the liberating army that swept across Italy. At Anfield he was commonly known either as 'gunner' after his exploits or 'rat' because of his Desert Rats connections.

When war ended he was back to Anfield to pick up where he had left off. Six years older, he went virtually straight into the first team, missing only the opening two matches of the 1946/47 season. By the end of the campaign he had landed his first medal as Liverpool clinched the championship. It was to be his only medal as a player. He might have picked up a loser's medal in the 1950 FA Cup Final but Paisley, despite hitting the opening goal in the semi-final against Everton, found himself relegated to the stands when it came to Wembley. Typically, he shrugged his shoulders and just got on with it. If nothing else it would teach him a valuable lesson. He managed a further four seasons but by 1954 he was 35 years old and was beginning to think about his future. Liverpool had just crashed into the second division and the omens did not look too good. It was the older players who were most likely to feel the cold wind that might blow through the club.

Paisley might easily have moved on somewhere else but the then manager Don Welsh had something in mind. Taking him aside one day shortly before the end of the season, Welsh wondered if he would be interested in doing some coaching at the club. Paisley had nothing else in mind other than playing out his days in the third division north or returning to his old trade as a bricklayer, so he accepted with more than a smattering of enthusiasm. The pay wasn't quite as good as he might get at Tranmere, Workington or Chester but the prospects looked more long term. Welsh would last only another two years in charge at Anfield, but in Bob Paisley he left a fine legacy that would take the club to glory over the next three decades.

Paisley's coaching responsibilities varied but in his earlier years he was primarily in charge of the reserve side. He would also follow up his interest in physiotherapy by taking a course at one of the top Liverpool hospitals. And, as many testify in these pages, Paisley could spot an injury on a player a mile away. Indeed he was to become acclaimed for his astute comments to opposition managers about injuries being secretly carried by their own players. They would look at him in astonishment that he had been able to detect an injury they either knew nothing about or had been trying to hide from the public. What's more, his training taught him how to deal with those injuries, and although it may seem outmoded by today's standards, Liverpool at the time had one of the finest physio setups in the league.

Liverpool spent most of the fifties trapped in the second division, never quite able to escape. They'd make the running every season until Easter and then they would panic and slip out of the promotion chase. It was appallingly frustrating. In August of 1959, just a few months before Shankly arrived, Paisley was promoted. Albert Shelley was officially retiring although he would still be spotted around the dressing rooms for another ten years and Paisley was asked to take over as first team trainer. Scotsman Reuben Bennett was brought in as chief coach while Joe Fagan ran the reserves.

The arrival of Bill Shankly later that year interfered little with the running of the club. Paisley took on slightly more responsibilities as he became increasingly involved with the first team, and in time, would be seen as Shankly's number two. But it is doubtful if that promotion was ever officially recognised. The only titles anyone cared about at Anfield were those with 'league' attached to them. It was not their style to worry about who was number one, two or even three. Everyone mucked in together. That in itself was one of the strengths of the boot room, everybody felt secure in their job. There were no threats and equally there were no personal ambitions. Nobody was looking for promotion or trying to outdo anyone.

Throughout the successful years of Shankly, Bob Paisley was always at his side, giving out the occasional advice, or more importantly resolving any problems. It was Paisley who would deal with domestic and private problems, discipline or whatever, rather than worrying the boss with such trivialities. Shankly never knew the half of what went on. If there were problems they had been long solved before Shanks ever got to know about them.

Paisley set up office in the boot room. It was somewhere where he and Joe Fagan and later Ronnie Moran could lock themselves away and have a quiet natter and a drink. Shanks didn't come down too much and the players never bothered them. They could close the door and if any of the players did come knocking they told them where to get off. It soon became their hidey-hole, their escape from the continual noise and demands of the dressing room.

While Shankly may have been the charismatic leader, Paisley was the tactical genius, though at the time few probably appreciated his input. There were few rivals with his knowledge of the game and the club's successes in later years would prove his genius. But in Shankly's time he would make the occasional aside while sitting in the dugout . . . 'maybe we should switch so and so into the middle, push up such and such a defender, or close down so and so.' More often than not Shankly would act on his word. Shanks would also send him on scouting missions, either to watch the opposition or to run the rule over potential signings. Few managers in the game had a better eye for a player than Paisley and with Geoff Twentyman as chief scout, the club had the two finest sets of eyes in football. The trophies tumbled in and then sensationally Shankly decided he had had enough.

Paisley admitted that Shankly's retirement was one of the biggest shocks of his life. It was so unexpected; he had never even talked it over with his colleagues. It came like a bolt out of the blue. Shankly had had his arguments with the establishment at Anfield but that was nothing unusual. He was a tempestuous character, always likely to fly off the handle, sometimes unpredictably. Even in his autobiography Paisley admitted to not knowing why Shankly quit so dramatically.

A few weeks later chairman John Smith asked Paisley to take over as manager. For a moment he hesitated. He didn't really want the job but someone had to do it. Shankly would be a hard act to follow but for the sake of the others in the boot room it was probably better that he did it than see anyone else drafted in. That would have meant new faces, new methods, uncertainty. And so, in June 1974 Bob Paisley was officially appointed manager of Liverpool Football Club.

Like Shankly before him, Paisley of course had his own office, but, unlike Shankly, he chose instead to spend most of his time with his old pals down the corridor in the boot room. It was where he felt happiest, mucking in with Joe, Ronnie, Tom and the rest. They carried on almost as if nothing had happened. But of course, it had. Shankly had gone and Paisley, the man in slippers and cardigan, was now the boss. And one of the first things he did was to promote Roy Evans into a more senior position. It was a case of everyone moving one rung up the ladder. Joe Fagan effectively became Paisley's number two with Ronnie Moran also moving up while John Bennison joined the coaching staff on a full-time basis to work with the youngsters alongside Tom Saunders. The coaching staff was Liverpool through and through with a combined total of almost 200 years' service to the club.

Over the next nine years Liverpool would go on to unprecedented success. They had already picked up three league championships, two FA Cups and the UEFA Cup under Shankly but Paisley would better even that by winning a total of six League titles, three European Cups, three League Cups and one UEFA Cup. The only trophy which would elude them was to be the FA Cup. It was to be an astonishing record that has never been bettered by any league manager.

And all the time the boot room ticked over like clockwork. Nobody can ever remember any rifts or major disciplinary problems. Often it was the players themselves who solved those dilemmas. A senior professional would be detailed to go and have a word with whoever was causing unrest. 'This is Liverpool Football Club. We don't do things that way here,' was the usual blunt message passed on to the victim. Throughout the period the boot room became more the fulcrum of the club. Shankly tended to keep out of the way, whereas Paisley was always down there, having a cup of tea or something a bit stronger and mulling things over with its incumbents, especially after training. They'd return to Anfield after the morning session at Melwood, sort players and injuries out, have a spot of lunch and then maybe settle down to record the day's work in those volumes they kept. Each day they would meticulously write up their training schedule, what they had done, the weather, any injuries and so on. Over the years they were to provide a valuable insight into their working methods. It wasn't just superstition that made them write things up each day, they had a genuine purpose.

After Joe had written the books up, they might settle down to chat about the forthcoming game, what treatment to give an injured player or maybe mull over a possible signing. Chief scout Geoff Twentyman would often drop in and they'd talk about the player he had been detailed to go and look at. Was he a serious prospect, should anybody else go and look at him?

It also became a tradition to invite their opposites into the boot room for a drink after the game. Managers and a coach or two would join Fagan, Moran and company for a whisky or beer. Paisley would nip in for a quick chat but on matchdays he had other responsibilities such as talking to the press, keeping the sponsors happy and chatting to the directors. It was a busy time for him.

But not so much for the boot room boys who would congregate in their room and would always begin by congratulating their opponents on their performance. Whatever the score, they always had something positive to say: 'you were unlucky, you played well,' and so forth. It was not their style to gloat. And yet all the time they would be gathering intelligence about their opponents, finding out how such and such a player was overcoming an injury or whether a youngster they'd been tracking in their reserves was really any good. Could he really use his left foot? What was his character like? But the seemingly generous hospitality offered usually had an ulterior motive. It was Lawrie McMenemy, the former manager of Southampton, who sussed out what was going on. He realised that as they plied him with drink they were also interrogating him in the subtlest of ways, making vague inquiries about a player's fitness or tapping his knowledge of players. 'Ah see you've got a good young lad called whatever. Ah hear he's coming on well?' was the kind of innocent question Bob Paisley might ask. Before he realised what he was doing, McMenemy had given them the run-down on the lad. After he'd gone they'd note it down somewhere and maybe, or maybe not, get one of their scouts to check out the youngster. In more rarefied circles they would call it intelligence gathering. 'God knows how many secrets I gave away,' he admits today. The questions may have seemed innocent enough but they usually had a motive.

Paisley strengthened his team with a magical touch, producing quality players like a conjuror pulling rabbits out of a hat. When Shankly's favourite, Kevin Keegan, left for Hamburg, Paisley plucked Dalglish out of Scottish football. Then came Graeme Souness, Alan Hansen, Mark Lawrenson, Steve Nicol, Ian Rush and many more. World-class players all of them. Indeed it's hard to think of any Paisley signing who did not make the grade. And for that credit also has to go to Geoff Twentyman. Ian Rush, for one, was signed on Twentyman's recommendation alone; Paisley did not even bother going to see him. There was complete trust.

At the end of the 1982/83 season Paisley retired. Typically it was with another two trophies, the League championship and the League Cup. After Liverpool beat United in the League Cup at Wembley, captain Graeme Souness ushered Paisley up the steps ahead of all of them to collect the trophy, such was the esteem and respect they held for their manager.

STEVE MORGAN
Sir Bob Paisley

It was a tremendously inspired decision to appoint Bob Paisley. I think Alex Ferguson getting his knighthood was very justified and very deserved and I congratulate him. I think he's done a fabulous job for Manchester United, but compare it to what Bob Paisley did for Liverpool – where's *his* knighthood? It's a disgrace that Bob Paisley was never recognized. They should make him a lord posthumously. Bob was quiet, efficient and, in many ways, ruthless. He didn't have Bill Shankly's charisma, Bill Shankly was a man of the people. If he walked into any room there would be absolute silence. People just wanted to hear every word he said. I can remember coming back on a train from an away match, it was just an ordinary league game against Chelsea on a Saturday afternoon. The Liverpool players were on the same train and I would have been about 14 at the time. I went down to try to get the players' autographs. In those days the carriages were like separate compartments. I never thought twice about going in the players' carriage, it was just 'Hi Roger, hi Saint.' But with Bill Shankly I was so nervous going into his carriage, I was shaking going in but I went in there and was with him for ten minutes. It's a treasured memory up to this day, such was the aura about the man. With Bob Paisley his feats, his achievements speak for themselves. They'll probably never ever be beaten in English football but Bob just quietly got on with it. I don't think he ever looked for accolades, he never sought the personal attention but just did the job. There was a difference in style and a difference in personality but he was hugely efficient.

IAN CALLAGHAN

Shanks And Paisley: Different Types

Although Bob Paisley always seemed to be super cool, deep down it wasn't always so. He was the kind of person who hung his emotions on his sleeve. And you could best spot this in the dressing room before kick-off. By 2.45pm you could tell what he was going through by just looking at his face. He would be pacing up and down the dressing room taking sips of water. He looked more nervous than the players, although he did his best to try and not show it. I don't think everybody realised that but I could see it.

He was a bit of a father figure to me. He was a good guy, someone you could go to with your problems. He was different to Bill Shankly in many ways. You couldn't always go to Shanks with your problems. But Bob would listen to your problems and offer you advice, you felt that you could talk to him. But it wasn't always so with Shanks. He seemed so important and never really understood people's problems. You weren't supposed to have problems. You also treated the two men differently. For instance, if you were messing about in the corridors, having a laugh, you immediately shut up if Shanks came by. But Bob was much more easy, he was a friendlier type of guy, he wasn't so authoritarian.

He was brilliant at man management. He realised that everyone was an individual and knew that some people would respond to a kick up the backside whereas others needed more understanding and an arm around their shoulder. I went through a particularly bad time at one point after a cartilage operation. I remember Bob pulling me to one side after a game and saying, 'Give it time. I know you're giving 100 per cent. Don't worry, it will come.' That was good. He knew I was feeling bad and to know that he understood and was backing me was so important. Nevertheless he could lose his temper and have a go at people, but it was always behind closed doors. We never let our rows go public. That was the way of the boot room. Keep everything in house. The players appreciated that.

He was a very uncomplicated guy, very different to Shanks who was such an extrovert. Paisley was more of an introvert. He never wanted the job and I don't think he ever came to terms with it despite all the success. In the end I think he was glad to retire and take a back seat.

ALAN KENNEDY
Boot Room Characters

I came to Liverpool in 1978. Bob Paisley had paid a record British transfer fee for a full-back and it was a big investment in those days because I think they'd just bought Kenny Dalglish a year earlier for £440,000 and I cost £330,000. That was an awful lot of money for Newcastle to get and for Liverpool to pay. So when I came to Liverpool, Bob Paisley said that you are joining a team that's just won the European Cup twice on the belt, you're joining a team that's hopefully going to win trophies. For me a great guy. I treated him like a father or a grandfather because his family were from the same area of the north-east as my family were and even the same village. I felt as though I knew him personally and I think he took it upon his shoulders to look after me for the first part of my time at Liverpool. I didn't like living in the city centre, I preferred living with a family. So after about eight or so months I ended up living out in the wilds really, with another family whom I met in Liverpool.

Bob took me into the ground and it was awesome going into the changing rooms and seeing such great players as Kenny Dalglish, Graeme Souness and Alan Hansen. In those days I looked up to every player on Liverpool's books. I thought, I'm joining a club that's rich in history, rich in trophies and I'm going to try to stay here as long as possible. Those were my thoughts at that moment in time, to stay at Liverpool as long as possible. But I felt as though I was always under pressure from various quarters. On the pitch there were a lot of players that I had to dislodge from the team, one of them being the great Joey Jones. People loved him, the Kop absolutely adored Joey, maybe not so much for his skilful technique of trapping a ball or passing a ball but for his 100 per cent passion for Liverpool Football Club. To replace somebody like him was always going to be difficult. Also in the team and playing full-back and centre-back was Emlyn Hughes. Emlyn was the captain and to displace him was always going to be difficult but I felt that if I got my head down and listened and learnt from Ronnie Moran, Joe Fagan and Tom Saunders I might succeed.

Reuben Bennett used to take the first team and he was instrumental in getting me settled in at Liverpool. He was the one who would tell me to get my boots on, hurry up, don't dilly-dally, get on the bus, get down to Melwood, get your training done. We called those words of encouragement but he was giving us a bit of stick really, saying, 'You lazy sods, you shouldn't be in the first team, you should play in the reserves for a couple of years before you actually attempt to get in the first team.'

Tom Saunders was doing a bit of scouting at the time and he used to go and watch the teams that we were going to play; he used to come back with a report but he'd only be away from Melwood for about a day or so. So he had plenty of time to come along and just observe and see how things were going. Generally speaking he used to get together with Bob Paisley and just have a little chat over things. How the performance on Saturday went, what the opposition is going to be like for the next game, and he would then offer his opinion to Bob as to how Liverpool should play. Bob would then have words with Joe Fagan, his assistant and Ronnie Moran, his coach. I am sure if he needed any help there were one or two others of the back room staff who would offer a hand as well.

Tom, I think, would help and give advice about the coaching, not help with the coaching. I think he was a little bit past his best when I first joined the club. But his advice was as good as being out there on the pitch, he was always helpful in his manner.

If you asked him any question on how you should develop your football game he would give you an answer, but I think because of his health he was more concerned about Liverpool off the pitch rather than on the pitch. It was Bob Paisley's job to get it right on the pitch and certainly Tom used his influence and experience to guide Liverpool through that period.

John Bennison took the youth team and the A and B teams and any other teams that Liverpool actually had at the time. John was an infectious character, a very funny man in a way but his basics were the Liverpool principles, what he'd learnt over the years. When Liverpool are not in possession of the ball you've got to get it and when you get possession of the ball you've got to keep it. The simple rule that Bob Paisley taught myself and every other player was to give and move and not let the opposition get the ball. John established a great youth team and then that helped the reserve team win the Central League ten times out of twelve. I remember Brian Kettle, who was the captain of the reserve team, saying how proud he was of that record. It was unheard of for Liverpool not to be in the top four or five again because the first team were doing so well and those players who played in the reserves knew their time might come to play in the first team. They had some great reserve team players: Steve Ogrizovic, Howard Gayle, Alan Harper and Bobby Savage. What John and Roy Evans did was to engineer the team around the better players. Every so often one of the first team players might come back and play in the reserve team. I had that quite a few times. A lot of players who came to Liverpool didn't start in the first team, they started in the reserves. It was up to John, Roy and any back room staff to help them through those early times.

I found it a great help that you had so many staff that could offer a word of advice. Right down from the manager to the youth team trainer, everything would be the same. They had this little book which they'd write things in every day – what happened ten years ago, what happened 15, 20 years ago.

ALEC LINDSAY
A Goal Disallowed

In the 1974 FA Cup Final I had a goal disallowed. I'm not one for hogging the limelight, that's not my scene. It didn't matter who scored as long as it was for us. But this was a one-off. Everything felt right as I just whacked it and it went in. It was the first strike on target. And everybody's going mad. There's me, Kevin Keegan, everybody celebrating; little did we know the linesman had his flag up. They'd taken the free-kick and were up the other end. They said Keegan was offside. It was like a one-two. I'm taking the ball up. Bobby Moncur was marking Keegan. I pushed it to him and they're more or less level but instead of Keegan laying it off to me he never even touched it, it hit Bobby on the shins and it bounced straight back into my path. Keegan couldn't have played it any better. I'm running on to it, I'm hitting the right stride and I just whacked it, edge of the box. It shot over Ian McFarlane right into the net. I'm jumping up and down. They quickly took the free-kick and nearly scored while I'm down the other end. We were just starting to get on top. We started playing, just pushing it about after that, and won 3–0. Malcolm Macdonald played in that game after saying what he was going to do to us. I felt sorry for him, every time he got the ball somebody was piling into him. We didn't give him a second. I think he had one shot all game and sliced it into the stand. He just stood there and shook his head. That team went on and won the UEFA Cup and the league, all in one season. We finished second or third the other seasons. We were robbed of the title at Arsenal, we had a goal disallowed. Toshack scored it with minutes to go. Derby had finished their season and were in Majorca. If Leeds lost and Liverpool won we would be champions. Leeds did lose. Nobody could understand why the ref disallowed that goal. So we drew 0–0 and Derby won the title.

ALEC LINDSAY

Goalkeepers

Bob was a bit shy. The thought of having interviews or going on television was his worst fear. He couldn't put himself over like Shanks, he couldn't communicate the same. He used to get a bit frustrated over that but he knew football, he knew the ins and outs of the job, he knew everything. He knew every player's weaknesses and strengths. If anything, and I'm not taking any-thing away from Shanks, he was always behind Shanks, prodding and probing. Shanks knew his football, but Bob would see things in players that nobody else ever saw. He was good like that.

We just played the same. We never played to a plan. Play the ball simple, keep possession, while we've got the ball they can't score. There's no rush to get it up there. They go on today about three at the back but we used to always play three at the back. If I wasn't up against a winger, I'd push up, leaving the two centre-halves and Chris Lawler or maybe Tommy Smith at the back. We'd do that automatically. It would be pointless four of us staying back. We always had two against one or three against two but nine times out of ten we had a full-back spare. Chris liked to go forward as well so if he wasn't playing against a winger, he'd go up. And when he did, one of the midfielders would drop in behind him, so you wouldn't be thinking about having to get back as quick as you can. I knew there would be someone defending for me so I could concentrate on the job of going forward and not worry. Everything came automatically to us. They said if you are going to go forward you go forwards. We were doing it 25 years ago. And the goalkeeper used to play sweeper, he'd push up towards the halfway line, or near as damn it. All right, we got caught once or twice, but we won more than we lost, so it must have worked.

Ray Clemence used to always play out and he was the dirtiest player going, typical goalkeeper, always think they are centre-forwards. He wasn't a bad outfield player but he used to whack a few but not meaning to. He was a bit clumsy more than anything. I'll tell you what though, he was a good keeper. If there was a free-kick or a corner going anywhere near the six-yard box we used to scatter because he used to come out with knees, elbows, chin, everything pointing at you. He used to command that six-yard box. I'd just glance at Ray, he'd be judging it and he was out, if anyone was in his way he'd scatter them. We'd played with each other that often, we knew each other that well. If the ball came over he'd shout, 'My ball!' We didn't hesitate, we just left it. Hell of a keeper.

BARRIE HOLMES

Bob Paisley: Who Is This Guy?

I would say Bob Paisley was probably the driving force behind the boot room. Because although Bill Shankly came in and turned the club around with his vision and his charisma, Bob Paisley in many ways was the constant thread right through it. He was there when Shankly came, he had been there as a player. He had given Shankly tremendous support which wasn't really acknowledged at the time. When Bill Shankly announced that he was going to retire, I amongst many others was concerned when they said Bob Paisley was going to take over. Who is this guy? He's been there in the background but what has he been doing? It was only when he took over and had the opportunity to build on what Bill Shankly had started that we saw his true character and true ability. I think he used the boot room very well. I always got the impression that he did take account of what Joe Fagan, Roy Evans and Ronnie Moran said. Okay, he made the final decision but it was done in a quiet and consultative way. Even when Kenny Dalglish took over, he was still there giving advice and support.

BARRIE HOLMES

Old-Fashioned Values

To me the boot room represented the way Liverpool went about their business, very professional, but when you look at the boot room it's a combination of old-fashioned people with old-fashioned values. You got the impression that they loved football and if they weren't employed by Liverpool Football Club they would be quite happy to do what they were doing in the park with any amateur club. There's almost an old fashionedness and underneath that a degree of cunning. I've heard stories that they used to have people back in the room after the game and they would crack open a bottle and talk to the opposing coaches. I heard Ronnie Moran at a meeting once saying that there was always something they would pick up about a player or training. Afterwards they'd note it down. So although it was very much a social thing it was also an absorption of what was going on elsewhere. It was very down to earth.

Bob Paisley was once about to go out at Anfield to pick up another trophy and he was talking to Ronnie Moran before in the dressing room and it was as if he didn't really want to go out. It was not important. It was a case of, well let's get this out of the way and then we can carry on with the important business, winning the next match. He didn't want to parade around.

The boot room was very much the engine room. It was where all things were developed, where ideas came from. It was a place to talk things through, try out ideas. I think at that time, certainly in the sixties, the culture was different from now. There clearly was not the same amount of money, the hype, the media exposure. I think loyalty is the word that springs to mind. The fans were more loyal, you never used to hear booing in those days; if your team got beat that was it, you still supported them. I think the players also were more loyal, they would spend 15 years with one club, now you're lucky if you get 15 months.

And it was the same with the managers. I think the secret of Liverpool was that element of consistency although at the same time you need the right people.

BOB GREAVES
Fancy A Drink?

Bob Paisley was much more quiet, more taciturn but a very amusing man whom I never met in depth. But I do remember once being in a hotel in Cheshire. I was guest speaker at the Daresbury Hotel. I didn't know but at that stage it was Liverpool's hidey-hole, where they took the players before home games. I had left this big dinner for a 'comfort break' as they like to call it on these occasions. We had all gone either to the bar or the loo. I went to the loo and into the loo came Bob Paisley and Joe Fagan. I had seen Liverpool players wandering around. It was about 10 o'clock. I had heard Bob Paisley say to the players, 'That's it, off to your rooms.' I said to him, 'Can't they have a drink?' He said, 'No, Liverpool don't drink before games, the players are in their rooms now.' Then they opened this very large travel bag which they had with them. I assumed it would be full of socks, shin pads, jock straps and so on. They gleefully unzipped this bag and inside there were about ten bottles of whisky. 'Do you want to join us for a drink, Bob?' they asked. And I thought poor sod players sent to bed like schoolboys, while the big men sup a few bottles of whisky!

BOB PAISLEY
The Diaries

So many people have asked what has been the secret of Liverpool's unprecedented success. There isn't one, except that we acknowledge you can never stop learning and putting it to good use.

In the filing cabinet of my Anfield office I have built up a collection of desk diaries for each season in which all sorts of details were noted, ranging from weather conditions for a match in September to the fact that a certain player was late for training on a day in March. Nothing can be discounted as unimportant. But as I said earlier, no one man sitting in the manager's seat can successfully run a club like Liverpool. It has to be a team effort on and off the field, and the back room staff are key men. When you have to contend with so many factors such as training, travel, hotels, food and the like, their foresight to sniff out any problems before they arise is absolutely essential.

The best planning and preparation in the world, of course, is useless without the raw material of the championship business, the players themselves. I have often been quoted as saying 'you can only play with what's available', and another comment of mine that has been printed time and time again is that 'Liverpool are a good team when they play well.'

What I am driving at is that a manager has to cut his coat according to his cloth, he has to mould his team's style of play to the players he has available. None of them is perfect, so you have to develop their strengths and cover or reduce their weaknesses. It is up to the manager to study players, to recognise certain factors in their playing ability as well as their characters and personal makeup.

An extract from *Bob Paisley, An Autobiography* (Arthur Barker).

BOB PAISLEY

Just Like Popping Down To The Local

We have a marvellous back room team at Anfield who share the workload wonderfully well. No club has a more able and closely-knit staff than ours. The Anfield 'boot room' has become legendary, and we have a full and frank exchange of views in there in a leisurely atmosphere every Sunday morning. It's just like popping down to the local. But despite all that, there are times when the manager has to stand alone and take a decision.

Sometimes you can deliberate on them for days, even weeks. But others have to be snap decisions, made spontaneously when the game is under way. If you don't possess that spark, that feeling deep inside for the game, that I have never lost and Bill Shankly never lost, your ability to make those decisions is impaired.

An extract from *Bob Paisley, An Autobiography* (Arthur Barker).

BRIAN HALL

A Collectiveness

There was a collectiveness about the boot room. It's very easy to stand back after all these years and say, 'Oh yes, when we pulled on the red shirt we went out there and forgot all our petty differences, and it was all for one, and one for all.' It's very easy to say that. And you know, that's exactly how it was!

There was something in the ethos of the place that made it one for all and all for one. I can't really explain it. I can't explain how they instilled into us a system of play, a pattern of play and the role of each individual within that. It became almost instinctive, you didn't have to think about it. After a while you just knew what your job was. I was never told too deeply what I had to do when I went out there, you quickly learnt it. You knew your little role within the system. It's blatantly obvious to anyone that if you have 11 individuals running around in different ways, it won't be as good as 11 guys pulling in the same direction.

I never had any real friends in the dressing room, they were colleagues at work. I was always conscious that there was a rivalry in the dressing room, that there were 16, 18 team players for 11 places. We were highly charged, highly competitive, fit young men. Inevitably, in that kind of close-knit community the sparks would fly. It was aggressive and at times people would square up to one another and punches would get thrown. Yet we all learnt to live with one another. The key to that was the management and the leadership, pulling all these highly charged fit young fellas in the same direction.

It was amazing considering all those arguments, petty jealousies and so on among those players, that when you went down that tunnel, they disappeared and it just worked. I think the sense of humour and banter helped enormously. If you couldn't hack it, then you were in trouble. It's also part of the Liverpool culture, learning to live with the banter and give it back.

BRIAN HALL

Tosh and Keegan

I'll tell you a story. I can't remember the game. Kevin and Toshack were a great partnership, they complemented each other so well. Tosh was through one on one at the Anfield Road in the first half. He was one on one with the keeper. Kevin came up alongside him. It was a tap to Kevin and an easy goal but Tosh decided to shoot and the keeper saved it. Kevin went ballistic, on the pitch. At half-time Kevin went mad with Tosh in the dressing room. Tosh answers back aggressively and there's a real confrontation. In the second half the roles are reversed, but this time Kevin passes it to Tosh and Tosh puts it in the back of the net and immediately puts his hands up to Kevin to say, 'Yes you were right!' Now that makes the wee man a bit special to me when he does something like that. He could so easily have said, 'Sod it, he let me down before, I'll have a go myself!' Tosh knew straight away that he should have done that in the first half. That little cameo sums it up for me. Despite so many things which pull that harmony all over the place, it still came together on the pitch, week in week out, year in year out.

DAVID FAIRCLOUGH

Reuben Bennett And The Fantastic Stories

I got to know Reuben Bennett really well because I used to take him home every day. He lived in West Derby near me. He used to drive Shanks in the early years but as he got older he stopped driving so he always asked me for a lift. Him and Shanks were born out of the same pod, exactly the same mentality.

On my first Tuesday training as a 13-year-old it was hard. Then on the Thursday night Reuben took it. He was mad, he used to tell us these fantastic stories. He was taking us and he was bawling at me and giving me a lot of stick, telling me not to do things this way or that way, telling me I couldn't kick a ball. There I was, a top Liverpool schoolboy, and now I'm being told I can't kick a ball! But that was part of a true apprenticeship. He was fantastic. He was always the first in every morning and he'd make the tea. He never knocked around in the boot room much, he was Shanks' right-hand man. But he'd be there to take the mickey out of the lads. He was a huge part of it all. You could always go to him for advice; he'd tell me things when I drove him in the car. They brought in this retirement age but they let it go for Reuben. John Smith said he could stay as long as he liked.

DAVID FAIRCLOUGH

No Nonsense Bob

Bob Paisley was very much a boot room man, far more so than Shanks. I rarely saw Shanks in there. I don't have any memories of seeing him sitting there on the skips. Joe very much was also a boot room man; it was his territory and Ronnie's as well. I got the impression that when Bob Paisley was mulling things over he went to them rather than them going to him. They wouldn't spend time in the boss's office. If they had their meetings they took place in the boot room.

My impression was that Bob would take no nonsense from anybody. He took a shine to me in my early days and he used to take me aside. He would be the goalkeeper for the staff team. I nearly always guested for the staff in our five-a-side games. I could never escape playing on their side. People used to make a point that I was a bit of a blue-eyed boy for the boss. Some players would call him but he was very good with me. It did change later however! No one would cross him, there was a lot of respect and fear of Bob Paisley. He was the one who sorted the problems before Shanks ever found out about them. Shanks never had to get tough with players, Bob had already sorted them all out. I think that's where Roy Evans made a bit of a mistake. When Bob Paisley was the manager, Joe Fagan did all that. He had enormous respect. He was tough but he was fair. That stood him in good stead when he was manager. You knew that you didn't mess with Joe. Ronnie did a bit of this role. Even Ronnie did not speak when Joe spoke. When Joe had to speak or he raised his voice it was serious stuff. I don't remember anyone ever speaking over Joe. Ronnie Moran had the utmost respect for Joe, they were big pals.

Bob Paisley was brilliant at tactics, so astute at identifying things. He rarely came out to training, he'd stand by the radiator by the window. He'd be looking out and we'd be saying, aye, there he is by the radiator but he was taking it all in as he watched. He knew everything. He was a fantastic observer of strengths and weaknesses. I remember when I was coming back from a knee injury. A pal of mine was a close friend of Bob's and he'd be singing my praises with the boss, get Dave back in and Bob said 'he's not moving right'. That's what he was there for, he was standing by the window not just to warm himself. He was there to observe and see little things to pick up what was going on.

He was never really the most comfortable in group situations but he would give you bits of information. When we were playing Norwich he came up to me before the game, and said 'This keeper, he's got short arms on his right-hand side.' And I thought, what a stupid thing to say. I'll never forget it. Anyway, I got a run in on goal in the first nine or ten minutes and as I approached the keeper, I thought, 'He said to me he's got short arms on the right-hand side,' so I put the ball on his right-hand side and it shot past him. Later on in the second half the same thing happened again and I scored another. That was his style, his gift. He was great at identifying injuries as well, even before they were out in the open. He was a bit of a witch doctor.

DAVID FAIRCLOUGH

Supersub

One of my key memories of the sub thing is this. Bob Paisley would come down sometimes from the stand and look around the dugout and say, 'Get Toshack off or whatever, get Dave on.' Sometimes, and this is why I always thought the Houllier/Evans thing would never work, he'd say what do you think, what about so and so? Bob would say to Joe Fagan, 'I'll leave it up to you'. At that point I knew I wasn't going on because they couldn't make up their minds. They had a different relationship. If he was decisive when he came down and said, 'Get McDermott off' then I knew I would be on. No chance for Joe to turn round and say anything, I'd be on. That's what always made me think that when he gave anyone time to reconsider, it was a bad sign.

DAVID FAIRCLOUGH

Tom Saunders: The Deep Thinker

I knew Tom Saunders as a schoolmaster. As an aspiring Liverpool schoolboy you'd heard of him as the manager of the England Schoolboys. There were two main managers at the time, a guy called Frank Cassidy and Tom Saunders and they alternated. My year fell to Tom Saunders. I thought this is going to be a test, he knows his football, I'd heard of his reputation. I was a bit frightened. In fact he didn't do it in the end because he joined Liverpool and someone else came in. It was a bit of a relief really. But then I met him within the year. I was already signed on with Liverpool by then as a 13-year-old. But when Tom got into that job as youth development officer I came across him. I had an immediate respect for him.

I had been at a grammar school and I had played for Liverpool Schoolboys which was a bit unusual for my school as they didn't play football. I remember Tom saying to my parents that I should stay with the Schoolboys and that's what I did. Then he asked my dad if I could become an apprentice when I was 15-and-a-half. My dad spoke to the school and they didn't feel that I should leave. They wanted me to do 'O' levels. I remember on the Saturday the decision hadn't been made and I had played for the Liverpool B team, Tom saying to my Dad, 'we agree with your decision, don't worry, there will be something for him next year'. It probably wasn't a good thing because I knew I was going to be a footballer and didn't work so hard.

My dad had booked a family holiday and the pre-season training had started. He had asked if I could come on this family holiday. So I had done a week's training and then I was going off. And I remember Tom Saunders saying to me, very steely, 'Going off on a bloody holiday? Well I hope you come back with a rebore,' you know, get a new engine. I thought I've got off on a really bad foot here. He could be a hard, unforgiving type. But that was Liverpool's way, knock you down and see how you come back. You either throw in the towel or make a conscious effort. Now I look back on it, I know I had something inside that didn't give up. They never really knocked me down or knocked my confidence. They knock you and knock you, it's a tough method to come through. I see Tom Saunders as much now as I did before. A deep thinker, he knows the Liverpool way. You can't underestimate his role.

DAVID FAIRCLOUGH

Boot Cleaning

In the early days there was a little bit of mystique about the boot room; not that it had the attention then that it got later. The trainers always went into the boot room and you wondered, what do they do in there? They were always there first thing in the morning. You'd walk past and they would be in there. There's no magic about it, it was just a box room full of skips, and a few cases of beer. It was a place where they could unwind. I don't think they even had a locker each. They didn't invite players in really, there was no need. My involvement at an early age was just to pop in and ask for a new pair of boots or something like that. But when you did ask, they'd take the mickey out of you, saying 'New pair of boots? You must be playing well.' You were on their patch. They had their own mentality around their environment.

The Liverpool thing was always to keep your feet on the ground, there were no big 'I am's'. When you are a young lad, if you had to ask for anything you'd have to find one of the coaching staff in the boot room. One of them would be sitting on a skip in there and you'd go in. You'd only be there a minute, there was never any reason to spend longer in there. I think at the time I came through, it was still developing. Later they began to decorate the place and get those calendars. If we went in it was to look at the calendars more than anything else.

One of the things I remember about the boot room was that, as an apprentice, I used to be on boot cleaning on a Monday morning. We'd be in at 9 o'clock and had to take the mud off the boots. We had to do everything in twos. Two would take the mud off, two would put the polish on, two would do the polishing. The door would be closed and we'd be spending time earwigging what was going on in the room itself, trying to find out what they were talking about. We'd hang around doing our jobs. Liverpool's games were always on a Tuesday night so we might find out who was going to be playing. I always remember that, hanging around and listening, hoping to find something out. Then I could go out and tell whoever it was that they were playing for the first team or the reserves.

GORDON BURNS
The Liverpool Way

Liverpool were a magical club for me when I was producing football for Granada. Of all the clubs I dealt with in the north-west, Liverpool in those days were the nicest club to deal with. From chairman right down to the tea lady, there was a wonderful atmosphere in the club and you were always made to feel welcome which you weren't at some other clubs. It was a joy to be there, plus of course it was the Keegan era and they were winning in Europe. I used to go to the matches on a Saturday if I wasn't working and I would bring my wife, who didn't like football, but she loved the atmosphere at Liverpool and the way we were all looked after and treated and I brought my son who became a Liverpool fan because we used to go there all the time. He was about ten or eleven. I remember specifically going to a Liverpool-QPR game. A friend of ours from London was a QPR fan and he came up with his son Eddie and I took them to the match.

We watched the match and then after we got tickets to go into the trophy room to have a cup of tea or whatever, look at the trophies, wait for the crowd to disperse. The kids had a look at the trophies and then I showed them where the players' lounge was downstairs. It was the holy of holies, nobody else was allowed in there. We couldn't get in, they had a big burly commissionaire on the door. Anyway the kids went and stood outside to try and get the players' autographs.

After a while we went downstairs to pick up the kids. They weren't there and I panicked. I had no idea where they had gone, if they had gone outside or got lost in the crowd. I was searching around when the commissionaire said, 'Are you looking for someone, Gordon?' I said, 'Yes, I'm looking for my son and his mate and I don't know where they are.' He said, 'Describe them,' so I said, 'Well, my son has blond hair and has a Liverpool scarf on and his mate is a bit larger with a blue and white QPR scarf.' And the commissionaire says, 'Oh aye, they're in the players' lounge.' I said, 'They can't be, nobody can get in there'. He said, 'Oh yes, they went in with a couple of players'. I said, 'I can't understand that,' and he told me that if I wanted to get them, to go in.

So I went in and there were these two sofas opposite each other with a little table in between. And there was Kevin Keegan, my son, Phil Thompson, Ray Clemence, my son's mate Eddie, and a few other Liverpool players. And these two young lads were looking at each player as they spoke. I knew Kevin Keegan because I had interviewed him a few times. I said, 'I'm sorry about this,' and Keegan said, 'Oh, is this your lad? He was standing outside getting autographs, so we just told them to come in. They've been sitting here, very well behaved.'

Those players didn't have to do that, they could have ignored them, they didn't know who they were. Now those kids will never forget that for the rest of their lives. And then as if that wasn't enough, we came out and I said to the kids, 'Would you like to see the dressing rooms?' and they said, 'Oh yes.' I said, 'Well, we might get thrown out but we'll see.' So we walked down there past the boot room and had a look round the dressing room. Suddenly the dressing room attendant, a man of about 70, came in. 'Oh no,' I thought. 'I'm sorry,' I said, 'I just wanted to show the kids the dressing room.'

'No problem,' he says, 'I'll show them.' So he took them in and showed them where each player sat and he gave them both a bottle of mineral water. Then the lad from QPR says, 'I'd like to see where the QPR players were.' So the attendant says okay and takes him in there. I'll never forget it because he was shown the big bath where all the players go. It was still full of water with mud and grime. Around the edge was the soap. This lad Eddie picks one up. I said, 'What are you doing with that?' He replied, 'Stan Bowles might have washed with this,' and he stared longingly at it. Then the attendant said, 'Look kids, the floodlights are still on, do you want to run down the steps under the famous sign and go on the pitch?' So down they went and ran down the Kop end and nodded in a few imaginary goals. You would not imagine a club, doing as well as Liverpool were, that they would care about kids but that was an example of the way the club was.

IAN HARGREAVES
A Corporate Effort

Paisley was remarkable. I've never known him or Joe Fagan ever claim credit for anything. With Paisley it's well known that he missed the 1950 Cup Final because they had two England centre-halves, Laurie Hughes and Bill Jones. You might have thought that Paisley, having played in all the previous rounds and having scored in the semi-final, might have been gutted not to play in the final. Well, he was, but he later said to me that he was disappointed but admitted that they were probably right to leave him out. You tend to forget these things, he said. But, he said that he had been out for three weeks with a hamstring not very long before and that he was not fully fit and in those days you did not have substitutes. Wembley was notorious for injuries. Realistically, he said, they were probably right not to pick him.

The great success of the boot room was that there was no *one* individual. It was very much a corporate effort. I know you've always got to have somebody who says, this is the way we shall do it. Certainly when Bill Shankly was there, he was the one who had the final word. But this was where Bob was so good. He never wanted to take anything away from the boss. He was telling me once, 'I didn't want Bill to retire, I tried to talk him out of it. I said, "Bill, for God's sake, go and have a holiday, I'll look after things until you get back, I don't want the job."' Bob hated dealing with the media.

Bob Paisley was the nitty-gritty man, the thorough person, no glamour about him. He was also the tactical man. He'd have discussions with Bill and it became very obvious after Bill had gone that Bob was a tactical genius. The team played more advanced football than any team had played in England or Europe. He taught his players patience whereas Shankly's teams were up and at them, hit them with all you've got. Paisley didn't, he told his teams to be careful, don't let your heart rule your head. Bill would get them going, Bob would calm them down. And then there was Joe Fagan in the middle of it all, loyal and doing the routine things. They'd lock up, open this, bollock anyone who was out of line, make sure everything was in place and ready. And then they'd all move up a notch when someone moved on.

JOHN BENNISON
Moving Up

I'm doing my coaching and one night I hear this voice, 'Hello John,' and it's Tom Saunders. He was teaching at the time and he said, 'I've been offered this job at Liverpool as youth development officer.' Tony Waiters had done it previously but had left to go back to Burnley and then to Canada as national coach. So Tom, when he came here full time, packed up as chairman of the Liverpool Coaches' Association and I took over. So he comes through one night and he says, 'I've got this job ... do you fancy coming there in a part-time capacity?' Well, I said, I was quite happy at South Liverpool, there was no way I was going to bust a gut because I had a good team there and I would only be in the same league here. But after thinking it over, I came to Liverpool.

From 1970 to 1974 I was here on a part-time capacity but with the hours you put in, you might as well be full time, and it was seven nights. If you weren't coaching, you were knocking on schoolboys' doors. So I came, first to look at players, then to coach the schoolboys on a Tuesday and Thursday evening and basically to get the players from there into the next team, the A or B team and the reserves. And once you were in the reserves it was out of your hands then.

Tom also got Ronnie Moran and Roy Evans to help because

of the experience they had. If you were going to a kid's house, they would go as well and that was a great help. I was doing that for quite a while and had considerable success in getting players through to the first team. If you were taking a kid around Anfield and Shanks saw you, he'd say, 'John, how are yae?' and that would raise your image in the kid's eyes. That would help a little. Then Shanks moved out, he'd had enough, and that created a vacancy on the staff. Within a week Roy Evans and I started. I moved up when Shankly moved out. I took the A team, then and all the apprentice professionals. I was full time and it went on from there.

We had a meeting in the boot room when Bob was moving. We were all going to move up one. I had been kind of promised the reserve job and Ronnie would become chief coach, but that did not materialise for some reason best known to the club. Joe became manager but I didn't become reserve boss. So I went to see them and said it would have meant more money and prestige, trips to Europe and so on. 'Well,' Joe said, 'I'll take you to Europe.' So I went on all the trips to Europe, helping out.

After that first UEFA Cup Final Shanks was on the steps at St George's Hall in Liverpool and he had a multitude in front of him. The whole square was full. Tom turned to me and said, 'If Shanks says we're going to march through the tunnel and take over Birkenhead, everyone will follow him!' There were thousands cheering and cheering. It was a tremendous cup to win against a strong Borussia Moenchengladbach side.

Anyway I came in and it's gone on from there. I was with the youth team from 1970 until halfway through the eighties and then Stevie came in the late eighties and I moved up to the reserves with Chris Lawler. After a few years he left and Phil Thompson came in. In my first year, 1970/71, he was captain of the youth team, now suddenly he's my boss. But we worked together. Then eventually Phil went and Sammy Lee came in. Sammy was a lad I brought here when he was 15. I had a look at him and one night he played in a local final here. He was outstanding so I went knocking on the door and he came in and just took over the whole club with his enthusiasm for the cause, a bit like Joey Jones.

JOHN BENNISON
The Daily Routine

The boot room basically was about eight feet in length and much the same across. On the table was a little mug, like a plant pot. Any visitors had to put their spare change in there, only coppers, for the staff night out. Now that went on for years although I don't ever remember the staff night out! Now that pot was covered by a fez, a little red fez like Tommy Cooper used to wear. Visiting managers came in, whoever, anybody, celebrities. Elton John was in once, and Rod Stewart. We'd get those types of celebrities and we'd make them put something in the pot. It was only coppers, or foreign notes that you brought back from your holidays or trips across Europe. I don't think it was ever used.

Reuben had his own room but he'd come in. Shanks, Tom Saunders and Geoff Twentyman, all had their own offices. But in the boot room was Joe Fagan, Ronnie Moran, Roy Evans and myself. Now Bob would come in but he had his own office and he wouldn't hang his coat up in the boot room. Then Joe moved out and for a while there was only three of us in there and then Chris Lawler came in.

On a typical morning there'd be eight or nine youngsters wanting to get the kit out, balls, boots, tracksuits, nets, it all had to be taken out. Each player had his own number. Now that kit had to last all week. You're over there lying in the mud and you get the same kit next day. The kit would go off on a Friday to be returned Monday or Tuesday. You'd then get another kit, just two kits for the week. The kit wasn't washed, just dried in the drying room.

We'd all go off to Melwood, leaving at 10.15am, warm up and always have a walk around the pitch. We'd have a small-sided game, a bit of shooting, very uncomplicated. A similar system day after day. They wrote down every day in the boot room what we did. Ronnie would get his book out, write down what we had done and invariably it was the same as they had done the previous year. These were the training manuals and everything was written into them: what time we started, was it sunny, cloudy, any injuries and so on.

In the boot room we had a cupboard which was a bar with glasses on the top and a bottle of Scotch for the visitors. In the afternoons it was a workplace where you'd do all your jobs. When the kids had gone home and you'd done all your work, the baths cleaned, steps and passageways scrubbed, you might just lock the door, put your feet up and have a wee dram. Then there'd be a knock at the door. 'Shhh,' we'd go, and they'd think we had gone. Joe would be puffing away. When Joe was manager he'd say, 'That kid's ankle, keep your eye on it.' He worried about the kids. He took his responsibilities seriously. 'He's come from Ireland. He's a long way from home, you know.' You tend to forget that someone of 16 or 17 thinks he's a man but he's not, particularly if he's had a rough morning out there.

The boot room was about many things. It was your office, your workshop, and after the game on a Saturday an entertaining room. Visiting managers would come in with their assistants. Sometimes you'd have 18 people in. There'd be a smoke-laden atmosphere, glasses clinking. And they all came on Sunday, especially if someone was injured. We were always a day ahead. Most clubs come in Monday but we worked Sunday, trying to solve any problems then rather than wait until Monday.

PETER ROBINSON
After Match Drinks

They established a great rapport with other clubs through this socialising in the boot room. Prior to that I think there was a tendency for a manager to go into a very formal boardroom session and for the assistant coaches not to meet. So they'd created something that was quite unique to Liverpool where they said to the opposing people, 'Please come in and have a drink with us.' That never existed at other places. And a lot of managers wouldn't go up to the boardroom. The place to be was the boot room, not the boardroom, after games whereas prior to that it had been the boardroom. So they'd go straight down there. Even people like Brian Clough did that, always going down there looking for a bottle of beer rather than come up to the boardroom.

It invariably went on until something like 7pm. It would be a couple of hours after games and they'd still be in there. It would gradually build up because they'd be involved in the dressing rooms in different ways. One would eventually come in and open up what would be termed the bar but would be nothing more than open some cans of beer. There was an old cupboard and somebody had to have the key to the cupboard to open it up. But someone would come down when they thought that the visiting people were ready for a drink and it would gradually build up. In the early days, if Joe was coming back from a reserve team match or whoever was coming back from an A team match, he would come in and there'd be this general discussion. Then that continued into the Sunday when I think the main discussions went on in the boot room. On a Saturday it was more entertaining, with the football gossip.

PETER ROBINSON
The Officers' Mess

How would I define the philosophy of the boot room? I think it was right for its time. They did have these meetings where they could exchange their views in a frank way.

The boot room was initially an entertaining room for matchday. Incidentally the beer that Joe obtained, and there are many stories about this, was exceedingly strong beer. It was some export beer that wasn't available in this country. I know there was one which went to some of the African countries that was about three times the strength. I remember one afternoon a certain manager who was having trouble with his board of directors drinking about four or five of these cans of beer. I don't think he knew how strong it was. Apparently, on the way back he had a fall-out with his chairman and got sacked. We all thought that was a result of the boot room beer.

Sometimes during the week they would have a beer as well. I think on Saturday the number of people who eventually got invited in there grew. There were people like John Bennison and others and it became the meeting point after the game. Joe would come back and he'd go in and tell them how people had played, one thing and another, and it developed.

I was privileged, I was always invited in there if I wanted to go in and often in those days I did go in. I didn't think it was a place I should go in too often, though. I would tend to go in more on the Saturday evening just for a glass of beer with them. But it wasn't a place for players. It was a place where players were discussed; it was the officers' mess. I think that's a good description.

PHIL NEAL
The Diaries

My first memory of the boot room is having my photo taken in there, just after I had made my debut. They wanted a picture of me cleaning my boots. I always remember going in there, the smell of 50 pairs of boots hanging up, match boots.

I arrived in October 1974, I was Bob's first signing. It seemed that any time after you got back from training and went down the corridor to go out, the staff would be in there sitting on skips discussing things, from how we were playing to who do we replace some of these older players with. I think Bob Paisley joined them in there as often as he could. He wasn't an office man, he was more attuned to sitting with his staff in the boot room to chat about things. We all knew it was like a social club after games. On the Friday afternoons after all the jobs were done they'd see it as a social gathering place, looking forward to Saturday.

I was one of the first into training every morning and if you walked past the boot room, Ronnie would be looking into his annuals. He kept these volumes throughout the footballing year, recording everything we had done in training. He would draw diagrams and so on. He would know all the time what had been done the previous year, and probably the previous ten years. He'd keep five or six volumes around the boot room. Ronnie was there so long, he's probably got 30-odd volumes at home. Joe might say to him, 'Have a look, see what we did this time last year,' if we gave the lads a sauna and a massage, so we'd try and match what had been done then. It was an annual for success and they didn't want to break that success. The silverware kept coming in, so it must have been right. Before we went down to Melwood they would always check what they had done before. Then after training they'd write it up. After Melwood we would come back to Anfield on the bus and Ronnie would sit down and write what we had done in training that day; who had broken down; details beyond the training schedule such as Graeme Souness looked good today in training; a dispute between Graeme Souness and Phil Neal in training. But it was only for his own record, it was for no other use. From the annuals he would know when to give the lads a break or when to ease up on the training.

After a game the boot room became a hospitality suite. There were times when the internationals after a game would often have to go in and collect their match boots. We'd be going to join up with the international squads. That was the time when you interrupted their party. The opposition was being entertained by our staff. They were great hosts, they made them feel welcome. As we collected our boots we would see what good hosts they were. It was as if to say, 'Hey, the game's over, let's have a drink together irrespective of the result'. I think they also used it as a way to find out about players. If they fancied someone from Blackburn Rovers and they'd just played them, they'd somehow got some insights from the opposition coaches. It was intelligence gathering, in the loveliest way. It was an efficient way of getting information.

PHIL NEAL

A Nerveless Debut

I remember my first game for Liverpool. Now that would have
been very much a boot room decision. Alec Lindsay was carrying
a bit of an injury and they weren't sure how it was going. In
truth he never had a chance for the game which was the Liverpool
Everton derby. But Bob would have told them all in the boot
room to keep quiet about it. So nothing was said. I was due to
be playing on the Saturday for the reserves in the mini-derby
against Everton. Now they obviously made a decision about Alec
on the Friday. It would have been taken by the boot room staff.
Bob would have asked Ronnie and Joe, 'What about Nealey, is
he up to it?' And they'd have said, 'Yeah, he's probably good
enough, he's doing well in the reserves.' So they'd have decided
to take a chance. But they didn't tell me. They let me carry on
thinking I was playing for the reserves. I turned up at Anfield,
all ready for the reserve game. I went into the dressing room and
all my kit was laid out, went into the boot room to get my boots
and there they were, sitting there before going off to Goodison.

'You're coming with us,' they said, 'you're playing for the first
team. Tom, you walk him over Stanley Park to Goodison.' Now
all that would have been a boot room decision. It was very clever
and cleverly worked out. It meant I got a good night's sleep and
hadn't done any worrying about the game. I didn't know until
2pm. By then it was too late to worry. I had to say to myself,
'Right this is it, this is what I've always wanted, to play in the
first division.'

PHIL THOMPSON

Geoff Twentyman and Ronnie Moran

Some of the greatest players came as cheap buys, some of the greatest names in the history of the club, and that's why Geoff Twentyman's role will always be important. He helped identify that crop of players and bring them through: Keegan, Clemence, Rush, Dalglish, Heighway, so many of them. They were always looking for players who could be part of a team, and not just great individual players, part of a jigsaw. It's that little bit of extra character. Look at how many of them are working in the media today, it's quite extraordinary. You might get on television once in a while as an ex-Liverpool player, but not all the time. It's all about having that extra bit of character. Look at Graeme Souness, he had everything as a player, especially character, he could grab a game by the scruff of the neck, now that's character. He was probably the greatest midfielder this country has ever seen.

Ronnie Moran is as big a name as any of the others. He was the driving force. He would bring you down to earth. He probably did more for me than any other person because I had him in the youth teams as a 15 year old. He'd bash into my head good habits all the time. I went through the B team, the A team and reserves with him. You can spot a Liverpool player who's been through the ranks. With players coming from other clubs, you can see that they need a little bit of teaching. It's these values which you are taught at Liverpool.

There was also a peer factor at the club. There were no written rules. Obviously you had your three committee members, three players, and if we met and decided something we would go and see the manager or the board of directors. I looked up to people who were on the committee. Later I became a committee member; it was nice because the players have to judge who they want to be their representative.

I remember playing in the first team when I was 18 or 19, and

Liverpool goalkeeper Tommy Lawrence looks on in despair as Alan Ball sneaks the ball past him in the FA Cup fifth round at Goodison in 1967.

Bill Shankly leads Liverpool out at Wembley for the 1971 FA Cup final with a host of new faces that would go on to dominate English football.

Record goalscorer and World Cup winner Roger Hunt, one of the most popular strikers in Liverpool's history. Dubbed 'Sir' Roger Hunt by the Kop.

Bob Paisley knew what it meant to wear the red of Liverpool, going on to win league championship honours in 1947.

Former midfielder Brian Hall later returned to the club as Community Development Officer.

The boot room at its height, from left to right – Ronnie Moran, Roy Evans, Bob Paisley, Tom Saunders, Joe Fagan and John Bennison.

Joe Fagan and Bob Paisley celebrate Liverpool's 1974 FA Cup victory while Bill Shankly pondered his future.

Former player Chris Lawler was appointed reserve team trainer by Bob Paisley but was later sacked by Kenny Dalglish.

One of the boot room's great characters, trainer Reuben Bennett (far right). A hard man but highly respected by all. Seen here alongside 'supersub' David Fairclough, Ronnie Moran, Roy Evans, Tom Saunders and Joe Fagan.

Kenny Dalglish, perhaps the finest player to have ever worn the Liverpool jersey.

Supersub David Fairclough in his greatest triumph, scoring against St Etienne in the 1997 European Cup Quarter-Final, second leg.

Peter Robinson, former club secretary and now executive vice-chairman, has been the pivot for stability and continuity in the boardroom.

Kevin Keegan, one of the many great and cheap signings from the lower divisions, usually spotted by Chief Scout Geoff Twentyman. Keegan went on to help Liverpool to league, cup and European honours before joining Hamburg for £500,000 in 1977.

Joe Fagan, the man widely regarded as the founding spirit behind the boot room.

Bob Paisley, player, coach, manager and director, with just one of the 13 major trophies he picked up during his nine years as manager.

Attacking full-back Alan Kennedy storms down the left wing to win the 1981 European Cup for Liverpool with his goal against Real Madrid.

The new boot room lineup including manager Kenny Dalglish, Roy Evans, Ronnie Moran and Phil Thompson.

Another trophy, another triumphant homecoming. The 1985/86 League Championship and FA Cup Double winners celebrate in style.

Graeme Souness' arrival as manager in April 1991 was to bring significant changes to the boot room tradition but brought little in the way of success. He left in January 1994.

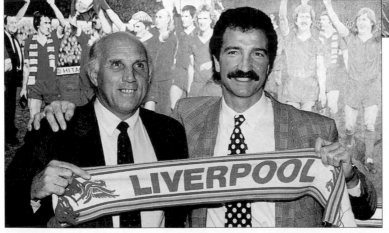

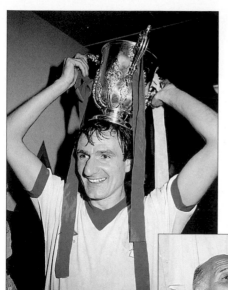

Phil Thompson, fan, player, captain, coach and now assistant manager. Sacked by Graeme Souness in 1992, he returned to the club at the end of 1998, bringing his enormous enthusiasm to the boot room.

Ronnie Moran, Kenny Dalglish and Roy Evans celebrate another championship triumph during Dalglish's reign as Liverpool manager.

Like so many former Liverpool players, Danish midfielder Jan Molby has gone on to become both manager and media pundit.

The Kop, always ready to play its part in the jigsaw that is Liverpool Football Club.

Roy Evans takes over as manager in February 1994 with a policy of back to basics.

The joint managerial team of Frenchman Gerard Houllier and Roy Evans never worked, and in November 1998 Evans stepped aside. It marked the end of the boot room.

the likes of Tommy Smith or Ian Callaghan, if they wanted something you went and got it, you did it. It was a learning process. They taught you all the good habits. They'd like to enjoy themselves but they knew when to stop. If anybody stepped out of line they would sort it out. We had controversy and problems but we didn't have the media focus that we have now.

ALAN HANSEN
Quit While You're Losing

Phil Thompson and I had a formidable partnership. It was like telepathy. Neither of us could head it, neither of us could tackle, my missus was quicker than he was, but we did all right. Bob Paisley's philosophy was simple strengths and weaknesses. We played to our strengths and exploited their weaknesses. Now I hear things about different philosophies and it's mostly a lot of tosh. I hear people saying 'the way the game should be played'. Rubbish. That's the worst saying in football. You win the game, then worry about the way it should be played. It's absolute folly to say 'Here are the tactics, now let's look at the players.' You look at your players, then decide your tactics. Take the sweeper system. In the eighties everyone was saying that you can't win the World Cup without a sweeper. Then Brazil in 1994, and France in 1998, win it with a flat back four, so where does that leave us?

In 1982 we tried it for four games at Liverpool, with me as sweeper. I could give you a day-long seminar on the sweeper system, but on the pitch we couldn't do it. We didn't know when to come or when to stay. We had problems with marking. In the end, Joe Fagan decided we didn't have time to mess about with it. Quit while you're losing, that's another important message we got from the boot room.

IAN RUSH

Boot Room Advice

To me Bob Paisley was the boot room. He was so canny, so clever. He understood footballers so well. He would say different things to different people. He wouldn't treat everyone the same. His man management was great. He didn't say much to me in the two or three years I played under him, but when he did say something he said it privately and it was always good advice.

The time I best remember was when I went in to ask him why I wasn't playing in the first team. I'd played seven or eight games without scoring but I felt I'd been doing well enough to keep my spot. I plucked up the courage to see him and he told me I was out of the side because I wasn't getting the goals. He said he'd seen me in training and I was passing the ball too often. I told him I was doing that because Liverpool were a passing team. But he said that sometimes I had to be greedy and go for goal myself. If I didn't then I wouldn't have a future at Anfield. Bob kept stressing the importance of scoring goals. I thought Bob would put me on the transfer list but he didn't. After that talk I became more selfish. I scored something like six goals in two or three reserve games and when David Johnson got injured I was in the first team again. That shows the way he knew how to handle people. Telling me to be more selfish was the best piece of advice he ever gave me. In fact, it was probably the best piece of advice anyone in football ever gave me. It shows how he knew. People say Kenny Dalglish's man management was great, and it was, but I think he learned that from Bob Paisley.

ROGER HUNT

Bob Paisley Never Changed

The secret really is the down-to-earth nature of the characters. They knew the game and were happy to be in their job. They weren't looking to become managers or get promoted. Bob Paisley never wanted to be a manager when Bill Shankly retired. It shocked me when he was appointed. I could see the sense of it with Shanks retiring. He was 60, he'd built two teams, just built another and I think he felt, I've been here 15 years at the top, time to go. Bob Paisley was pushed into that job, he was desperate for Bill to stay on. I was surprised when he took the job, he's a quiet behind-the-scenes man. He wasn't the best communicator, he didn't want it. He had always been a second in command. He was going into the unknown when he took over.

The secret was that he never changed much. The philosophy was, give it to the nearest man in a red shirt, keep it simple. I think Bill would have been a success without Bob Paisley but Bob Paisley and Joe Fagan obviously helped enormously.

STEVE HALE

Taking Photographs

Paisley never really wanted the job, he was quite happy where he was but if he could be of any assistance to the club he would do anything. Even he at the time thought that Shankly would have second thoughts and come back but of course that did not happen. It did later get embarrassing. Joe Fagan was given the job of telling Bill. He used to come to Melwood long after Bob had taken over but eventually he was told, 'Bill, it's best that you don't come because Bob's boss now and that's it.' It must have been very hard for Joe and for Bill. He took it badly. I always felt that Bill Shankly regretted what he did five minutes after he walked out of the place. I think he needed a rest. Even in those days the pressures were immense. He was an extrovert in many ways but he kept things to himself.

Bob certainly utilised the boot room far more than Bill did when he was the manager. I certainly saw him coming in and out of it far more than Bill. He invited me in, through Roy Evans, to take some photographs. They'd just won the league championship. We knew that was our opportunity to get a picture that no one else had got and there were 60 or so photographers at that game, so just a couple of us went in. We were very privileged, one was the club photographer, one was the staff man on the *Echo* and the other was me, a freelancer – it was a good deal for me.

While Shankly was there the boot room had not developed, it was just a place to go for some peace and quiet. But by the time Paisley had become manager it was being talked about. It was by then becoming the stuff of legends. And certainly once they started winning European trophies it became even more important. I remember saying to a group sitting behind a goal that this team could have taken on the 1970 Brazil side, they were that good, it was perfection. You just went every week, and it wasn't a question of whether they would win, but by how many. When they did lose it was headline news. There was an arrogance, it's not like these days.

TOM SAUNDERS

Joining The Boot Room

I joined the club on a full-time basis in 1970 but prior to that I was head teacher of a school in Liverpool West Derby Comprehensive, the lower school. I played as an amateur player for New Brighton when they were in the football League Northern section, that's going back a long way, before they were thrown out of football. They went bankrupt if you remember.

I got very interested in coaching and became a staff coach with the Football Association and at the same time I was manager of

Liverpool Schools Football team. I went on to manage the Schools International team for a number of years. At the same time I kept on playing and played for non-league clubs such as Fleetwood for about four years, Clitheroe, Marine, you name it, anybody who would pay my expenses I would play for.

I finished playing when I was about 33, 34 years of age. But I was so involved in the football with schools international matches, both home and abroad, that I found it difficult to get time off from running a big school. At that time Tony Waiters was in charge of the youngsters here and I'd developed quite a relationship with him through coaching and he was going back into the game as a player. He went to keep goal for Burnley and he suggested to Liverpool when they asked him about a replacement that they should try me. I was 47 years of age I think then. I had always hankered after doing something full-time in football and felt the temptation to come here. The director of education was horrified that one of the head teachers should consider joining the rat race of football with all its ramifications but I'd decided that's what I wanted to do. For his part he was very decent. He said that should it not work out there would always be a job in Liverpool for me, albeit starting at the bottom again! Armed with that assurance I came here.

I started here in 1970 so it's nearly 30 years and in that time I've done a variety of jobs. Apart from coaching the young ones I was used in various capacities during our very long and success-ful run in European competitions. I used to go and watch the opposition, that was a most interesting period for me because I went all over Europe on my own doing the spying job, as it were. I had some experiences, particularly in the Iron Curtain countries because in the early years they didn't really want you there and didn't make you very welcome either. Particularly I can remember five very lonely days in Russia when I went to watch Dynamo Tblisi play. They played two games in five days and they weren't very hospitable. I don't know what it's like now, probably vastly different, but in those days it wasn't easy to get about.

I had a bit of a setback in 1985 when I was coming up to 60, I had a heart problem and I had bypass surgery. I had five bypasses done and it was thought that I should retire. But I never lost my appetite for football and as soon as I was well again I was back here. The chap who filled my position as youth development officer left rather suddenly and so they invited me back to hold the fort until they got someone else. I was invited on to the board of directors in Graeme Souness's time.

I've enjoyed every minute of my association here and I've a host of interesting memories of this place. I've never lost my appetite or addiction to this game and people now say to me, 'well, you're 78 in a matter of weeks' but I can't lose this appetite that I've got for footballing people and the game itself, even though it's changed dramatically since I first joined this club.

TOM SAUNDERS
A Good Buffer

Bob Paisley was a very good buffer between the players and the manager which assistant managers ought to be. Shanks made the bullets and Bob fired them.

We used to get changed at Anfield and come down to Melwood and I'd be there about 8am but there would always be one fellow there before me and that would be Shanks; he'd be in a tracksuit by 8.30am. He would stand at the far end of the corridor where the players would come in about 9.30am and he used to look at everybody and he'd say to me occasionally, 'Tom, did you see that one, did you see his eyes, he's been out all night. He's not looking after himself.' Now he didn't go to the player and confront him with that, Bob was the man. He'd say, 'You get after him,' and Bob was very good at doing that. It wasn't an easy job because it was a job that produced people who thought 'well, you're having a down on me', that kind of thing, but that was the way it operated and at that time very successfully.

TOM SAUNDERS

The Talking Shop

The boot room really arose out of a need for somewhere to be on a Sunday morning. Players who were injured on a Saturday had to report on a Sunday morning and all the staff also came in on a Sunday morning. What was tremendous about that place was that in the early years you tended just to listen, you didn't make much of a contribution unless you were asked. But the interesting conversation that emerged about the previous day's game, about individual players and the team as a collective item was tremendous because at the time we were the most successful club in European football.

People presumed that there was a lot of magic here but in my humble opinion whilst management was very important, more important than that was the quality of the players that Liverpool had at that time.

Somebody has to choose those players and develop them but not only was the choice important but the continuity. Once you have that position that you've got good players and they're successful, other people want to join you and you have a certain continuity. The art of the business is maintaining that continuity so you've always got a residue of good players available to you, that's the important thing. It's about looking at the team and the individuals that make up the team and assessing how long they're going to be able to play at the top level.

Bob Paisley, for example, often said that a player could play in top-class football, barring injury of course, for a ten-year period but with the mental effort required to stay at the top and the physical effort, that was about it. You really had to say, hey, he's nearly at the end of the road. Now I think that was a very difficult thing to be able to do because there's an emotional aspect. You know you like to see a player, you're only a spectator but you have a particular feeling for a player and there's no way that you can see the football team playing without this particular player and there's an emotional involvement. It's difficult to see and to say, but how long is he going to be good enough for us to win things, and winning things is the important aspect. Bob Paisley was very good at looking at his men and saying, yes, he's a good player but I'm not sure we'll win anything with him because he's short of certain qualities that I think the top-class competitor needs to bring to the team in order to win things. So it really is about the players.

On Sunday mornings they would ask me or John Bennison, for example, how the junior teams got on. I remember only too well if you said you'd lost with the A team or the B team or whatever, that often was the end of the conversation. If you said you'd won, they'd say, well, how did he play and so on. In those days the training involved the staff playing the young players so they were well aware of the young players' capabilities and they were obviously interested in their development. But it was all about winning. That was what the boot room was about.

Now times have changed a bit, I think. Today the development of young players is much more enlightened and progressive and it is probably a much more intelligent approach. Now they have all sorts of embargoes on them. They can play only so many games a week and do so much training and coaching and all the rest of it. But in the old days they played every day and competed every day. Time will judge which is the better way. The way in which the professionals now approach the game has changed dramatically in the last 10, 15 years, both on the medical side, the fitness side and training. It has been revolutionised and probably we'll reap the benefit of that. I like to see a very competitive animal in a football shirt.

The other aspect of the boot room of course, which probably is more known to people, is that after the game on a Saturday or a week night or whenever, the opposition trainers and coaches were invited into the boot room for a drink. They seldom discussed the game which had just taken place other than perhaps to mention an indifferent refereeing performance. It was an opportunity to talk about football in general terms and it was very illuminating and interesting. If you were a youngster like I was in those times, you tended to listen and you learnt a good deal. I'm talking about the people like the Cloughies of this world; it was a focal point after the game. Those were the only people who ever came into the boot room, the staff of the visiting team and our own staff. We were the first club, I think, to institute a place where the staff could get together after the game and enjoy a half-an-hour chat about football in general. Gradually the others followed suit. And so I suppose it's true to say that the boot room was the starting point for such activities to develop in other clubs.

There was another thing about the Sunday morning dialogue which was interesting. You'd got 24 hours or so to have thought about your games. I think today it's a mistake often for people to be forced into a position to talk about what's happened only half an hour after it's finished. You went away either dispirited or on a high. If we'd had a bad result Shanks used to go home and clean the cooker, that kind of thing, everybody had a different type of activity to do. If my results weren't that good I listened to music, particularly opera, and I could get lost in that but only for a period of time and when the music switched off you were back. I think the boot room on a Sunday gave you an opportunity to put the whole thing in perspective. You know there's a danger in football of losing and thinking it's your fault as an individual but that's not the case, you were all involved, the team's involved and everybody else. I think that people could talk much more coherently about the game given 24 hours or so.

My philosophy has always been about any successful organisation that it is the people in it and the people who run it. The more diverse they are in many ways, the better it is, providing someone is at the helm who can keep pulling all the strings. Shanks was a very charismatic figure who showed tremendous emotional enthusiasm for everything that was part of Liverpool. But he needed direction and he needed someone to lean on and he leaned on his men, all of them. Whether he did knowingly or not, I just don't know, but he was the boss man. For example, nobody gave an interview, I couldn't talk to you now if Shanks was here without going to Shanks for permission.

WILLIE STEVENSON

Gunner Paisley

Gunner was his nickname after the time he spent in the war. He knew the game inside out, though he was not so good on players' names. Some people would go all around the houses to get to their point but Bob would cut through the long grass, straight to the point.

There was no animosity between Bob, Bill, Joe Fagan and Reuben Bennett. That's unusual with four people who were all personalities in their own right to get on so well. That was the most remarkable thing as far as I was concerned.

Although Bob was not bombastic he could make his point. He would stare at you and when you got the stare from Bob you knew you mustn't overstep the mark. Bill was the manager the whole time I was there. He pulled the strings, but Bob was given the bullets to fire.

I remember one little story. We were up in Blackpool. It was a bit of relaxing, a spot of fresh air, some training. We had been given £3 per day, for the three days. That was £9. Anyhow, after the first day Shanks was not happy with the hotel so he decided we would go back home. He then sent Bob round to each of the lads, telling him, the lads owe us £6, go to each of them and get it back. Well, we told him to bugger off, we'd already spent it all on the Saturday night. He had no chance of getting it back. We just stayed the one night and went back on the Sunday! It was so funny to see Bob having to get that £6 back off us!

He was a great tactician, not over-elaborate. He wouldn't do things with the drawing board or moving players around. No, it was mainly verbal. He would know that one or two players would make the opposition tick. If you were playing United, for example, they would have Best, Law, Charlton, etc, so who do you mark? Bob would say, look at the goalscorer, Law is getting 25 goals a season, so watch him. That way you cut out 50 per cent of their scoring chances. It's not that he would say Charlton couldn't play but he would see Law as the man creating 50 per cent of their goals.

Bill would take team talks but he would always ask Bob afterwards 'Right Bob, what do you think?' and Bob would have his say. Shankly's team talks were fairly brief, they did not get over complicated. But he would always ask Bob for his opinions. But he had to be careful. I can remember Bob coming back after seeing a European side. Bob was very impressed by them but before he could get too deeply into it, Bill said, 'Hey Bob, that's enough, let's talk about our players.' He'd sent this guy abroad, put him up in a hotel and when he mentions two or three of their players, Bill shuts him up.

ALAN KENNEDY

Geoff Twentyman: The Vital Cog

I think there was a consistency. Liverpool never really changed formation throughout the youth teams and the first teams and the reserves. They kept the same system all the way through and they didn't like playing players out of position. If they'd bought a player to play full-back then he played full-back, if they'd bought a player to play centre-back, or centre-forward, it didn't matter. But I liked the way that they nurtured the players through.

Ian Rush really had a pretty bad time when he first came to Liverpool, playing in the reserves, and probably wondered why he had joined from Chester City, but Bob saw something in him. He had him watched by Geoff Twentyman who brought some great, great players. He stayed in the reserves for a little while but got his chance in the first team. And that was always going to come but you had to be patient. Some players wouldn't actually make a great impression on Liverpool as a regular first team member but you felt as though you'd made a contribution. Players like Michael Robinson and David Hodgson, they didn't really have too many games for Liverpool but their contribution was vital at the time. I think Bob, Tom Saunders and Geoff

Twentyman could see players that would fit in. Now whether they fitted in for a year or ten years doesn't make any difference, they would make a contribution towards Liverpool winning a trophy.

Geoff Twentyman's contribution cannot be measured by anything other than he brought people like Kenny Dalglish, Graeme Souness, myself, Alan Hansen. The team was fashioned by Bob Paisley but it was brought together by Geoff Twentyman.

I think Bob would say something to Geoff like, 'Geoff, I need a right-sided midfield player who likes to attack down the right, would you go out and find me one?' He probably didn't have to look very far, he probably would have got Jimmy Case for the job. But if he wanted a left-sided player who could score a few goals and was neat on the ball, he looked at Ray Kennedy. He's not quite a centre-forward, let's bring him back and see what he's like at left-half. It was up to Bob to mould him into that left-sided midfield position and he did ever so well.

ALAN KENNEDY

Solving Problems

Bob used to put the fear of God into you when on a Saturday or a Friday we'd have our team meeting. He might say something that he didn't really mean, like he was going to change the team around. We would be wondering who was going to be left out and when we arrived at the ground on Saturday lunchtime he had put all the boots in the middle, rather than by your strip, so nobody knew who was going to play. But really he had only got 13 or 14 to choose from because in those days it was 11 outfield players and one substitute, so only 12 could play. I felt terrible on several occasions when I was left out as being part of the 13. On some occasions he played Emlyn Hughes at left-back instead of me. I think on one or two occasions he played Alan Hansen instead of me and I was disappointed but the one thing I didn't do was to go crying to the manager. I just felt if I got my head down, if I listened and I learned then I'd get back in the team.

Bob never liked anyone to go to his office. If Bob wanted to see anybody he would call them to his office through Ronnie Moran, and Ronnie would come into the first team dressing room. He'd say 'Alan, the manager wants to see you.' You knew you were either going to get transferred or you were going to get a rollicking. You always felt as though you were going to get a put-down when you went into Bob's office. I went in several times because he called me. He would say, 'What's wrong with your game?'

Part of my game in the first stages when I came to Liverpool was based upon Newcastle where I used to hit the long ball. I had Malcolm Macdonald and a guy called Tudor upfront and, based on the long ball theory, I thought route one, get it over the top. Macdonald would maybe score a goal but that wasn't Liverpool's policy and it took me quite a long time to actually get into Liverpool's way, to build up patiently from the back. Then you get into a position where you can either cross the ball or maybe have a shot at goal. He called me in several times to re-emphasise the point that I wasn't playing for Liverpool, saying if I didn't buck my ideas up there would be somebody else in the team. He didn't actually say that but I knew what he meant and I tried and tried and tried.

After seven years at the club there were probably six people who tried to take the left-back spot from me. They brought in Avi Cohen, the lad called Richard Money, and they had a lad called Mark Lawrenson. He didn't start off as a central defender, he started off as a full-back with Phil Neal as right-back. Phil Thompson was also there and Alan Hansen and myself that came in and played full-back. And then there was Emlyn Hughes, as well as Joey Jones and eventually Jim Beglin. Jim was eventually the one that succeeded in taking the left-back spot from me. But going back to the earlier ones, they could play in several other positions as well. I think Avi Cohen was cover for anybody along the back four, so was Colin Irwin, so was Richard Money. Those two played against Bayern Munich in the semi-final in 1981. I didn't play and Alan Hansen didn't play, so they played and did their part to get us to the final. I think when Bob looked at the team and looked where his strengths were, he thought to himself, well, I'm going to play Alan Kennedy in the final. Fortunately it worked for him.

I think Bob had a good back room staff. Not one of them worked against each other and they all got on well and once the manager or the assistant manager spoke, that was it. Generally speaking Ronnie Moran was the taskmaster. Bob would say 'Right Ronnie, you're taking the lads out, I want them to have a quick warm-up, a little game and then we're going to go for a big run.' And he was the one that would do it. He'd say to us 'Right, you're doing it, simple as that.' We'd moan a little bit and we'd say, we played a game a couple of days ago, we need a rest, but generally they knew how far to push us and we knew how far to push them. The general opinion was that if you push players too far they rebel in some way but they did give us the freedom to express ourselves at the training ground and on the pitch and that was the good thing about it.

I think a lot of Liverpool's play was off the cuff. It was just what you thought and did at the time. They allowed you to be men, to be professional, to look after yourself and to know that you are a professional footballer.

ALAN KENNEDY

Discipline

In those days you could probably get away with doing what we did. We were never told to go home, relax, get your feet up. We were told, 'you've got a training session tomorrow, you've got a match on Saturday, look after yourself' and that was it. Some liked playing golf, some liked to have a beer to relax and some liked to do other things. The family men would probably go home to their families, they had young kids to bring up. Myself and a few of the lads who were single tended to wander off and do our own thing. As long as we didn't get into trouble and as long as we didn't disgrace the name of Liverpool then the club were happy. You wouldn't last five minutes at the club if they thought you were trouble. There were a couple of occasions when Liverpool did have a few problems and those players were quickly ousted from the team and out of Liverpool Football Club. You have to say that experience tells you it was probably for the better.

JOEY JONES

Joining Liverpool

I joined in July 1975. I only stayed three years or so. But it was the time of my life and with the family being from Liverpool that made it even better. My dad's family was from the south end of Liverpool. I was brought up supporting Liverpool even though I was born in Llandudno which was full of Liverpool Irish and Welsh people. I joined Wrexham when I was 15 but I have supported Liverpool all my life. Whenever I had the chance I would go and watch them and stand on the Kop, going on the train with all the lads. I can remember being in the boys' pen as well before I went on the Kop. This would be middle to late sixties.

I never, ever dreamed I would get the chance to play for the team I supported. I couldn't believe it when I found out Liverpool were after me. There was talk at the time that a few clubs were interested. Everton were said to be one and there was the possibility of a swap deal with Sheffield United with Len Badger. They were in the first division then, it was £100,000 plus Badger. But to be perfectly honest I didn't want to go as I was perfectly happy at Wrexham. The only club I would have left Wrexham for was Liverpool. When I first signed I was overawed. I couldn't believe I was in a club where the players were the ones I had cheered from the Kop. So it took a little bit of time to settle.

Bob Paisley was the manager. Reuben Bennett was still there, John Bennison, Geoff Twentyman. An ex-Carlisle player, he was the chief scout. I know his son now, he was assistant at Bristol Rovers. Geoff was always popping in and I found myself chatting to him a lot, particularly about the lower divisions. He bought a lot of players from the lower divisions such as Kevin Keegan, Ray Clemence, myself, Alec Lindsay and so on. A lot of them came through Geoff Twentyman. He didn't really train with us but he'd be down at Melwood in a tracksuit. I always found that most of them were hands-on. They weren't office types. They'd all have tracksuits on, and give you advice. Coming from the lower divisions, he'd sometimes ask me if I'd played against so-and-so, what do you think of such-and-such a player. I'm sure he had an input into signing not just the top players but the lower division ones as well. They had complete faith in him and you certainly can't knock his record.

I was one of the few who did the opposite to the norm. They usually signed players from the lower divisions and then put them in the reserves for a season or so. But I did the opposite, I came straight into the first team and then ended up in the reserves! When I signed I went straight into the team and played against Utrecht in Holland and then Borussia Dortmund. I scored against them. They must have thought I was another Chris Lawler but it didn't turn out that way. I also played against Queens Park Rangers where we lost but we beat them to the league title. I remember having to sprint 30 or 40 yards to hook the ball off the line and it was the first time I heard Liverpool fans chanting my name. It made me feel ten feet tall. Although we lost, I remember getting back because I couldn't drive and I got the train to Wrexham and I got back into my digs in Wrexham in time for *Match of the Day*. It was the first time I'd been on *Match of the Day* and they showed the incident a couple of times. It felt very strange looking at myself on television.

Tom Saunders used to take us in training sometimes. He was the European scout. In pre-season we'd break into different groups and Tom would take one session where he would give us a series of exercises, good for the stamina or whatever. Again, he was usually in a tracksuit. He obviously didn't have the input of Joe or Ronnie or the boss but he did take sessions and had a lot to do with the youngsters. John Bennison was with the B team when I was there. He too would be out in his tracksuit and he spent a lot of time with the younger lads. He had a lot to offer them and lots of them came through. For every one or two who did come good there would be ten or a dozen who didn't. You can't get everyone through. But he played a big part in the club along with Joe, Ronnie and Tom, and they were influential in what happened. I always found it easy to talk to them for advice or whatever. Now that I'm on the coaching side that's the way I would like to be. If any of the players have a problem I'd like to think I could talk to them.

Another lesson I learned was the determined way they go about things, the commitment they demand. I think you have to have someone on the side who is enthusiastic as well. You could constantly hear the coaches from the side giving advice, especially Ronnie who was always bawling. It helps. Phil's the same. It's part of the game, the shouting from the touchline. Even though the boss might sit in the stands for the first half he'd come down after the interval and let you know in no uncertain terms what he thought of you from the dugout. But Ronnie was the loudest. They told you good or bad and it didn't matter if you were a superstar or a kid. It made you feel better to hear them. They didn't go overboard if you made a mistake. They'd tell you the right way. It was positive. I think that's why it was successful.

Everyone knew about the boot room and wanted to know its secret. All I ever saw of the boot room was crates of ale, or bottles of coke. If I did have to go in they'd be sitting there on crates or skips, talking. I think that's where they did most of their planning. But I didn't go in there an awful lot, just the odd occasion. Being one of the younger ones, they'd take the mickey out of me. That was great and of course you'd give it back but you were fighting a losing battle with them. They'd heard it all before, they were wily old foxes. It was all part of the team spirit, character building. Part of the Liverpool thing, you've got to be able to take it as well as give it. We'd go to the Daresbury Hotel on a Friday night and you'd pop in the boot room to check in and then go and get the bus outside. Most Fridays we went to the Daresbury unless of course we were playing some distance from Liverpool. That was all different to me, coming from a small club.

JOEY JONES

The Brilliance of Bob Paisley

I remember Bob Paisley said to me, 'Joey, Clive Whitehead, if he plays on the right wing I want you at left-back, and if he plays on the left wing, I want you to swap with Phil Neal and go to right-back. You follow him everywhere,' he says. The next day the team sheet comes out and Clive Whitehead is sub. 'Joey,' says Bob, 'you're not playing.' I couldn't believe it. He dropped me because he wasn't playing. I'd arranged for my dad to come over and the tickets were there for him. The next thing is that I hear them all shouting, 'Joey, Joey, get in the dressing room, Alan Hansen's gone down with something.' So, I did play in the end but initially he wasn't going to play me because Whitehead wasn't playing!

I thought Bob Paisley was brilliant. He had a dry sense of humour. I had just signed and didn't have much European experience. We were in Barcelona for a UEFA cup tie. We won 1–0 and John Toshack scored. Now they hadn't been beaten at home in a while. I was one of the substitutes. We were sitting on chairs by the touchline. Liverpool were playing really well. Then all these things started being thrown at us. I thought it was stones. We looked around and it was hard-boiled sweets. So Liverpool are passing it round and playing really well. Tosh scores and it's getting better and more and more stuff is coming at us. It's the end of the game and the whistle has gone and everything starts coming out of the stands at us, cushions, the lot. I got up and started throwing these cushions back like Frisbees and they're bouncing off the Spaniards' heads. I was getting really good at this. The fans were looking at me in amazement. Bob Paisley comes rushing over, grabs me by the collar, and says, 'What the f*** are you doing?' I said, 'I'm not having all these fans throwing cushions at me.' He says, 'What, don't you realise they're not throwing them at us, they're throwing them at their own players because they're getting beat! Now get back in that dressing room.'

He had a right go at me. I hadn't done it on purpose, I was just trying to protect us.

Another time. A Good Friday at Melwood. I was in the second team and Roy Evans was taking us. We were at the top end of the field, I'd run, played the ball to Roy and he's laid it back, I've hit it and it's gone over the bar, over the wall at Melwood and through someone's window. I popped my head over the wall and this fella is going berserk. Not only has it smashed his window but it's taken half his frame out. So I asked for the ball back. Well, you can imagine what this fella thought. He wanted to fight me. So I said, I'll come round and get the ball right now. Anyhow, Roy comes over and says, 'Get down, I'll get someone to go round and get someone out to put a new window in.' Anyhow Bob Paisley was looking out of the window of the hut at Melwood. He comes out and he shouts, 'Joey, get in here!' So I thought, 'Oh hell, I'm in for another fine here.' So I went in and he says, 'Sit down there.' So I sit down and I'm expecting the worst and he said, 'I've been here over 30 years and nobody, but nobody, has ever done that before. You know your problem, don't you?' I said, 'What?' He said, 'You're leaning too far back, you want to get your body over the ball!'

He could be a hard man. You have to be if you want to be a manager. How can you leave people out of Cup Finals? You need to be hard, have a hard streak. You can only play 11 men. Someone has to be disappointed. I never saw him play but people tell me he was a tough one. He had the build for toughness. He certainly had a hard streak in him. He'd have no qualms about leaving a top player out as he would a young one. I was at his funeral and I was sitting having a cup of tea afterwards and Bob Paisley's son came over and said hello, and told me that his father had said a lot about me and liked me a lot. Now he didn't have to say that. I was just one of the ordinary players, no big star, but he deliberately came over to tell me that. I felt very humble that in my short time there he obviously thought much of me. Of all the people there, Tommy Smith, St John, all of them, he comes over to me and tells me that. I'll never forget that.

JOEY JONES
Training Was Never Complicated

I have to be honest and say that the training at Wrexham was a lot harder than Liverpool, a lot harder. I'd always had this image that the higher the team, the harder the training. But at Wrexham it was really hard. We used to do really physical stuff at Wrexham. I thought when I got to Liverpool that it would be tough going but I couldn't believe how easy it was compared to being here at Wrexham. Everything was more simplified, it wasn't complicated. I always remember Joe Fagan saying when we used to do running, as long as you put it in; not everybody can be first, somebody has to finish at the back, as long as you are not cheating yourself. I thought that was great for a coach to say that, because at many clubs the coaches say you've got to be at the front. But not everybody has the same pace. You can still get everything out of training if you are at the back. It's a lesson I've carried over now that I'm a coach. Everything was simple at Anfield, never complicated. I can't recall us doing any set-pieces. I think they had the players who were capable of doing things off the cuff, and just let them get on with it. I think what Ronnie, Bob and the others did was to give advice and let them get on with it. We had loads of five-a-sides and some board work, particularly to help Ray Clemence by having bodies in the way. But I honestly can't remember set-pieces.

SAMMY LEE
The Coach's View

When I first came to Liverpool Football Club in 1976, I was an apprentice. So part of my duties was to make sure the boot room was clean. It was actually then, as it was termed, a boot room. It was where all the boots were stored and where they were cleaned.

You'd always had the same crowd – John Bennison, Tom Saunders, Joe Fagan, Bob Paisley, Roy Evans and Reuben Bennett – all crammed into that small room. Then on matchday, there would be the opposition management staff in there, as well as other guests. They would all fit in, no problem. It used to astound me how they all got in there.

The boot room was one of those places that was always revered, and after games people would want to go in and talk about the previous 90 minutes. You'd be walking past it and in that small space you'd see the likes of Dave Sexton, who was a manager then, Don Howe, and Ron Atkinson. If you had a job to do with the boots as an apprentice you'd do that outside, but you wouldn't just walk into the boot room. You'd ask before you entered and then you'd go and put the boots back where they belonged. There was a definite mystique about the place, it was sacrosanct.

I think what made it so unique was that the back room staff started it. I think Liverpool were the first club to initiate post-match discussions by inviting other teams in there for a drink. Win, lose or draw, you entertained people, just to chew over the game. When I joined the coaching staff, I found it very beneficial to talk to the opposition in there. Sometimes it's not very easy if you've been beaten, but you still have to put on a brave face, albeit when you don't want to. I think people have respected Liverpool Football Club for that.

After every training session, in the afternoon the Liverpool staff were in there talking for three, maybe four hours. They never used to leave until 5pm. They certainly held tactical discussions about players. I'm sure they did.

There were slight changes when I came back under Graeme Souness as a coach. The main nucleus of the boot room staff was still there. Graeme wanted to keep them there, so it was still a meeting place where you went and chatted about things. We then moved away from the system of reporting to Anfield, changing into our gear, going to Melwood, training, then coming back to Anfield and changing back. So the day-to-day things altered a little.

You can't say that things haven't gone well because the boot room has gone. The Kop has gone as well, there have been all sorts of things and many reasons why Liverpool haven't done so well in recent years. People have their own theories and solutions, but I don't think the disappearance of the boot room has had anything to do with the club's problems. We still hold discussions. The fact that we don't go back to Anfield after training doesn't mean we never meet. We still try to plot the downfall of the opposition.

I can understand why people link the demise of the boot room with the problems at the club; it's to do with tradition. You go to many clubs now and things have moved on, but there is still a role for that boot room philosophy. At Liverpool we have meetings all the time which you could term boot room meetings. They are staff meetings. The actual venue may be different but we have pre-match and post-match get-togethers all the time.

Personally, I think it's the characters that make up any meeting or committee who are all-important. So whether it be a two-man committee or a 22-man committee, it's the individuals who determine the input.

Bob Paisley was the constant throughout. I still don't think he has been given the full credit; I don't mean by people at Liverpool FC, but from outside the club. Bob was an extremely talented man, very knowledgeable and wise. I think he suffered sometimes because he was perceived as not being able to get his point across as eloquently as some people. But he was vitally important to the club. He's been the one common factor and that in itself speaks volumes for the man.

Joe Fagan was another important figure. He was in the background when Bob was manager, very quietly spoken, but when he did raise his voice you knew that he meant it and that something was wrong. He led with a rod of iron but in a quiet way. He didn't rant and rave, yet everyone had so much respect for him. When he gave you that glare, you knew you had to get yourself into shape.

Ronnie Moran was also vital. He was different to Joe. That's what makes a good team – everyone was different. It's that mix and blend that you have to have. Ronnie was the man who kept on reminding you of your responsibilities. He was crucial to the makeup of the boot room. Then Roy Evans came in, and being younger than the others he acted as a bridge between the boot room and the players. It became a breeding ground and you could see the continuity which I think was vital for the changeover of players.

There's no doubt there was a change when Phil Thompson left in 1991 and I came back. Strictly speaking, I did not take Phil's job. But he was absolutely brilliant about it at the time, he was terrific. It was a difficult period for me because I was close to Phil, and I still am. The way he conducted himself was first-class. To me that showed the true strength of his character. It would have been easy for him to be bitter, but he wasn't. I can't praise Phil Thompson enough for the way he handled things.

The actual boot room was still there when I returned to the club, but plans were afoot to change things. Everyone at Liverpool appeared to be very philosophical about it going. They didn't see it as the end of an era, they just said time moves on, things progress. The end of the boot room didn't seem to have any great effect on them.

CHAPTER THREE

Joe Fagan

If anyone can be regarded as the founding father of the boot room it is probably Joe Fagan. The rubbery-faced Fagan was the man who established the tradition, bringing in the crates of Export Guinness, and inviting visiting managers and staff in for a drink after the game. Shankly was manager then but it was the boot room staff of Fagan, Paisley, Ronnie Moran, Reuben Bennett, Albert Shelley and later Roy Evans who did the entertaining. After each game at Anfield, including reserve matches, they would invite the visiting staff in for a bottle of Joe's famous Export Guinness. Shanks would pop down and say hello, but it was basically left to the others.

Born in Earlstown in 1921, Joe Fagan might well have joined Liverpool as a youngster after impressing the then manager George Kay with his ability in a trial game. But instead he surprisingly opted to try his luck 35 miles down the East Lancs Road at Manchester City. Sadly, war was to interrupt his career, postponing any league appearances until New Year's Day 1947.

A centre-half, he helped City gain promotion to the first division that season and went on to give sterling service over the next couple of seasons as City consolidated their place in the top flight. Then in 1951 he moved briefly down the road to Altrincham and then Nelson before returning to league football with third division north Bradford Park Avenue. In 1953 that was followed by a spell as trainer at Rochdale under manager Harry Catterick, the man who would later lead Everton to championship success.

Fagan had more than witnessed the underbelly of English football and so, in a way, it was surprising that in 1958 Liverpool should pluck him out of the obscurity of the third division. But Phil Taylor, the then manager, must have spotted something in Fagan. When Shankly arrived he merely reminded Fagan that he had tried to sign him for Grimsby. Therefore, as Shankly put it, 'You must be good.' He was, and for 25 years he proved it in the back room staff at Anfield, always eager to do any chore.

Fagan didn't shout often, but when he did the players jumped and took notice. Generally he was a quiet, unassuming man. If he was your next-door neighbour you would probably have never known he was a football manager unless you yourself were interested in Liverpool. His bark was worse than his bite, says Roger Hunt, even though he gave the appearance of being a strict disciplinarian. Others tend to agree that he was never as hard as the likes of Shankly, Paisley or Reuben Bennett. Like Paisley before him he was a father figure. Hunt, for one, benefited enormously from Fagan's understanding approach. So too did many others. His finest quality was perhaps his ability to interpret Bob Paisley. Paisley was well known for his incomprehensible and often muddled team talks. He was not the greatest communicator but Fagan understood him and could readily impart his meaning on to the players.

Joe Fagan's moment arrived in the summer of 1983. He had been promoted to Bob Paisley's assistant when Shankly retired but with the departure of Paisley, Fagan was promoted to the top job, although he shared the same reluctance as Bob Paisley to take on command. He was to hold it for just two seasons. At 62 years of age he was probably the oldest manager in football. What's more, you would be hard pushed to think of another man getting his first managerial job at such an age. But he'd served his apprenticeship and the board had every confidence that he would carry on just as normal. Joe was never the kind of man to upset things.

As usual everyone moved up a notch with Ronnie Moran becoming assistant and Roy Evans taking over as first team trainer. Former full-back Chris Lawler was drafted in to look after the reserves while Tom Saunders and John Bennison continued to spend most of their time with the youngsters.

Dalglish felt that Fagan, like Paisley, never really wanted the job.

'Joe was a wee bit similar,' he says, adding that 'he was great in the first year but didn't really enjoy it. Management wasn't Joe's scene.' Ronnie Moran is, as ever, full of praise for his friend. 'I have known Joe since he arrived from Rochdale and I have always looked up to him. I have never met a nicer, more straightforward fellow. He was what the boot room was all about.'

And yet, Fagan's first season turned out to be one of the most successful in the club's history as they lifted three trophies, the league title, the League Cup and the European Cup. It was the first time any English club had claimed three major trophies in one season. It was also their third title in three years, a feat matched only by Arsenal and Huddersfield Town.

Liverpool's victory over Roma in the European Cup Final, albeit on penalties, was one of their finest, particularly as the game was played on Roma's home ground. The shrewd Fagan reached the highest pinnacle primarily with the side he had inherited from Bob Paisley but Ronnie Moran feels that he ought to be given more credit for winning the treble. 'He was a marvellous tactician,' he says, 'it should be appreciated more widely that Joe did an enormous amount towards getting that team together and then developing it.' And yet Fagan, unbeknown to himself, almost scuppered the entire occasion.

Dalglish and Souness were rooming together the night before the final and had gone to bed early to get a decent night's sleep but were awoken by a terrible racket coming from the room next door. They banged on the wall but still the noise continued. Souness was all for going next door to sort the culprit out but Dalglish calmed him down and instead phoned reception and asked them to telephone the room next door and tell them to switch their radio off. A minute later the radio went off and all was quiet. The following morning at breakfast they discovered that the occupant of the room next door was none other than Joe Fagan!

Fagan will probably never be given the credit he deserves. There will always be that argument that it was Paisley's side and that he only had two years in the job. Yet Fagan did venture into the transfer market. Paul Walsh, a big-name signing from Luton Town, joined in the summer of 1984 to provide the tasty prospect of a Dalglish, Walsh, Rush trio upfront. Strangely, the three were to play together on only a handful of occasions. The bubbly Michael Robinson, a surprise £200,000 buy from Manchester City, also joined along with Gary Gillespie from Coventry and later that season John Wark from Ipswich. Robinson turned out to be a disappointment who lasted little more than 12 months, while Wark was an inspiration. There were only a few notable departures from Anfield, mainly ageing players like Terry McDermott, Phil Thompson, and David Fairclough. Steve Nicol also became a regular but apart from that there was little meddling with the format. The only other major change in Fagan's stewardship was the departure of Graeme Souness for Italy in the summer of 1984, the European Cup final win over Roma marking his swansong.

Fagan's second season in charge was to be a story of personal tragedy as well as humiliation for Liverpool Football Club. Liverpool had geared their entire season towards winning the European Cup. You could always sense that the league was not top of their priorities and they finished in second place, a massive 13 points adrift of neighbours Everton (and reached the semi-finals of the FA Cup, only to lose to United in the replay). Dalglish called it 'a dreadful scason'. He'd also had a disagreement with Fagan when he was dropped. 'I had no problem with him leaving me out,' claims Dalglish, 'what upset me was reading about it first in the papers.' Dropping Kenny Dalglish was unheard of. But at least it demonstrated that Fagan could be ruthless when it came to doing something which was in the best interests of Liverpool Football Club. In truth they missed Souness and the authority which he had brought to the midfield; Jan Molby, delightful player though he was, could never replace the hard man Souness.

Yet, if ever there was a European campaign aimed at bringing success, this was it. They had already won the European Cup four times and the anticipated fifth victory would make them the most successful club in European football behind the great Real Madrid.

Towards the end of the season Joe Fagan indicated to the board that he wanted to retire. But it had never been made public. He would be 64 years old by the end of the campaign and the club's policy of retirement at the age of 65 meant it would be his final full season. With a March birthday he could probably have wangled a few extra months until the end of the following season but this seemed as good a time as any to depart. To go out in the blaze of glory of a European Cup triumph had its appeal.

But it was not to be. Instead Joe Fagan departed a broken man, his moment of glory robbed by the mindless stupidity of hooligans and the authorities who refused to listen to Liverpool's warnings that the Heysel stadium was not equipped for such a game. In the event 39 people died and with it much respect for Liverpool and their fans. It was a nightmare and utter humiliation. Instead of returning to a tumultuous reception along with the accolades of the world's press, Fagan trudged down the steps of the plane at Speke Airport with tears in his eyes and away from football. He would rarely return to Anfield.

ALAN KENNEDY

Heysel

Bob moved out in '83. Joe took over and really, I don't think things changed. We still saw Bob every so often. The only thing about it, we couldn't call him 'boss'. He was now a director of the club and Joe reluctantly took over as manager. Two seasons, five trophies, not bad. He might go down as one of the greats as well. Nothing changed . . . Roy Evans moved up from Central League to looking after the first team and they brought in a couple of other ex-players. I think Chris Lawler came in, Steve Heighway came back from America and although one or two faces might change, the policies didn't change. They were still 'Let's get out there, let's beat the opposition. If we score more goals than the opposition, we'll win the game.'

But of course it all ended tragically with Heysel. I don't think Heysel did us any favours. I think the five years out of European football did a lot of damage to Liverpool Football Club. We

weren't allowed to play in any European or any world competition. I don't think it helped Liverpool Football Club or the likes
of Everton who won the European Cup-Winners' Cup. I thought
that was very extreme considering what happened at Heysel but
when they came back into Europe we were sadly lacking and
behind European football. Although Liverpool were still domin-
ating English football, it then became in the nineties Manchester
United who dominated and Arsenal to a certain extent.

IAN HARGREAVES

The Clever Joe Fagan

Now Fagan to me was the cleverest. He gave the best interviews
of the lot. He gave the press everything and nothing. He was
always available. There were a lot of good things about Joe
Fagan. I don't think his best friends would claim that he was a
tactical genius or the inspiration behind Liverpool but he was
one of the most underestimated of men. He was totally honest,
totally decent. People would play for him, they'd die for him.
His interviews were hilarious. If he knew you, he'd make sure
he really knew you. He'd remember your Christian name. But
if you said anything against him he'd remember and he'd let you
know and you'd get no more out of him.

   After a match he was brilliant. He was always smartly turned
out, probably the smartest of Liverpool managers, always in a
suit. He'd come up the steps, saying 'How are you, how's the
wife, like a drink?' He'd always take the initiative 'by Jove, that
was a good game.' He was never involved in bad games, always
a good game. 'But Joe,' we'd say, 'you were beaten.' He always
prefaced things with 'Well, I said to Ronnie beforehand, this is
a good side we're up against.' At the end of it there was not a
thing you could use. Then he'd stop and say, 'Anything else?'
Nobody could fault him, he was always available but you got
nothing you could use.

PETER ROBINSON
The Unsung Hero

When Joe took over Bob was still around. Bob would still tend to go there for a drink with them. Tom Saunders did as well, because Tom was always part of the inner circle. I think if there is one man in this club who has not had the credit he deserves it's Tom Saunders. He's always been the unsung hero. He's made an enormous contribution but because of the nature of the man, he's never sought any publicity. I think it's never been recognised but I think if you could go back even to Bill and to Bob and people who are no longer with us and they would all tell you about the contribution that Tom made. Tom was very much the man who made a lot of the decisions about recruitment of new players. Tom would go and see them and Tom's word would be accepted by all of them.

PHIL CHISNALL
Down to Earth Joe

Joe Fagan was a nice bloke, he was the same as the others, down to earth. He'd tell you straight, but there was never any malice, you're not playing well son, and so on. Ronnie Moran was still playing then. It was mostly Shanks, Bob Paisley, Reuben Bennett. Tom Saunders came in occasionally but I didn't really know him. Those four were the main ones. Roy and Ronnie came later. They'd just come in, sit down and have a cup of tea and natter about what had happened that morning. I'd go in, take my boots in, and so on. You'd hear them laughing, talking about the five-a-side, Joe with the reserves, what happened Saturday, games in the week, and so on.

PHIL NEAL

John Bennison, The Local Lad

JB lived in there really. He was on the periphery but he was training every day, working with the youths, the YTS kids. He was never around the first team but he was always there, travelling on the bus with the young lads. He was a valuable member of staff. He'd tell me how he had brought such and such players through. In a way I was a foreigner coming to the club and didn't know all the detailed history. JB was a local lad, as was Ronnie Moran and Roy Evans. John would tell me these tales. One of the things I remember about John was that he was given the task of training the Liverpool ladies, that meant my wife, Kenny's wife and so on when they played charity games, usually against the Everton Ladies. They'd be trained for six weeks beforehand. For some reason John got this job of training the women, God knows why, but he had to train them, 15 girls for six weeks or so, followed by an outing to the sauna and pub. He was always around to pack skips, carry skips, and generally be on hand. But really he was training the youngsters. He was there every day but I didn't come across him so much.

PHIL NEAL

Have A Word

Once a player was accepted into the first team Joe would ask you to have a word with him. It would be better from a senior player and once a senior player said something to you, you listened. It was better coming from us rather than from Joe all the time. Joe was very diplomatic but he encouraged us five years down the line to become a senior and gave us the responsibility to put a young lad in order. And you'd go and sort it out. It was always better if it was done that way. There were eight or nine senior players with the rest coming up the ranks but you had to qualify for that. It worked very well. It helped them do their jobs. For me, Joe gave us that. There was very little trouble.

When I walked into the dressing room after I arrived I was in awe. Tommy Smith was three pegs away, Cally was right close to me, Chris Lawler was two pegs away. All of a sudden I'm looking in awe, so it took me five years before any youngsters came to me. I think that's the thing the boot room had, that discipline. They were good at having their board meetings in that eight by ten room. There was a cupboard as you came through the door and pegs all around with 40-odd pairs of boots. It was just like a warehouse, a place for kit, there were crates, empty bottles and a large waste bin outside the door. Had it been inside they wouldn't have got in.

GRAEME SOUNESS

The Agent Provocateur

Inside the boot room you will find Ronnie Moran, Roy Evans, Tom Saunders, Reuben Bennett, Chris Lawler, John Bennison and Geoff Twentyman, though rarely all at the same time. I must be honest and say that I have had more rows with Ronnie 'Bugsy' Moran than anyone in football. But when I sat down to analyse how I felt, I realised what a remarkable job this man does for Liverpool Football Club, albeit in an unusual manner.

I am not the only player to have had words with Bugsy but it was a long time before I discovered that it was all for my own benefit. He is deliberately antagonistic, a personal device used only to motivate players. There are no pats on the back, no congratulations, in fact, in the end you feel that you have done it yourself in spite of him rather than because of him. He is the club's *agent provocateur*, the man who gets everyone working, not just the players I played with at Liverpool but those who went before. It cannot be a coincidence that he has overseen all the great teams. His mate Roy Evans is just the opposite. He reminds me of a young Joe Fagan in that he is the perfect diplomat, always ready to talk and listen. He is everyone's friend. Tom Saunders probably knows more about the club and how it works than anyone else involved below stairs because he is the go-between who travels without the hitch or hindrance between boot room and the offices. The funny thing is that Tom, as far as I'm aware, is still officially called 'youth development officer' as he was when he left his job as a headmaster to join the club. He is a clever and versatile man who handles such matters as cautions, writing dinner speeches for Bob Paisley and spying on our European opponents. The job of watching our domestic opposition falls on the capable head of Reuben Bennett. Reuben is another popular figure and particularly among the old boys who come to visit. They call him the 'Fighting Scotsman' in reference to the dirty work he used to do for Bill Shankly.

An extract from *No Half Measures* by Graeme Souness (Collins Willow).

RICK PARRY
The New World v The Old World

The great thing about the boot room, when I started watching Liverpool, was the great mythology which was built around it. In a way that kind of contrasts with football now, it wouldn't be the same today because it would be completely exposed to television. Sky would have been in there every week. Maybe we are stripping too many layers back now. Is there no room for mythology any more? Do people know too much about the inside, about players? Was it not better in the days when we were allowed to form our own individual illusions? I guess everybody had their own notions of what the boot room was and maybe that was the best way. If you were inside it with a television camera every week, would it lose that mystique? It probably would.

I guess as a fan, and I'm going back to 1963 when my proper interest began in the boot room. It was what made Liverpool successful. It was where it all emanated from. Where all the planning and plotting of the great triumphs happened. It probably didn't but that was our perception. That was what we wanted to believe. And it obviously worked because we won everything in sight and the boot room distinguished us from every other club. We were doing it right and others weren't. I suspect the reality was a long way removed from that. But it probably symbolised more than that too. I actually think it was at the very heart of Liverpool as a family club. Anybody, any fan, could relate to the boot room because it was such a simple concept. It wasn't that plans were being hatched in great boardrooms across Europe. It was just so simple, you thought you could readily touch and relate to it. I think it symbolised family, and also continuity, the promotion from within, from within the boot room, that was the perception. It was perceived as a dynasty. It was where the continuity was created and nurtured and where the short-term and long-term plans were hatched.

I think it was largely the personalities. It must have been the personalities because without the personalities it would never have happened. It could have been anywhere. It was the boot room because there was nowhere else. What it was really about was the simple concept of people talking football, of like-minded people spending hour upon hour talking football and hatching their plans.

When I was at the Premier League I spent a lot of time with managers and when you talk to the likes of the Bobby Robsons of this world they felt that in their era, there was a greater community of spirit and a much greater opportunity for them to spend time with the great and legendary managers, listening, drinking in their ideas, just a great willingness to sit up until all hours of the morning exchanging ideas. When they were on the coaching courses at Lilleshall, for example, they talk very fondly of many hours spent in discussion. Dave Sexton and Terry Venables would say much the same thing of their early days as coaches, spending time with the likes of Malcolm Allison, exchanging ideas. They didn't have a boot room as such but it's the same sort of idea. It's about having a thirst for knowledge, about exchanging ideas and a desire to move on.

Although I did not know the man, Shanks was a great innovator, a great leader. He was never afraid to try new decisions, and to move on. But you do not do that in isolation, you do it by testing your ideas. It's all about having that chemistry of people, who you can bond with. They would bring the likes of Roy Evans in and thereby continue the dynasty. It's on-the-job training if you like.

I think to an extent it has gone but I don't share the view that it has no place or that because life is now different that you throw out all that is good. You can't however run football clubs like you did in the seventies, that's gone whether you like it or not. But my own view is that there is a business around football. I don't necessarily say football is a business because football to me is a game but you have to be businesslike. My own view is that we can be very businesslike without losing the essence of what Liverpool is all about. We talk about developing clubs as global brands which is a phraseology I hate, but let's use it as it does encapsulate the notion. I actually don't think we should lose touch with our roots or what is attractive about Liverpool. We don't have to be big and brash, or be what Manchester United are. What makes Liverpool attractive is the very essence of what Liverpool is all about. So I don't think you rush out and over-commercialise. You can still be very professional in a business sense without losing what the heart of Liverpool is. Its very attraction to the five million people worldwide who support Liverpool is that it is not brash and over commercialised. Somebody recently said to me that if you are looking at Liverpool and Man U in brand terms then maybe it's a bit like Avis and Hertz, the 'we try harder' philosophy is maybe not too far from the truth.

There is a paradox for United in that they are both the most loved and hated club. Liverpool don't have that, and there's no reason why we should become over-commercialised. It's a challenge but to me there is still a family feel about Liverpool, though I think we have maybe lost touch with supporters to an extent. I think that has drifted but it is not irreconcilable. We and United are the two national, indeed worldwide, clubs. We are successful; people want to share in our success. You don't knock that. It's a success that came from that special relationship. Shankly defined that with his relationship with the fans and in creating an image for the club. You can't replicate that. You can't constantly look backwards but if you could just bottle that essence and define what that essence really was. It's not easy to define what that special relationship was because it is different to everybody. And, as I say, in the sixties and seventies it was a lot easier because you were able to keep things secret. When all the layers are peeled back there is no mystique any more. People have to build their own image of what the club is about.

It's hearsay, as I was not here then, but it's not just that Bob Paisley could spot a good player. Many can spot a good player but what Bob had, which was a tremendous gift, was that he could spot the players who were going to win championships for you which is what it is all about. Now if we all had that secret this game would be easy. What Liverpool was all about was the right players which is why the coaching philosophy was so simple. You get the right players with the right attitudes and they will go far. Players imposed their own discipline, for example. You set the standards and people appreciate them. Of course it's so much easier to do when you have that winning habit. United to an extent have that. Fergie has been enormously successful in imposing that discipline. Like Shanks, Fergie has been ruthless and has been prepared to move players, top players, on when it has been demanded. That you can do when you are on the top of the pile. That's what sets standards when players know there is a line they cannot cross and you either want to go with those standards or you go somewhere else. And when you are on the top of the pile, there is nowhere else bigger to go. It becomes a clear message.

When did the boot room end? I don't think we're talking about when it was physically knocked down, no. People would say it was in the Souness era or maybe slightly before that in the Dalglish time. I don't think the physical disappearance had anything to do with it at all; that was an irrelevance. But somehow we lost that continuity, that stability. It was bound to happen one day, it's exceedingly difficult to perpetuate because in a way it was not planned or pre-ordained that those people would come together. It was one of those happy accidents of fate, so replicating that is difficult. There was equally always going to be some accident of fate that would break that continuity at some time. But my perception, and I was an outsider at the time, is that it was around then that it happened.

RONNIE MORAN
The Diaries

I learnt about the training books from Joe Fagan. After lunch Joe would get his book out and write in it what he'd done that morning, treatment of players, what training we'd done and so on. I followed suit and started keeping notes about what the weather was on the day, what we did for warm-ups, treatment and so on. The pre-season format was written down properly. We didn't do exactly the same each year but we always started training five-and-a-half weeks before the start of the new season. We always started on a Thursday morning. We'd have all day Thursday and Friday morning. It wasn't gruelling stuff, some players would be fitter than others at this stage.

MARK LAWRENSON
Fagan Ages

When Joe Fagan took over, he kept things ticking along pretty much in the same style as Bob Paisley. But he was a different type of person, always ready for a chat about anything under the sun. This bubbly character never looked his age in his first season in charge but he looked considerably older in his second. Something happened to Joe in that second season, and it happened long before Heysel. I think he just got tired of the job and of the daily routine and was happy to get out. I hope that he didn't get a premonition of the terrible events which were to come at Heysel, but certainly he was not the same man. He started to look old, and age was something we never associated with him, even though we all knew he was older than either Bill

Shankly or Bob Paisley when he became manager. In fact, Shankly was younger than Joe when he retired. The enjoyment seemed to have gone out of the job in that second year.

Joe was a happy man but he could be hard as well. He only needed to show this hard streak twice, as I remember, to get his message across. The first time was after we had lost at home to Manchester City. He really hit the roof. Even the top players like Kenny Dalglish and Graeme Souness and Ray Kennedy were silent as he read the riot act. The other time was at Melwood. Ronnie was away at a funeral so Joe was taking training. We were doing some simple exercises involving two people at a time and had to pass the ball to each other a distance of 20 yards. Terry McDermott and Phil Thompson were the two involved and, as ever, Terry was up to something and drove the ball too hard at Phil. That was okay because Phil managed to control it and then sent one back just as hard back at Terry. Unfortunately, Terry couldn't control it and the ball went skidding away, bringing a temporary halt to the session. Thommo started laughing but Joe was not amused. He just glared at him and said, 'Don't ever take the mickey out of me again.' That was it. There was a silence and we continued with not a word more said.

The boot room was always Joe's second home and he didn't change when he took over. It was in there that he spent his happiest times and he liked nothing better than to chat things over with the rest of the back room staff in that little room. Joe was an easy man to talk to and probably allowed us more freedom than any other Liverpool manager. He trusted us more than anyone else, allowing us to our own ways as long as we did our best on matchdays.

One of the saddest sights I've ever seen was when our plane touched down at Speke Airport in Liverpool after the Heysel disaster. Joe Fagan looked like a broken man and Roy Evans had to help him across the tarmac. Apart from the tragedy, I think it finally came home to Joe that he was not returning as Liverpool manager, even if it was his choice. It was a long time before we had any contact with him again. It was as though he wanted to purge himself of football.

ALAN HANSEN
Boot Room Psychology

The thing which the boot room really taught me was that being second is no good. You have to win and you have to be a professional. I think when I arrived at Liverpool I did not have that kind of attitude. I was too casual. In a way I'd drifted into the game to escape working in an insurance office or whatever but at Liverpool the boot room staff taught me differently. They taught me about winning and that football is not about playing and then picking up a cheque at the end of the week. There's more to it than that. It's about pride and about winning.

I remember one incident in 1982. I'd missed the Milk Cup Final against Spurs because of injury and had missed about six or so league games as well. Anyhow, I was coming back from injury and the boot room boys had had me training hard. I played against Huddersfield on the Tuesday night in the reserves and the next morning Joe Fagan came up to me and asked me how the knee was. I told him it was okay. That night the first team played at Old Trafford and won 1–0. I had gone home after training before going to Manchester to watch the game but while I was at home I dropped a glass in the kitchen and it fell on my knee and gashed the knee badly. Suddenly there was blood seeping through my trousers. I went to the hospital and they promptly put half-a-dozen stitches in my knee. Because of that I couldn't train on the Thursday morning. But no one from the boot room bothered to come up to me to ask me how the knee was. Joe Fagan ignored me, so too did Ronnie Moran. I was left on my own walking around Melwood. I remember thinking, they might at least come up and ask me how the knee is. But they didn't, they just left me to my own devices.

The next day I was working out at Melwood when Joe came up and asked if I fancied playing the next day, Saturday. Just like that, out of the blue. We were playing City at Maine Road and although the team was playing well, they wanted me back in the side. I could hardly say, 'No, the knee's still a bit bad,' because that might have ended my Liverpool career. So of course I said yes. But that was typical of them, leave you brooding one day and then lift you the next. It's the kind of psychology they use all the time.

They were always great at keeping players slightly on edge. You could be going through a really bad spell, not playing at all well, and then one of them, usually Joe, would come up and tell you how well you were doing. Then, of course, when you were playing well and were feeling cocky about it, they'd come over and tell you how rubbishy you were and bring you down to earth. It was little games they were playing but with a serious end product. After a while you recognised what they are up to but you could never be certain, there's always that element of doubt. It was their way and it nearly always was Joe who put his arm around you and dropped these words of wisdom into your ear.

Bob Paisley could be totally ruthless, especially when it came to the best interests of Liverpool Football Club. He would always go on about how he'd reached the FA Cup Final in 1950 and had even scored a goal in the semi-final and had then been left out of the final at Wembley. When he became manager he always maintained that the lesson had stood him in good stead when it came to making vital decisions about team selection. He knew in his heart that it had been right to leave him out of the final. So, sentiment did not come into it. If it was necessary to leave a player out, then so be it. It was tough and it was tough telling a player that he might not be playing in an important game, but he wouldn't lose any sleep over it. If the decision was right for Liverpool Football Club, then it was right and that was it. He knew that you could not afford to allow sentiment to interfere.

He also did his share of shouting in the dressing room. Not that he was one for blowing his top all the time. That was not his style. But I well remember one incident. It was not because we had played badly or because we had just lost a game at Villa Park over the Easter, it was because Alan Kennedy had predicted that we had already won the championship. This came after we had beaten Manchester United 2–0 at Old Trafford. The newspapers had all carried stories with headlines about 'we are the champions: Alan Kennedy'. Bob went berserk. I thought he was going to have a heart attack. His hair was all over the place and he could hardly get the words out. He was raging. The view from the boot room was simple: let others do the shouting off the field, we'll do it on the field. At Anfield you keep your mouth shut until you have achieved something. Don't tempt the fates.

WILLIE STEVENSON
Heysel Changed Fagan

Joe Fagan was looking after the reserves at the time. He was a quiet fellow. He seemed to change when he became manager. He just stepped into it as if he was made for it. I didn't think Joe would do particularly well but he did. Although everything was in place I was surprised at how well he took to it. I didn't think he was going to be a particularly strong manager but he was. I think Heysel knocked the stuffing out of him. He seemed to have that lost look in his eyes afterwards as many others did. Very sad.

STEVE MORGAN
A Dark Era

Heysel was one of the darkest hours at Liverpool Football Club. We can blame the stadium, we can blame the Belgian police, we can blame the fact that there was no segregation of tickets and you can say I don't think a single Liverpool fan who was involved in the rumpus ever meant that to happen, but the fact remains Liverpool were out of order and the fans were out of order. But I thought the club handled that situation with dignity. Hillsborough was horrific, the darkest hour in Liverpool Football Club, but again it was handled with dignity.

Heysel was a dark era for the club in a totally different way to Hillsborough. Hillsborough was a tragic series of mistakes by the police that led to disaster. At Heysel certain individuals were just totally out of order, and quite frankly there could have been many hundreds of Liverpool fans who could have and perhaps should have been charged with manslaughter.

LAWRIE McMENEMY
The Third Degree

Back in the 1960s Liverpool was undoubtedly the place to be. You had the Beatles and all that music, Merseybeat, and of course you had the comedians like Jimmy Tarbuck, Ken Dodd and the rest. Of course, Bill Shankly had a wonderful sense of humour. There was that lovely story of when he signed Ron Yeats. When all the football journalists came to see his new signing he invited them to take a walk around him because he was so big.

Bill Shankly had a tremendous team and he had a tremendous passion which he introduced into that team. I think the important thing was the continuity and the stability. If you look at any great side you will see continuity and wherever a club has had this continuity and stability, you will also see success. You never get lasting success where there is controversy. The secret is simplicity. Shanks made it look easy, pass and move was his motto. Pass the ball, then move into space. So why can't every team do it? Well, admittedly it does take other things. You have to have the players who can control the ball and have the intelligence to be able to move into space. And with Liverpool you had those players. Often they were players who had not performed that well elsewhere but when they came to Liverpool they were playing among giants and that would rub off on them and they too soon became stars.

When I used to take teams to Anfield, Liverpool used to leave their dressing room door slightly ajar. They did it deliberately because they wanted to scare the opposition. My players would look in as they walked past and they would see all these famous faces, players who were giants in the game, and yes, it used to scare them.

Anfield is a magnificent ground. I can remember the first time I went there with a team. I was all dressed up in my suit looking very smart and after the game they said, 'Come in the boot room and have a drink with us.' So I went in, and I was really looking forward to it, going into the boot room. 'Come in and sit down,' they said. Well, I looked around and it was a bit tatty to say the least, things all over the place, a bit small. Of course they're testing you. All that there is to sit on is an upturned crate and it's a bit dusty. So there I am in my best suit, thinking, what is this, and they're looking at you to see how you'll react. You know, 'Is it a bit too dusty for this man with his suit on?' Well, if you do react, they'll slaughter you, so you just have to get on with it.

Then they offer you a drink and you're looking around think-ing, where's the drinks cabinet then? So one of them stands up and opens a cupboard and there's an old bottle of Scotch in there or they open the other cupboard and there's a few cans of lager. Of course there aren't any glasses. You either drink the lager from the can or the Scotch from a cup. If you ask for a glass you're a sissy. All the time they're testing you.

Then they start talking about players, bits of gossip here and there. The next thing is they're asking you about some of your own players and you're innocently answering their questions. Is he any good they ask, what's his left foot like, has he got a bit of character. All done very innocently, of course! But it's when you get out and are halfway home that it slowly dawns on you what was going on. You've been getting the third degree without realising it. If you've said anything positive about the player in question then you could expect Geoff Twentyman or Tom Saunders to turn up the next week at your home game, or even expect to see a bid on the table by the time you've arrived home.

I always thought they were the worst losers. The abuse you used to get from them from their dugout during the game was something awful. We had the temerity to go there and win once, something which doesn't happen very often, and the abuse I got was unbelievable. I remember asking a policeman to go and tell them to calm down. But as soon as the game was over, they shook hands and then they had me in the boot room and it was all forgotten. It was as if it had never happened. They congratulated me, praised the side and so on. Amazing. They couldn't have been more friendly.

The other thing which was important was the continuity of goalkeepers. Over a period of about 25 years they had Tommy Lawrence, Ray Clemence and Bruce Grobbelaar and that was it. Three goalkeepers in all that time and all three of them were terrific keepers. Down the years they've had their bad patches and usually these have been at the back. But astonishingly they never seem to have had any problems upfront. They've nearly always had a strong midfield general who has usually also been captain, Emlyn Hughes, Graeme Souness, Steve McMahon, someone who leads by example.

JIM GARDINER
Honesty And Simplicity

I suppose I was aware of the boot room from the start, when I first started watching Liverpool on a regular basis in the seventies. You knew it was there and I suppose, to a fan, you could compare it to the Pentagon in Washington or the Kremlin in Moscow, you felt it was the place at the club where a lot of the decisions were made that really mattered. I know the boardroom would be where the important decisions overall were made but you got the impression that the decisions affecting the team were made in the boot room. This was where the coaches lived, this was where day-to-day decisions on the club were made, on who was going to play, what transfer targets there were. You never got to see it, you just heard about it, just this mythical place where everybody met but it was very jealously guarded and no one could get in there, even within the club, unless they were invited. Stories built up. You knew it was there but nobody knew what it was really like because its secrets were jealously guarded.

There probably was no secret, it was just a group of very knowledgeable like-minded people that knew what they wanted and how to get it and were all thinking on the same wavelength. I suppose you can trace it back to the man who set it up, Bill Shankly. He gathered his entourage around him, the people that he could trust, Bob Paisley, Joe Fagan, Reuben Bennett, Ronnie Moran as his playing career stopped and Roy Evans later on. The boot room started from that. It was Bill Shankly's philosophy and then these other coaches came in on the same wavelength. I don't really think of it as a physical place, in many ways the boot room was a way of operating. The boot room was just a place where they all met but it was the spirit of the boot room, the continuation of Bill Shankly's philosophy through his coaches and people that came on after he went.

I would sum up the philosophy of the boot room as knowledge and honesty and simplicity. They didn't have any fancy ideas. They knew that football was a simple game, that it was a matter of bringing in good players, making sure that they had good habits and providing them with the facilities to be able to produce their best form week in, week out. Making sure that they were fully fit, making sure that all their needs were catered for on and off the park, bringing in discipline where it was needed and making sure they put good habits into players, building them up when they needed building up, a kick up the backside when they needed it.

JIM GARDINER
A New Manager

It was certainly a surprise at the time. I can recall the day hearing that Kenny had got the job. We were in a bar in Brussels on the day of the Heysel disaster and the rumours were going round that it would be Joe Fagan's last game and that Kenny Dalglish would be taking over as player-manager. I can specifically remember just laughing out loud, saying 'There is no chance.' Player-managers were just coming in at one or two clubs and the idea that Liverpool, on the verge of a fifth European Cup that morning, would appoint a player-manager was just unthinkable. I suppose the club probably looked at and considered the knowledge that Kenny Dalglish has got and his abilities. They'd obviously spotted something in there and decided they wanted to keep Kenny at the club. Rather than bring in a new manager at that stage, if they were looking ahead, to say, Kenny will be our manager one day. If they left it with Kenny nearing the end of his playing career and brought in another manager, knowing that Joe Fagan had asked to go, then another manager might have been there for five years or longer if he'd been successful. Perhaps they saw themselves losing Kenny so maybe they said 'Right, we're going to have to do something a bit dramatic here, let's go for him. We want Kenny as manager, let's make him player-manager.' I take my hat off to whoever in the club made that decision.

JOHN BENNISON
The Same Era

I don't think Kenny came in much when he took over. Of course he had his own office. But he was a different era. Bob, Shanks, Joe, although a bit older than me, were all of the same era; we were pre-war. To be honest I don't think Joe wanted the job but he took it because I think he thought if a stranger came in we might all be out, they'd bring their own people in. So he took the job as much for us as anyone else. Kenny didn't come in. His friends and guests would be in his office. Joe and Bob didn't really have guests.

ALAN KENNEDY
The Little Books

When your time comes, you're off and away, and you have to go. When Liverpool say, 'well, I'm sorry, lad, but we've got another player who's better than you who can take your position,' you have to move on. The club was always bigger. It was always told to us by the staff: 'The club is always bigger than the player and that should always be the case'. It stemmed obviously from the boot room with Bill and Bob and Joe and Ronnie. If you had to add up all the years they actually stayed at the club, it's well over 250 years. I think a lot of players, no matter whether you only played a few games for Liverpool or thousands of games, can all hold their hands up and say they made a contribution to that. Whether you scored a goal in a Cup Final or cleared one off the line, whether you did what Ian Callaghan did, 800 appearances, it doesn't make any difference, you contributed towards that team.

I did find a big difference coming from Newcastle, not so much in the training or how hard it was, but by how organised it was. It was very organised. Everybody, every part of the boot room staff was on the same wavelength. I think that was important because if Ronnie and Joe were with the first team and they were taking training, they knew what was going to happen. They would look in their little book and say, right, this was what we did last year on 22 July, this is what we're going to do today so you basically knew what was going to happen. If they had a shock in store for you, then it would be a little bit of extra running. In my seven years there I knew what was probably going to happen the following day. Why change something that has not gone wrong?

They always had the same comments, Ronnie and Joe: 'Look after yourself, game on Saturday.' After a midweek game on a Wednesday night, they'd say 'Any injuries, see you tomorrow, straight home. Don't go out boozing, gallivanting with the girls, anything like that, don't do anything like that.' Well, you did but they said that at the end of it, it would be you that was the problem, not them. If you disgraced the club, see you, bye.

ALAN KENNEDY

A Simple Room

I always felt apologetic going from the first team changing room to the boot room. Supposing I had to go in to get a pair of old boots, to make sure my boots were fine for Saturday, I always felt as though when I stepped up to that level, stepped up the step, stepped into the room, I always felt as though I shouldn't be in here, I'm only a player. There's pictures on the walls, there's boots all over the place and it's not the tidiest of places and they've got their little stash of memorabilia. I always felt 'Blooming heck, this is the boot room.' Nobody steps inside it unless you're a coach, unless you're a manager, unless you're a physio. I never, as far as I can remember, went in socially. It was always, 'I need my boots doing for Saturday. Can I change them for these ones?'

I think most players were in awe of it because it was only a simple room. Later on it had a fridge in it for cold drinks. I'm sure many a time managers have come in there after a game and they've talked with Bob and Joe and they've probably thought to themselves, 'I wish that I had that job that Bob has and that Joe has, describing how Liverpool played well again, didn't they. They only won by three goals, three clear goals. They were lucky to get none, the away team.'

You think to yourself, 'What's the mystique about it?' I think it was actually just the people who were in there. I think the staff realised we were human beings as well. They didn't treat us like kids, they treated us as professionals but also as human beings. There were times when we needed knocking down a peg or two, there were times when we needed building up and Bob and his staff were pretty good at that.

CHRIS LAWLER

Working In The Boot Room

I joined the staff, 1983 I think it was, when Joe Fagan brought me in to run the reserves. I had been over in Norway and he asked me to join him, so I packed in the job over there and came back to Anfield. Nobody talks about Joe Fagan, he seems to have been overlooked really. He was a very straight and honest man. People might say that it was not Joe's team that won the European Cup and did that magnificent treble, but you could say that about most managers and certainly you equally could say that Kenny Dalglish's team was really Joe Fagan's. Joe was the boot room. He had been there since I was a kid in the early sixties. It was Joe, Bob Paisley, Ronnie Moran. It was never really Bill Shankly, it wasn't his room, it was the other lads', those I've just mentioned.

Nothing changed when Joe Fagan took over as manager, they just continued pretty much the same. I spent a lot of time in the boot room. On matchdays I would be there pre-match and then after the match and also through the week. And even on a Sunday. On a Sunday morning we would be in there and Joe would be there as well, even when he was manager. Nothing changed at all with Joe. He could be hard as a manager but generally he was easy going. Everyone knew exactly where they were with Joe because he was so straight. I never knew he was going to pack in at the end of the season, none of us knew. We never expected it at all. None of us, Roy Evans, Ronnie Moran, we were all surprised when he decided to quit, there were no clues.

When he had the manager's job he had a lot of pressure and he was getting on a bit. It was his age and the pressure. He used to say to us when he came down to the boot room, 'It's a lonely job up there.' When he went into his own office he was a lonely man. He had to spend time up there as he had things to do. But, of course, he would still come down to the boot room.

I never really went in the boot room much as a player. I'd

knock on the door occasionally for something but you never got invited in. We had our players' lounge and that's where we went. I think the thing about the boot room was its friendly atmosphere, particularly after the game. We'd have discussions about players, training, and we'd also be writing up the books every day. That was usually Ronnie; Joe Fagan had started it and it just went on. All that would be done after training when we got back to Melwood. On a Saturday the visiting coaches would be invited in and after they had gone we would stay on and chat about the game. On a Sunday players who were injured came in for treatment, then after all that had been started, we'd settle down and discuss the various games of the previous day, how the reserves had done and so on.

But these things can't go on forever. I don't think there is a place for a boot room nowadays. Our boot room was unique, you couldn't create something like that again. It wasn't purposely built, it was just the way things happened. It was the people who made it so important.

JAN MOLBY

No Team Instruction

It was common knowledge that I was due to leave Ajax in the summer of 1984. I had spoken to a few clubs, some of them English like Sheffield Wednesday and Crystal Palace had shown an interest as well. Tom Saunders phoned me up on a Friday afternoon and asked me if I'd like to join Liverpool for a ten-day trial, from the following Monday, culminating in going down to London for the Charity Shield against Everton. Although I knew I wasn't going to be involved in terms of playing, he said it would all be part of the trial. I spent the ten days with them and Joe Fagan decided to give me a three-year contract. Joe was in his second season then as a manager.

In the boot room was the manager Joe Fagan, Ronnie Moran, Roy Evans, Chris Lawler in charge of the reserves and John Bennison. I've got the greatest respect for Joe Fagan, not just because he bought me but I just think he had such a simple way of doing things. He had a simple way of keeping the discipline, he had a simple way of keeping, at the time 15 full internationals, quite happy. I always think that in itself is a skill. I know it was different in the eighties but there was never anyone looking to move away. I remember just after I'd joined, we sold Dave Hodgson and Michael Robinson, and they didn't want to leave. They were going to go to other first division clubs and be guaranteed first team football and they didn't want to go. They would have struggled to be in the twelve at any stage of the season but they would have rather stayed at Anfield. That was the kind of club it was and I think that was all down to people like Joe Fagan.

I remember the first game I played down at Norwich when I made my debut. At Ajax and Denmark we had 45-minute, perhaps hour-long meetings, before games. But not at Liverpool. I said to Joe Fagan 40 minutes before the game, 'What do you want me to do?' He said, 'Listen, we've signed you because you're a good player, just go and show us what a good player you are, whatever you want to do.' That was basically him introducing me, saying, 'Don't worry about it, he'll do his job. You'll have an area where you do your job. Just get on with it. Show us that the faith we put in you is right.' I think if somebody tells you that just before your debut, you want to go and play. Although during that only season when Joe was my manager I missed a fair amount, I think I had 22 games, I still had the greatest respect for the man. I think he had a fantastic way of doing everything. I used to love the way he'd join in the five-a-sides although he was 60-odd. There was an immense respect for the man. Although he might not have been the greatest player in the world, I think people had a lot of respect for the way he did things. Everything was so simple.

People said sometimes it was a case of trying to complicate things as much as they could. Now you come to what was the greatest club in Europe at the time in the early eighties. Nobody could get anywhere near them. Then you realise how simple it is. I know Bob Paisley, although I've never worked with him as a manager. I know of him and I think he was very much of the same type as Joe Fagan.

I had never heard of the boot room but I read a lot of magazines when I was a kid. I kept hold of those and although Liverpool held a little bit of an interest for me, I was an Arsenal fan. If there was an article in the paper about Liverpool, I wouldn't necessarily read about it. I kept them all and since I joined Liverpool, I've read back through all this. There are a lot of mentions of the boot room although it didn't have any interest for me. But it had been mentioned in magazines in Denmark in the seventies and the early eighties. Everybody was trying to look at Liverpool and everybody was trying to come up with 'What is it that makes this club what it is?' People would come and watch the training and say 'Is that what you do?' There was no magic there so everybody looked a little bit deeper and that included the boot room. It is fair to say that people abroad were aware of the boot room in the seventies and eighties.

JAN MOLBY

Visiting The Boot Room

The first time I ever went into the boot room, I think, was in 1987/88. I'd broken my leg pre-season and I used to spend quite a bit of time at Anfield, unsociable hours either having treatment or doing a bit of work. The boot room was for the back room staff and we'd never go anywhere near it. There were only a couple of us at Anfield and I needed to speak to Ronnie Moran. I shouted to him from outside the boot room and he said, 'Come on in, son.' These are the kind of things that people would do at Anfield. And then, as you go in the boot room, they fly at you and say, 'You're not allowed in here.' I said, 'Are you sure Ron, can I come in?' And I walked in. This was the first time I'd ever been in the boot room. There were a couple of chairs, a table, all the boots and the skips for the away games and there's calendars everywhere and that's basically the boot room.

I thought, 'Someone's taking the mickey here.' Ronnie said, 'What do you think?' I said, 'Not a lot.' He goes, 'Many a battle's been won in here.' At the time I wasn't in a position to appreciate it. I can appreciate it now, I had a little spin as manager myself and I know it's the funny little places where you get an idea or discuss a player. They must have had some fantastic hours in there, especially when they were winning European Cups and leagues.

It was possibly another two or three years before I went in again. Although I'd been in there and broken the ice, you weren't going to push your luck and go in again the next week. It was theirs. I wonder what they did in there, apart from having a beer and discussing probably nothing magic. But I think it was a place where they all felt comfortable. It's not like coming into the manager's office where he sits behind a big desk and he's in charge. I think they all felt equal and although John Bennison was in charge of the youth team and Kenny was the manager, in there it was like an unwritten rule that no one's in charge and we can all have our say. I think that's what made the boot room a great place for the likes of John Bennison. It gave him a chance. When they were outside the boot room or at Melwood, we all knew that there was the manager and there was Ronnie Moran. Ronnie was in charge, he would tell John Bennison what to do but I think once they got into that boot room, they all had a chance to have a say. That's what made it special.

CHAPTER FOUR

King Kenny

It was hardly the most auspicious of starts, coming as it did, on the back of the Heysel disaster. It was meant to be a glorious day in the history of Liverpool Football Club; a fifth European Cup victory followed by the dramatic announcement that Kenny Dalglish was to take over from the departing Joe Fagan. Instead it was the most shameful moment in the club's long and rich history.

While the world's media grilled club officials at Speke Airport, seeking an explanation for the tragedy that had taken place in Brussels, another group from the club sat in the lounge at Anfield introducing a weary-looking Kenny Dalglish to the sporting press. It was a bizarre juxtaposition. Somehow you felt that there were more important things on people's minds than who was to be the next manager of Liverpool Football Club. Dalglish was set to take over as English football sank to a new low, and with it the name of Liverpool was to become synonymous with hooliganism.

It was chairman John Smith who first suggested Dalglish. Whether or not he was unhappy with the prospect of Ronnie Moran as manager will never be known. Perhaps he felt that Dalglish represented the new face of football, or maybe he believed in what one manager called Dalglish's natural good luck. Whatever it was, it was to prove yet another masterstroke from the Liverpool chairman. Roy Evans was also overlooked as Smith decided to sweep away the tradition of the boot room and appoint a player rather than someone from the coaching staff. There was also no discussion at board level, although John Smith may well have taken one or two directors into his confidence. Although secretary Peter Robinson knew, it is certain that there were a number of directors who did not know of the appointment until they arrived in Brussels for the European Cup Final. Smith had made his mind up. The boot room wasn't exactly being dismantled but it was being overlooked for the first time in decades.

Dalglish had been offered the job more than a week earlier when Smith and Robinson visited him at his home. He had few doubts and accepted immediately. Few others knew of the decision. The rumours began on the day of the final. One newspaper even floated the name of Dalglish but it was one of many names being tossed in the air by the tabloids.

The official announcement had been planned for the Friday when Dalglish and Fagan, flanked by Smith and company, would sit proudly with the European Cup alongside them to tell the world that Kenny was the new player-manager. But it was not to be. The appalling disaster at Heysel and the deaths of 39 Juventus fans saw an end to that scenario. Instead, the news filtered out on the Thursday morning. Ronnie Moran and Roy Evans were called over to John Smith on the plane returning home and informed. By the time the plane had landed back at Speke Airport everyone in the club had been officially told that Dalglish was taking over.

The party went straight to Anfield where Smith decided to make an immediate announcement about the succession. It was possibly the crassest piece of public relations in football history. While one press conference at Speke Airport was questioning the deaths of 39 fans in front of millions of television viewers, another party was applauding the arrival of a new manager.

At least one concession was made to the boot room: Bob Paisley was to be an adviser, ready to give help whenever called on. Tom Saunders would also be available. But it was all so messy. Throughout the summer there were accusations about Liverpool fans, tough talking from the Prime Minister, a European ban for English football, and a slide into shame and humiliation. English football was at as low a point as possible.

Yet oddly enough for Liverpool things went on as before. Dalglish stuck with much the same side as Joe Fagan's and despite a sluggish campaign, ended on a high note, emulating even the great Shankly and Paisley by winning the Double. Dalglish was the toast of the football league. One season in the job and he had achieved what only two managers this century had managed. He'd even scored the winning goal at Stamford Bridge to clinch the league title. On the surface little had changed. They were still winning trophies and the boot room was still ticking over. There was Ronnie Moran, Roy Evans and Chris Lawler while Bob Paisley, Tom Saunders and John Bennison could often be spotted on a skip or two, offering the occasional word of wisdom.

But changes were beckoning. Dalglish was getting more confident and two trophies in one season allowed him to flex his muscles. The first was the sacking of Chris Lawler, the former full-back who had joined the boot room under Joe Fagan in 1983 as reserve team trainer. In that time he had won two Central League titles and been runners-up once. After the Cup Final he suddenly found himself out in the cold. Dalglish no longer wanted him running the reserves. Into his boots stepped Phil Thompson, a popular choice that hid the fact that Lawler was the first boot room person to ever be sacked.

Also out was Liverpool chief scout Geoff Twentyman, the man who had unearthed the likes of Kevin Keegan, Graeme Souness, Mark Lawrenson, Alan Hansen, Ray Clemence, Ian Rush and a host of other world-class players, many of them bargain basement buys from the lower divisions or Scotland. Twentyman had been doing the job since 1967 and in almost 20 years you could count the number of questionable signings made by the club on one hand. Both Lawler and Twentyman were devastated. It sent shock waves around Anfield.

Into Twentyman's shoes stepped big Ron Yeats as the new chief scout. Dalglish claimed that Twentyman had arthritis and that he had been released because of his medical condition. Twentyman did not agree. Whatever the reason, it signalled not just a change in personnel, but more importantly a change in attitude. Lawler and Twentyman protested but the rest of the boot room bit their tongues and just got on with the job. At least in appointing Thompson and Yeats, the new manager had wisely brought in a couple of legendary names; anything else might have caused severe ructions within the ranks. Nevertheless, something out of the ordinary had happened and there was no escaping it.

The following season, 1986/87, did not go quite so well for Dalglish. With much the same line-up Liverpool failed to take the title, trailing champions Everton by nine points. They were even beaten in the League Cup Final at Wembley by Arsenal. It was the signal for a change of team personnel. John Aldridge had already been signed as a replacement for the Juventus-bound Ian Rush but during the close season John Barnes arrived from Watford and Peter Beardsley from Newcastle. Ray Houghton was also signed from Oxford United. It was the biggest shift of personnel in the side for many years. The old Liverpool adage of one out, one in each season was flung out of the window. Jan Molby, John Wark, Craig Johnston and the departing Ian Rush were the biggest losers. Criticise Dalglish if you wish, but Liverpool then stormed to the title, playing as attractive a game as they had in their entire history. They simply took sides apart and ought to have won the Double but lost wretchedly in the FA Cup Final to Wimbledon. Dalglish may have made a few changes to the boot room here and there, but if anything it seemed to have improved matters.

No one could argue that this was Joe Fagan's or even Bob Paisley's side. It was undeniably Kenny Dalglish's team. But there was talk of a rift with Paisley, that the former manager had been increasingly ignored as Dalglish had grown more confident. Perhaps that was inevitable although Dalglish denied any such rift. Tom Saunders meanwhile took up residence in Dalglish's office. He was just there to answer the phone and generally help out. He didn't offer advice but if Kenny asked for any, Saunders would throw in his knowledgeable twopennyworth.

Dalglish may have made some questionable changes behind the scenes but equally there were positive improvements. He identified the lack of youngsters coming through the ranks and brought Steve Heighway back from America to unearth and train up a new generation of young players. Over a period of 15 years or so Liverpool had brought on surprisingly few youngsters from their youth sides. Apart from Phil Thompson, Jimmy Case and

Sammy Lee, there weren't too many others coming through the ranks. It might not have shown any dividends in Dalglish's time but other managers would benefit as Robbie Fowler, Steve McManaman, Michael Owen, Jamie Carragher, David Thompson and others would emerge in later years.

And so it went on until that fateful day in April 1989 when the heart was ripped out of Liverpool Football Club at Hillsborough in the semi-final of the FA Cup. Heysel had been bad enough but Hillsborough, coming so soon afterwards, was a fatal blow. The club would never be quite the same again, and nor would many supporters and families who suffered losses. The players too lost their edge. They struggled on, even winning the FA Cup, but ran out of energy and adrenalin at the last moment, falling to Arsenal in an epic title decider at Anfield. They picked themselves up to win the league the following season, 1989/90, but it was to be the last time they would be called champions in the twentieth century.

In February 1991, festering under the strain of running a machine like Liverpool and still suffering the stresses of Hillsborough, Dalglish sensationally resigned as manager. They had drawn 4–4 with Everton the previous evening but his mind had already been made up. Tom Saunders could see the suffering he was going through yet even within Anfield nobody could quite believe it when Dalglish resigned. The papers swelled with conspiracy theories galore; there was a rift with Peter Beardsley, the team had grown too old, Dalglish had realised the enormity of the task ahead, he had been offered a multi-million pound job elsewhere, and so on. But none of them were true. The truth was far simpler; Dalglish had basically suffered a nervous breakdown and needed a rest from the game. He had been under pressure since the age of 17, first with Celtic, winning titles and trophies in Scotland, then in England and Europe. It had been pressure football, day in day out. And now he needed a break from the game. He wasn't the first to succumb to the pressures. Shankly too had quit in similar circumstances, and similarly, after a long rest, had recharged his batteries, ready to return.

As Dalglish trundled out of Anfield for the last time clutching his holdall, and saying his final farewells, more than a few around

Anfield must have quietly realised that it would probably never be quite the same again. Too much had happened: Heysel, Hillsborough, the sackings of Lawler and Twentyman and now the sudden resignation of Dalglish. But then maybe change would not be such a bad thing. After the two tragedies football itself was set to undergo a major transformation. The question was: were the boot room staff, the players and everyone else at Anfield ready to confront the changes?

STEVE MORGAN

An Inspired Choice

Kenny taking over was a big surprise. I don't think it was a big surprise that Joe Fagan stepped down because he was never really suited to the role. But I thought it was quite an inspired and very brave decision to put Kenny Dalglish in charge because he was still a player. It's happened since then on a number of occasions but at the time it was almost unheard of to make a player a manager. I think that came as a big surprise to most people, it certainly did to me.

What Kenny did was to bring in more of a player's perspective. Prior to that there was a generation gap between the managers and the players. With Kenny, he was still one of the players and I suspect he was still thought of as a player initially, and then as a manager. Even though Kenny is not a person for making big press statements, more was said under that Dalglish era than had previously been said, particularly with Fagan and Bob Paisley. I suspect there was a sea change in the dressing room that wasn't necessarily seen by the fans or by the public at large.

MIKE BERRY

Kenny's Humour

I don't think it changed when Kenny Dalglish took over, I think
he carried on with the same basic principles which Shankly,
Paisley and Fagan had set, the same sense of humour. A lot of
people in the media think that Kenny Dalglish is very bland and
boring, but he's not; he is one of the funniest men I have ever
met. He has quick, sarcastic comments that put you in your place
but is very nice with it. I always remember an interview he did
with Barry Davies when he first became manager and Davies
said to him, 'Don't you think you are going to have trouble communicating with the players because your accent is so difficult
to understand?' And he went on and on about this and Kenny's
reply each time was 'Pardon.' Very funny.

Kenny Dalglish would pop in the boot room as a manager
and have a drink. He would tend not to dwell in there. But when
he was in there he was just one of the lads. I wouldn't like to
say that the sackings of Lawler and Twentyman were the beginnings of the change. After all, he brought in Phil Thompson and
Ron Yeats. I don't think it had any effect. After he had sacked
them Liverpool still went on to win things.

I suppose the start of the demise was the Arsenal–Liverpool
game at Anfield when all we had to do was lose by one goal to
take the Double. But Michael Thomas's goal sealed a 2–0 win
for them. I went into the sponsors' lounge at the end of the
game and it was stacked with bottles of champagne all ready to
celebrate. But no one was drinking. I was in there with Roy
Evans. Roy and I went back to my house afterwards and we sat
in our house until five in the morning talking and drinking and
singing old Liverpool songs as though we had cracked up. It
must have been the pressure. It had a terrible effect on me so it
must have had an even worse effect on Kenny Dalglish and Roy
Evans and Ronnie Moran.

Then it started to go wrong and that was when I had my first official trip to the boot room. That would be '91. I was invited in by Roy Evans after a match. I remember sitting there listening to Roy, Kenny, Ronnie Moran, John Bennison, Tom Saunders, Alan Brown, and instead of being my normal talkative self, I sat there saying nothing. I was in awe, listening to these legends talking about Liverpool Football Club. I was waiting to hear what the secret was, sitting on tea chests, a cold beer and a good chat for an hour and then I went home. I went in there after most home games for five or six years then. All the personalities would come in: Dave Bassett, Ron Atkinson, Alex Ferguson. Again I just sat there as a fly on the wall. I always treated that as a bonus, knowing that after a match I could go down there. It was great. I was friendly with Roy but I was also doing some of the high-profile testimonials: Ian Rush, Steve Nicol, Bruce Grobbelaar. Great times, legendary players.

To me the boot room was a special place with special people. The spirit of the boot room was ordinary people with, as they say in Liverpool, no side, talking in simple language about the game in a relaxed fashion whether they had lost or won. And whether they lost or won, it was always the same atmosphere, it was never heated discussions, there was no gloating if they won and no arguing if they had lost. No ranting and raving or throwing cups around. It was like an oasis of calm after the match. I remember we beat Man United, winning 4–0. I went in the boot room after the game as a gloating fan, with sounds of 'Always Look On The Bright Side Of Life' ringing in my ears and yet in the boot room it was calm. Maybe that was the secret, I don't know. It was always calm, no anger, no gloating, and that sums it up for me.

ALAN BROWN
Sundays At Anfield

Kenny had his own office so he started entertaining his own friends in there. Bob and Shanks had their own office but it was only small. They built an office down the bottom for Kenny, a big one, he had a bar in it so he could entertain in there. His wife, children, friends and so on would go into his office. The visiting managers never went in there, they still came to the boot room. Kenny would pop in for a few minutes and then go back to his own office. Kenny never really came in on a Sunday. The younger generation had taken over then. The players used to come in for treatment on a Sunday with Ronnie or Joe Fagan. We never had a physio in those days and that's why everything was focused around the club. The players would come in for a rub down or a wax bath. Then after that Joe and Ronnie and others would go back to the boot room and have a drink, talk things over. But the new ones, Kenny and Souey, had a different outlet, they were a different generation and neither of them came in on a Sunday. Even in midweek it was rare for Kenny to come into the boot room. He never drank. He'd come in and say hello and have a few witty remarks with the visiting manager, but then he'd shoot off. Bob was still coming in then. He had his little office upstairs because he was looking after Kenny for two years, that was part of the deal and he would come down to us. He was the most successful manager of all. He knew how to run a club, he didn't go around shouting. I don't think he ever shouted. Others would shout in the dressing room but never Bob, you never heard him shout.

ALAN KENNEDY
The Leaving Of Liverpool

I left in September '85 and went to Sunderland. I read in the paper that Newcastle were interested and Kenny told me that they'd had a bid and they'd accepted it. Although I'd played the first eight games of the season in that campaign, I think Kenny thought Jim Beglin was a younger player, slightly better and probably worth a first-team place. But talks broke down at Newcastle and then Sunderland came in. I thought, Lawrie McMenemy is the man for me. Although it didn't work out at Sunderland I probably wasn't wanted at Liverpool even though I still had 18 months of my contract left. Looking back, I probably should have stayed because Liverpool won the double in '86 and I'd only played eight games so I didn't get a league championship medal.

I remember Kenny in his pre-season talk saying, 'Well, I've taken over now, nothing will change.' But there obviously were personnel changes because I left two months later, Phil Neal left four months later, so really he got rid of two stalwarts, I was 31 and Phil was 34, 35. It probably seems old in terms of footballers but we still felt that we had a couple of years left at the very top. But Kenny said, and I'll always remember it because it was in the home team dressing room, 'I've got the job, I'm here to do a job not for you. There will be difficulties throughout the year but I want you to give me 100 per cent for Liverpool, for the football club.' So things didn't change.

I always felt under pressure under Kenny because of the availability of Jim Beglin to take my place and Jim knew that eventually he would take over that left-back role. I think Kenny had decided to make a couple of changes and see how it went. And just look at him, he won the Double and you can't argue with that, facts are facts.

Bob didn't spend all of his time in the boot room either. I remember Bob on quite a few occasions being down in his office taking telephone calls. You have to have a bit of privacy and Bob and Kenny liked to go down to their offices. Bob would still come in and offer Kenny advice even when Kenny was the manager. When Kenny took over you felt there would be new personnel and inevitably there were.

BOB GREAVES

Interviewing Kenny

When I was a newspaper Saturday match reporter, either for the *Mail on Sunday* or before that for the *Telegraph*, I and many others had the experience of trying to get an interview out of Kenny Dalglish when he was manager of Liverpool. In a sense it was a farce. I've never gone along with the thinking that Kenny Dalglish could not speak English that was understandable, because I've heard him speak perfectly normal Scottish English that was perfectly understandable on other occasions. But he did, I'm sure, very deliberately put the accent on when he was having to conduct his post-match press conferences, even when there wasn't very much controversial to discuss. I just think he took the piss and he was very clever at it.

People who don't know how journalism works in football might be surprised to know that after a match there are radio, print journalists, anything up to 30 press people, and with Dalglish if you weren't within two to five feet of his face you simply could not hear what he said. Now I think that was deliberate. He knew with a crowd of 30 people that if he raised his voice, everyone would be able to hear him. But he never did. So you had to try and get in the front line, cock an ear to literally hear what he was saying but also to try and understand it. He would reply to pretty straightforward questions like, is the new so-and-so signing playing next week? The reply you would get would be, 'Y pixdateem.' You would then have to think, what did he say, because it was in a sort of verbal shorthand with lots of letters missed out. Then you'd have to get together with some of your press mates and try and work out what he had said, like 'Y picks da teae.' Eventually we'd put it all together and come up with 'Wife picks the team.' So, you're not going to quote him because he's taking the piss. Well, you might quote him once, but only once. I've also heard him say, when asked if so-and-so would be fit for the game, 'Amneed'ctr.' Again you would think, what did he say? And you'd say to your mate, 'What did he say?' 'Don't know, didn't hear it.' Then you'd find someone who did hear it and again you'd go into a little committee. What did it sound like? 'Amneed'ctr.' 'Am Nee doctor.' Oh yes. 'I'm no doctor.' So, again you would not quote him because he wasn't saying anything.

There was one press conference I was at where we were awaiting Kenny Dalglish and someone from the opposition. There were 20 or 30 of us at the top of the stairs in the Main Stand, hanging around at 5.30pm. Then suddenly someone spotted

Dalglish down the bottom of the corridor but we also spotted the fact that he was engaged in one-to-one conversation with our colleague John Keith of the *Daily Express*. They were having an animated conversation, with their faces eight inches from each other's faces. And we all knew that John would come back and in the nice old terms of the press pool he would share with us what Dalglish was telling him, unless it was a world exclusive. And he was with him for ages and we all hung about watching. It probably went on for eight or nine minutes. Then John came back and to a man we all said, 'What did he say?' And John replied, 'F**ed if I know, I didn't understand a word of it!' He'd had a ten-minute conversation nodding, agreeing and hadn't understood because Dalglish was in one of those moods. There was no world exclusive, he simply had not understood a word.

DAVID FAIRCLOUGH
Geoff Twentyman Cast Aside

There was no secret. It was all about the right selection of players, and not just ability but character as well. I think it was very sad the way Geoff Twentyman was treated. Geoff Twentyman was, in my eyes, a genius. He didn't discover me but Geoff was fantastic at finding players. I thought it was terrible the way he was cast aside. He was as much a major part of the boot room as anyone and he doesn't get the credit he deserves, he doesn't get a mention half the time. He knew Shankly's brain, he was probably a similar type of player to him and Bob Paisley. In a period of ten years you can count the number of bad signings on one hand. Just look at the last ten years by comparison! Geoff knew what he was looking for.

Me and Geoff got on very well. I talked to him a lot, he was fantastic to talk to. A good indication of that was the way Graeme took him to Rangers. He saw what had happened to him and thought, what a waste of a man's knowledge. He had his own methods; he didn't just go and sit in the directors' box, he'd go and stand on the terraces and listen to what the punters thought of a player, those who saw him week in week out, ear to the ground. I wonder how many people like Geoff Twentyman exist now. Scouts nowadays get calls from here, there and everywhere. Football hasn't changed in that respect; there is still the little diamond playing up in Scunthorpe.

I remember me and Geoff walking around the B team pitch and I asked him about this Rush fellow because there was a lot of talk about him at the time. He said, yes, he's got something, could be another Davey Fairclough one day, that was nice of him. He's got pace, an eye for goal. Now Rushie had been watched and turned down by a number of clubs but Geoff saw something. And remember in those days you spent a year in the reserves before you ever got near the first team.

IAN HARGREAVES

A New Team

Dalglish's early years were phenomenally successful. Admittedly the team he took over was a very successful one – Joe Fagan's European Cup team which they genuinely believed would have won the European Cup. Everything that year was geared to it and they were convinced they would win it a fifth time. Dalglish broke the team up but then produced a new one with Beardsley and Barnes – arguably that was the strongest team they had ever had.

Kenny never consulted the boot room as much, he was more his own man. He was no 'I am'. He'd been brought up in the Anfield philosophy. But if you ask the others he was full of innovations. They did a lot of new things under him. The boot room were full of admiration because they worked. He would only name the team an hour before kick-off and he wouldn't even tell the players until the final moment. They also stopped letting anybody on the coach. I used to travel on the coach but was told that it was stopping, it was the squad only, even Bob Paisley couldn't travel with them. The team playing away was certainly different. They were more flexible.

If Liverpool wanted a player then there was no doubt they

would get him. There weren't so many foreign players about then either. Football has changed, there is now so much more money in the game. It's far more difficult today.

IAN HARGREAVES
The Incredible Tom Saunders

Tom Saunders was a headmaster who ran the Liverpool Schools teams and also the England Schools team. Then he was persuaded to help out. He's been an incredible figure. He would always go out in the morning for a strict walk around the pitch half a dozen times, really concentrated. Peter Robinson once said to me, there's been no man done more for this club than Tom Saunders, including Bill Shankly.

He's been unbelievable, he's always stayed totally in the background. You probably know that after Kenny Dalglish became manager he asked Tom Saunders to sit in his office. I said to Tom, 'What are you doing there?' and he said, 'Nothing much really. You see, Kenny just asked if I'd mind sitting in his office taking the telephone calls.' He said that Kenny asked him things occasionally. I said, 'You mean you're a sort of adviser.' 'Oh no,' he said, 'I never offer any advice, I never say, why don't you do this, because people don't like that. I take messages and he'll occasionally say to me, "Oh, what do you think about this?" And I'll say to him, 'It's up to you boss, but you might just have seen that maybe he doesn't play well when we're playing away or he's a bit left sided or I think he may have got domestic troubles.'

Now I imagine some of that would be regarded as absolute gold dust as information about people. Tom always took a lot of interest in the people. He wasn't just looking to grab the best kids for Liverpool and if they didn't make it, tough luck. He wanted kids with promise but was determined that they just didn't play football but that they continued with their studies or were apprentices or moved to other clubs.

JOHN ALDRIDGE
The Gas Man

I joined the club in January 1987. In the boot room then would be Ronnie Moran, Roy Evans, and of course Kenny Dalglish who was the manager. Tom Saunders would be in there as well. Sometimes Tommy Smith would be around as well; he wasn't on the staff but he might be in there cadging a whisky or whatever. John Bennison was about as well.

I'll tell you a funny story about John. He gave me a trial for Liverpool. He was our gas man and he came to our house when I was young and he saw all the medals and cups that I had won and my Mum was telling him all about me. 'Oh,' he says, 'I'll arrange for him to come to Liverpool and have a trial.' So, true enough, he organised it and shortly afterwards I went up to Liverpool for this trial. We played their youth team, I really enjoyed it although we lost 8–1 but I scored our only goal. After the game Tom Saunders came over to me and says, 'Well John, we'll definitely be ringing you.' Anyhow it took them 20-odd years and cost them £750,000 before they got round to ringing me. But John was a well-respected and well-liked man. Everybody respected him.

The door of the boot room would always be open after a game and you would see the opposition coaches and managers in there having a drink. Kenny Dalglish would pop in as well but he had his own office upstairs. It's hard to say if it changed under Kenny as I didn't really know it before him. But I got the impression that things just went on the same, they just followed the line that had been laid down by Bill Shankly.

I have something similar now here at Tranmere. We get together after a game at Prenton Park. Oddly enough it was all done subconsciously, I didn't set out to deliberately do the same, it just happened. First of all we entertain the opposition, though not every team, there's one or two we don't like! But most of them are good friends and come and have a bevy with us. Then once they've gone we get chatting among ourselves. Sometimes it goes on so long you forget the wife is waiting upstairs to go home.

We also write up reports of our training just as they did at Anfield. Kevin Sheedy does that for us. The thing about Liverpool was that everything was basic. It was all about pass and move. People would go and see Liverpool train and they'd come away and say, 'Is that it?' They couldn't believe we didn't do something else.

So what is the secret of the incredible Liverpool success story? They have been asking that since the late and great Bill Shankly started this era of total dominance in English football. At the end of the day it's about good players, the right players. The game's changed now and it's not so easy. I think the boot room still has a part to play, definitely, but it's not so simple now. The game is more technical but it's still pass and move and still about good players, but you need a bit more now. The boot room was the heart of Liverpool Football Club, where it was all done and dusted.

The secret of Liverpool's success is simple. We are so basic, so simple in our approach to the game that anyone spending a week at Anfield would not believe how easy it all seems. There are no strong-arm tactics, no prima donnas amongst the players, no gimmicks, no big heads, just good habits, good sensible living and a manager who treats the players and the rest of the staff like adults.

If you play for Liverpool you join an exclusive club. The membership is only handed out to a chosen few and the rules are simple. Liverpool look after you off the pitch, you look after them on it.

The players and managers win the prizes; the back room staff make the club tick over like a machine. Peter Robinson, John Smith and Kenny Dalglish are the top men, but there are so many others who work hard for the cause that is Liverpool. You don't leave Anfield, you go reluctantly.

PHIL THOMPSON
Football Talk

It was a great honour when I first came back and to be part of the boot room scene. It was organised chaos in a way, everyone knew where things went. But when I did come back I realised it was more organised than I thought it would be. When I was a player and saw things lying around I wondered about it but it was organised in its own way, that was the one big thing I noticed. As a coach you went in there and enjoyed the football talk and the deep thinking and the meticulous organisation that went on, when to travel to games, when to give the players a day off, all these things were thought about in advance. They tried to make things as easy as they could for the players. I realised how the players were wrapped up in cotton wool. They barely had to think for themselves, it was all planned out for them. When I went back on the coaching staff it was Kenny Dalglish, Roy Evans, Ronnie Moran, John Bennison and Tom Saunders. Tom was always a vital link man between the staff and the directors, a very important link. A clever and important figure. He played a major part, he was a better communicator than Bob Paisley who was also involved as a link with Kenny. Bob was not good at communicating things but Tom could do that.

Chris Lawler went when I came in. Things moved on. It was a change but not such a major one. It was obviously sad for Chris but a great opportunity for me. Apart from that, things didn't change under Kenny. I was the youngest of the boot room, the next generation.

There were slight changes with Kenny. You had this younger manager and Kenny maybe made one or two small changes but it was still the old values. He was not stupid enough to change things too much. He maintained the boot room status and its organisational role. He allowed Roy and Ronnie to get on with it. His identification of players is legendary. The boot room continued much the same. There was a chart on the wall and it had

13 league championships and it just went on and every year, they would scratch out the number and add a new one. There were notes all over it and it was ripped but that stayed year upon year upon year. And someone had written 'just like Real Madrid' on it. It stayed there for years from 1978/79. It was looking at the things that happened before, that drove them on to succeed all the more. If you won 5–0 on the Saturday it would have been forgotten by the Monday morning. Ronnie Moran would be screaming at you and you'd be thinking, but we won 5–0. It made no difference. That was so vital. We criticised it as players but it was so important to have that driving force.

RONNIE MORAN
Kenny And The Boot Room

Kenny was appointed after Joe, after Heysel. The rumours were going around that day. Officially it wasn't said until after the game. We were ready to fly home the next day. Mr Smith the chairman, Peter and Joe and myself were on the plane first. We were driven right to the runway and we were called, Roy and myself, from the back of the plane and were told that Kenny was officially taking over as player-manager and that he wanted us to stay on in our roles.

Kenny was like Shanks in a way. He'd come down, go to the club first thing in the morning, then come down here to Melwood. By then we'd be out training. Not every morning but generally he'd do his work up at the club with Mr Robinson. He'd get changed and then come out training. We used to use Anfield then for changing. He'd drive down and join us, he knew what we would be doing that morning.

In the boot room we'd discuss tactics, new players. We went in every Sunday morning after the game up until Graeme Souness took over. The reason we went in Sundays was not so much to tidy up but to get the laundry ready for the next day and after we'd done that the main thing was injuries. You can go home after a game all right but then the next morning you wake up and your leg's swollen or whatever. But if you're not going in until Monday it's no good. We used to say to the players, if you feel anything, don't wait until Monday, come in straight away. We used to get in by 9.30am and we'd have everything cleared up by 10.30am and be in the boot room having a talk, waiting for injured players. We'd natter about all the results, or *Match of the Day*, talk about possible signings.

The boot room didn't change with Kenny. The philosophy of the boot room went on. Bob used to come down as well. It just carried on. Whoever was manager, we'd do the warm-ups and then split up into groups. The manager would come out training most mornings. Kenny would come in the boot room but the main things were done in his office. After the game he'd be in there with his wife and personal friends where they had a drink. But he'd come and talk to us at some point.

WILLIE MILLER
No Change

I don't think the boot room changed with Kenny Dalglish. He still had his back room staff, the continuity of Tom Saunders and so on. Tom would sit in the dugout with him and would still be there at Melwood every day. Roy was there as well. You still see that picture where they've just won the championship and Dalglish is sitting there with Roy Evans and Ronnie Moran in the boot room. Now Kenny Dalglish was not in the dressing room with the lads. The boot room was still there, it was part of the jigsaw.

He came in and made his own decisions. He got rid of Chris Lawler, and Geoff Twentyman, but he brought in Phil Thompson. He had his own ideas. Thompson was a good choice, red through and through. Now there's a man for you who as a player won 42 caps for England, captained his country, won seven championship medals. Now nobody can come up to him and say, show us your medals. I don't think it went wrong there at all.

JIM GARDINER

A Changing Game

You can probably trace the changes in the way the boot room operated to the mid-eighties when Kenny was taking over. But football itself was changing then. It was becoming far more commercialised. You suddenly had one or two of the big clubs starting to pull away. That was the first change from the game that had been there in the fifties and the sixties and the seventies. Suddenly the game was changing. You had far more powerful players who had more to say for themselves. They were more highly paid players and maybe management and coaches didn't have quite the same control over players as they did in the past. It was not down to Kenny Dalglish or anyone else, it was just down to changes in the way modern managers operated. Rumour has it that Kenny did not go to the boot room very often but from the mid-eighties you had managers taking on responsibilities that they didn't have before, for example dealing with the media, be it newspapers, magazines or television. The additional call on managers' and coaches' time meant that they couldn't spend the same time that they did before sitting with a cup of tea and a chocolate biscuit discussing what was going to happen on a Saturday.

I think any manager likes his own staff round him. Whether they were sacked or their contracts were not renewed, I'm not sure, it happens all the time. Managers are in there, they're highly paid to do a specific job and that's to be successful. If they feel that to be successful they need their own people in there, if they feel that the job could be done better by someone else, you have to be ruthless. You don't get to be a successful manager or successful in any line, whether it's football or business or whatever, without that ruthless streak. You have to have a ruthless streak to be successful and unfortunately people's fingers get burned.

LAWRIE McMENEMY
Hillsborough

When you talk about Liverpool you've also got to talk about a club that has had its tragedies. Bill Shankly was always known as a 'man of the people' who made his players understand that they were servants of the people, that the people pay their wages and that they are supporting them home and away every week. The fans are watching them perform on the pitch and the one thing they really want is to be playing alongside them out there on the pitch. So when the tragedy comes along it all comes together and the footballers come off the pitch and go among the crowd, the people. Kenny Dalglish supposedly couldn't communicate, they said, but he did it with his feet. After Hillsborough he showed how he could communicate. I was there that day at Hillsborough and he was genuinely distressed and later he went to all those funerals with his wife. Hillsborough had such an enormous effect on the whole world of football.

CHRIS LAWLER
Getting The Sack

We did the Double that first season and then I got fired. That came as a huge shock. I had no idea. I didn't get a large wage in those days, I had to rely on my bonus. We got this bonus for winning trophies. After the season ended I noticed that I had not been given a bonus. So when the new season was coming around and we had gone back to get ready for pre-season training I asked the others, Roy and Ronnie, if they had got their bonus. They said yes, they had. So I decided to go and see Peter Robinson, the secretary. I hadn't been able to get hold of Kenny because he wasn't in so I had gone to see Peter. He told me that Phil Thompson was coming in the next day to take the training. He more or less hinted that something was going on. The next day Kenny was around and I discovered that he didn't want me. There was no reaction from the rest of the staff. That's the way it is in football. You don't take sides, you just get on with it. I was annoyed at the time with the way it was done. I had not been properly told. In football you're going to get the sack sometime. I had been very successful running the reserves but managers want their own players, their own staff. But there's no hard feelings about it now. Geoff Twentyman was also given the sack. He'd been there a long time and was one of the best scouts in the business, if not *the* best. He knew all about players, that's for sure. But things change, even more so now.

KENNY DALGLISH

Changes at Melwood

I made only the odd change at Melwood. There were aspects of training which I didn't want to continue. In the past we used to come in and play mixed games on a Monday or Tuesday morning which were a waste of time. Then the staff and injured first teamers used to play the kids on our 'Wembley pitch'. So that stopped. The staff would still play the kids after training with the pros or if the pros were off. One popular move was bringing the lunches back for the players, which gave a social focus to the working day. Preparation for matches altered a bit as well. We started the journey to away matches earlier, instead of four or five o'clock in the afternoon. I was always worried about being held up by roadworks or bad traffic. On coach journeys that invisible barrier between me and the players was really in force. As a player I used to sit with the others. As manager I used to sit in the middle of the bus at a table for four by myself. Tom Saunders would occasionally come and sit with me and we would try to do *The Times* concise crossword.

Like Bob, Tom Saunders was very important to me. I kept the same people in place for my first year. Then I began to restructure the reserves. Chris Lawler went and so did Geoff Twentyman

... it was right for Geoff to leave. He had arthritis in the back. My decision had nothing to do with Geoff's judgement, more to do with his medical condition. Chris was very quiet and I felt I needed someone with greater charisma to bring on the kids and the reserves. It obviously wasn't a popular decision with Chris or Geoff. They had given Liverpool great service and indicated that they didn't deserve the decision I had taken. But that was their opinion. The only opinion that mattered was mine. It was in Liverpool's best interests. I asked Chris to stay for three months to work with Thommo. It was easier for us to help Chris if he was in employment with Liverpool Football Club than if he was on the outside. Chris did not think that he could do that. My only regret is the way Chris found out. He was talking to Peter Robinson about his bonus and Peter said that first Chris should see the manager. Chris came into my office knowing that something was about to happen. That was wrong. I should have been the one to give him the news about him going, rather than him coming into my office already realising.

An extract from *Dalglish – The Autobiography* (Hodder)

KENNY DALGLISH

Keeping The Boot Room

One accusation levelled at me is that I dismantled Liverpool's great boot room. That's utter rubbish. It was an institution, one I would never have meddled with. The boot room wasn't just a chunk of air enclosed within four walls or a store for boots. It was a symbol of Liverpool's approach to the game, the thinking and planning that brought victories. Ronnie Moran and Roy Evans were the guardians of the boot room philosophy and tradition. They were a vast library of information used for the club's benefit. As a player I had great respect for the boot room. I wasn't even allowed in, except to collect boots.

Contrary to the media's belief, my first act as manager was to keep the boot room intact. I had total respect for Ronnie, Roy and their boot room. A manager couldn't have asked for a better duo than Ronnie and Roy. I would never have done anything to compromise the boot room. It was special because of the people in it: Ronnie and Roy, Tom Saunders, John Bennison, Chris Lawler and Phil Thompson who were there during my time . . . It was Liverpool's heart. Like the club, there were no airs in the boot room. The room itself was nothing special. It was simply a room with four hampers to sit on. On the walls were rows of pegs, boots dangling from each, a bit of shelving and a double cupboard where Ronnie and Roy could keep their bottles of whisky. Eventually they put in a fridge, their one concession to modern life. The boot room was a university for football. It was a bunch of intelligent guys discussing football.

People who claim I tried to reduce the boot room's influence ignore the fact that I went in there every day of the week to talk to Ronnie, Roy and Tom. But I never went in after games for one very good reason: I wasn't clever enough. I knew what Ronnie and Roy did to visitors from other clubs whom they invited in there. After games, Ronnie and Roy would sit in their famous hideaway, chatting away, dispensing a little bit of liquid hospitality to visiting managers and coaches, who were always delighted to be invited into Anfield's famous boot room. But it was so cunning. All the while Ronnie and Roy were picking up little bits of information about players, perhaps even about tactics. They didn't miss much. New ideas, how other people were working, what other people were doing, anyone floating about in the lower leagues who was half-decent: Ronnie and Roy soaked up everything and anything. They were brilliant at getting information out of people.

An extract from *Dalglish – The Autobiography* (Hodder)

CHAPTER FIVE

Graeme Souness: Champagne Charlie

Graeme Souness's arrival to take charge at Anfield was greeted with universal enthusiasm. Initially he had indicated an unwillingness to take over. He was enjoying life at Ibrox, he insisted, and didn't wish to return to Anfield. Perhaps that was merely a cover as he negotiated a contract with Liverpool chairman David Moores. Whatever it was, when he finally did roll up outside Anfield he was welcomed by a large enthusiastic crowd. Of all the names that had been suggested as a successor to Dalglish, Souness topped the list by a mile. The prodigal son had returned and would surely continue the dynasty of success.

But to those in the know there were always a few doubts; his reign at Ibrox might have produced plenty of silverware but there were worrying stories of dressing room rows, indiscipline on the field, and transfer coming and goings that defied logic. Yet there was no denying that Souness had initiated a startling revolution at Rangers. In former Celtic star Mo Johnston, he not only signed the club's first Catholic but sent shock waves through the city of Glasgow. That in itself was enough to catapult him into Scottish folklore. On top of that he had also bought the club's first black player as well as signing the odd England international. It may have all been forbidden territory but Souness had not been afraid to venture in pursuit of football glory. Rules were made to be broken, seemed to be the Souness philosophy.

Graeme Souness had been the finest midfielder in Liverpool's history. Phil Thompson even suggested he was the most accomplished midfielder this country has ever produced. He was as tough as they come, the supreme leader both on and off the field, a player feared but also respected by every professional in the game. He had joined Liverpool as a player in January 1978 from Middlesbrough where manager Jackie Charlton had performed miracles in keeping the youngster on the straight and narrow. Charlton warned him that he had a choice of being a footballer or a playboy. Souness chose to be a footballer but a bit of the playboy was never too far away. Paisley had no such problems with him as Souness went on to captain the club and pick up three European champions' medals as well as the usual bagful of domestic medals. The Kop nicknamed him Champagne Charlie for his love of the high life. But in the summer of 1984 he left for the sunny climes of Sampdoria before sensationally joining Rangers as player-manager in 1986. In his first game he was sent off; his Ibrox career continued to follow much the same pattern.

He knew there was a huge task in front of him at Anfield. 'Things have been left to slip,' he said, the finger firmly pointed at someone or other. And so the Souness reign began. It was to prove a whirlwind. The press had made much of the fact that Dalglish's side was ageing and that Dalglish himself had failed to bring in the necessary youngsters to succeed them. The papers even suggested that Dalglish had resigned because he feared the prospect of creating a new side. It was wholly untrue as was the allegation that the Liverpool side was over the hill. Nevertheless Souness was quick to act. He'd only been there a couple of months before Peter Beardsley, Steve Staunton, Gary Gillespie and David Speedie were all packed off to pastures new. Steve McMahon, Gary Ablett and Glynn Hysen had also gone within six months. But into their place came a few relishing prospects, including England central defender Mark Wright, the goalscoring Dean Saunders, Michael Thomas and Rob Jones. It was only the beginning.

During his three seasons in charge the turnover in staff would be greater than at any time since the early days of Shankly. In all, Souness signed 15 new players, costing a then phenomenal £21 million and sold 18 others for £12 million. One senior player compared the Anfield dressing room door to the swing door of a department store with players flooding in one way while just as many were pouring out the other side. Even some players signed by Souness barely lasted a season. The old Anfield motto of one in, one out, each season had been tossed aside. The disruption brought chaos and what's more, it showed on the field. There were also injuries galore, many of them blamed on the introduction of a new training schedule.

In his first season in charge Liverpool crashed to sixth in the table, their lowest position since 1965, but there was some consolation as they went on to win the FA Cup, beating Sunderland in the final. Yet just weeks before the final the club was thrown into confusion when Souness suffered a mild heart attack and was promptly admitted to hospital for major bypass surgery. As if that was not enough, Liverpool fans awoke on the morning of the third anniversary of the Hillsborough disaster to find Souness's own exclusive story of his heart operation splashed across the *Sun* newspaper. Given that the *Sun* was the most reviled newspaper on Merseyside following its accusations after the Hillsborough disaster, Souness's story hardly went down well with those on the Kop. He eventually apologised and agreed to hand over his fee to a named charity. Some were forgiving; others not so. But at least Liverpool went on to win the Cup and with Steve McManaman emerging as the new hero of English football there was hope for the forthcoming season.

There had been plenty of reasons why the previous season had been so disappointing but things still looked promising. More new players were signed during the summer of 1992, including goalkeeper David James and midfielder Paul Stewart. Alas, it made little difference. Liverpool finished sixth again and the knives, put aside after the *Sun* exclusive, were now being sharpened again. The accusation was that Souness was trying to change things too quickly; what Liverpool wanted was evolution, not revolution.

But other things had happened as well. Most importantly, coach Phil Thompson had been sacked. The precise details still remain shrouded in mystery but it is clear that the two did not get on too well. Thompson was clearly upset at what was going on at the club and eventually Souness snapped and sacked him. An outraged Thompson threatened to take the club to an industrial tribunal in a case of unfair dismissal, but weeks before it was scheduled to be heard in court, a settlement was reached. Part of the agreement was that Thompson would not speak publicly about what had happened. In all the years there had never been such a public row at Anfield. Dalglish had sacked Chris Lawler and Geoff Twentyman. Both had gone quietly but that was clearly not Thompson's style.

Souness had also introduced a new occupant to the boot room, Phil Boersma. The former Liverpool player had been a colleague of Souness at Middlesbrough and Liverpool and had later joined the staff at Rangers. Boersma had trained and qualified as a physio and now he was back in that role at Liverpool. Bob Paisley, Joe Fagan and Ronnie Moran had always been the men working the magic sponge in the past but Souness decided to bring in his own medicine man. The other boot room members accepted it with grace but it's hard to imagine they did not have one or two concerns. Sammy Lee also moved in, replacing the departing Phil Thompson.

Training was also altered. New systems were put into place, and Melwood became the centre of the club. The daily trip from Anfield for changing and meals stopped. Instead everything was transferred to Melwood so that the players only showed up at Anfield on a matchday. It probably made sense and certainly found favour among the players, although Jan Molby for one missed the daily mickey-taking that always took place on the bus.

But perhaps more important was that the very soul of the club, the boot room itself, was torn down. With Anfield a designated stadium for Euro 96, UEFA had insisted that a press room be provided for the hundreds of journalists who would be attending the games. The lack of a press room had been a shortcoming at Anfield for years. Back in the 1960s post-match interviews were little more than a word or two from the manager. But in the 1990s the manager was subjected to a more rigorous questioning while players also had to be drafted in to give their reactions. A corridor had sufficed in the past but now a proper designated press room was necessary. A major renovation was needed and that meant ripping the boot room down as part of the rebuilding. In truth it was not a Graeme Souness decision, it was a board decision, but there will always be a feeling that it would never have happened if Shankly had been manager.

As the 1992/93 season drew to another disappointing close, it seemed the end for Souness. His extravagant signings had, for the most part, failed; Manchester United had won the title while Liverpool were in sixth spot. The Kop was baying for Souness's blood. The board met and duly decided that enough was enough. But then, in a remarkable U-turn a few days later, they changed their minds, reaching an unsatisfactory compromise with Souness. Souness pleaded for more time, the pay-off price was going to be costly, and regretfully the board backed down. Although Souness was still in charge there was a compromise; Roy Evans was to be elevated to assistant manager. It was a clear signal that Evans had been earmarked to take over. In the event he would not have to wait too long.

Souness was even given more money, signing Nigel Clough and Neil Ruddock for the new season. At the start it looked like it might be about to work out as Liverpool soared to the top of the table, but the optimism was short-lived. Souness panicked and signed Julian Dicks from West Ham, allowing Mick Marsh and David Burrows to move in the opposite direction. The Kop was staggered at the prospect of Dicks pulling on a red shirt. There was talk of dressing room rifts and then Ronnie Whelan was transfer listed. It simply went from bad to worse. The end came in late January 1994 when after a humiliating defeat in the FA Cup at Anfield, Souness saved the board the trouble of sacking him by promptly resigning. Into his shoes stepped Roy Evans. 'My job,' he said, 'is to get Liverpool back to basics.'

So, was the Souness era such a disaster? There are some who now look back and argue that he ought to have been given more time. His ideas may have ruffled a few feathers around Anfield but in the main part they were full of foresight and sense. Football was changing and the boot room mentality, while important, was no longer any guarantee of success. New fitness regimes were necessary with a more professional approach to treatment. The traditional five-a-side practice games might have been fun but football tactics had moved on. Modern players needed more specialist fitness programmes such as weights and more planned work with the ball. The decision to move the boot room was not his alone while the other crucial decision to shift all the training facilities to Melwood was greeted enthusiastically by the players. It made sense not to have to traipse back and forth to Anfield just to change and eat.

All this is true but the nagging doubts remain that the turnover in staff was far too excessive and vast amounts were lashed out on second-rate players. Let's not forget Mark Walters, Istvan Kozma, Torben Piechnik and Paul Stewart. Souness undoubtedly showed a pride in the red shirt and tried to instill some of his own passion into his players but in the end they were either not good enough, overpaid or simply incapable of performing with the same fire that Souness himself had shown on the field. Five years on, the innovative ideas of Souness might have been received with more consideration by the players and fans. As it was Souness and Liverpool were running out of steam and more than a few nails had been banged into the boot room coffin.

ALAN BROWN
Decline and Fall

Souness used to just pop in. He had his own room as well, he took over the office from Kenny. He had a security lock on his room and he used to invite his friends as well. He was courting then with his now wife. He'd come in, say hello to the visiting manager, and then away.

The boot room was only there for one year when Souey was around and then it disappeared and was knocked down. Everybody said we shouldn't have closed it down. Everyone was sad when it went, it just disappeared during the summer. I didn't know it was going. I don't think many of them knew. Things were just dumped, taken out. We were shocked because we would have liked to have kept some stuff for the new one. But the new one is just an office now. It still carries on, same system, but it's different. It's more crowded, more people come in. In those days not many came in. The Lord Mayor of Liverpool

used to come in and big Paul Orr, because he was big in the
Guinness company. But other than that not many came in. But
later it started getting friends and friends of friends. Souey sometimes wouldn't come in after a game because if they got beat he
would get very uptight and depressed.

MIKE BERRY

A Diabolical Mistake

Graeme Souness came in and everybody, bar none, in the city
of Liverpool said he was the right man for the job, all the press,
all the fans. They were all delighted. He came in on a tidal wave
of euphoria. He had been such a great player. For the first six
months everybody was delighted, then we started getting all these
comments that he was changing things too quickly, he was changing the training, pulling the boot room down, he was doing this
and that, lots of bad press. Now whether the press was accurate
or not I don't know but I suspect it wasn't. But it certainly had
an effect on Graeme.

   You started to get a split down the Kop. I can remember one
day half the Kop booing and half the Kop clapping his name. I
remember the last game of the season, playing Coventry at
Anfield. Everybody thought Graeme Souness had been sacked
because he was not at the game. There was all these rumours
going around that he had gone. Then there was a board meeting
the next day and there was an announcement at about 4.30pm
and that the board had agreed, everybody thought that's it, he's
been sacked but no, Graeme Souness was continuing in office
with Roy Evans coming in as assistant manager. Obviously there
had been some disruption behind the scenes. To this day I still
think he is a mad, passionate Liverpool person. Had he been
given more time, who knows? But he did do the honorable thing
and resigned after the Bristol City game. I have a lot of respect
for him. I think if you ask Liverpool fans you'll get a 50–50
split, half thinking he was good for the club, half thinking the
opposite. I think he was good for the club, I don't think he was

allowed to finish the job. Okay, he made a few stupid errors like being in the *Sun*. That was a disgrace. That could only be done through naivety or stupidity. That was diabolical. But after winning the cup in '92 things did start to go wrong. We had a Mickey Mouse Cup win in '95 and we've gone downhill since.

STEVE MORGAN

Injury Problems

When Kenny Dalglish walked out, after that cup match at Everton, there were things going wrong at the time the season wasn't going right. There were cracks showing and there were strains there. Then Graeme Souness came in. Though he was a great player, he was quite an abrasive character with Rangers up in Scotland. On the face of it he had done very well with them but if you speak to David Murray, he had his problems with him. With hindsight it was a huge mistake appointing Souness but the precedent had been set with Kenny, another tremendously successful player of the eighties. Souness had more managerial experience because he had a track record up at Glasgow Rangers. I think from a fan's point of view it looked like the right decision at the time but it was very obvious very quickly that it wasn't, from the changes that were made.

Liverpool had never really had huge injury problems. They had a set way of training. As soon as Souness came in it seemed like every other player was out injured all the time and we just couldn't seem to string the same 11 together for two matches on the trot. Everybody seemed to be injured. There were changes that I'm not aware of but there were obviously changes about the way things were done. There was a lot more mouthing in the papers, he seemed to have a lot to say, sometimes about nothing. The style of the club started to drift and we've never got back to the halcyon days of before.

ALAN KENNEDY

Our Little Differences

When I came back to the north-west I said to Kenny, 'I've got a serious problem with my knee, would you mind if I rebuilt the knee with the help of the physio and some of the equipment at Anfield?' He said 'no problem' so when Graeme came, I asked him 'Do you mind if I use the equipment at Melwood? So I used to go down there to Melwood. I think Graeme felt as though I was angling towards a job at Anfield. We had had our little differences over the seven years that we played together but he was very professional and very nice in allowing me to go to the training ground to keep me going in football. I was now playing non-league. My knee had been restored, not to full fitness but to a good level, so I still needed to keep myself going. If I had any problems I could go and see Phil Boersma for any sort of injury I may have. So Graeme was fine but I was probably putting undue pressure on Sammy Lee, Ronnie Moran and a few others by being down there so I had to think about not going down as much as I liked to do. I was coaching schools at the time, I had free time and all I wanted to do was just play football.

Since Kenny left there have been a couple of major trophies but where they've been in the league hasn't been as good as we did in the past. From 1977 all the way through to '89, I don't think Liverpool were ever out of the top four. That's not a slight on any of the managers because Roy Evans took over in '93 or '94 and again he was never out of the top four as a manager so you look at that as success. But Liverpool were winning trophies back in the eighties and they weren't winning them in the nineties. They were getting to finals but they weren't winning them.

BARRIE HOLMES
Not Quite The Same

I think it was in Graeme Souness's time that they pulled the boot room down and turned it into a press room. Not only did the boot room go but the spirit went as well. I think Souness had a different way of approaching things. We may look back in future years and say that, yes, those things did need to be done. Things do change, methods change, techniques change, and you have to keep up with change.

I think the boot room began to change when Dalglish took over because I think he was very much his own man. Although in the first couple of years he took a lot of advice from Bob Paisley, I got the impression he was moving more and more towards the way he wanted to do things and I think that was accentuated when Graeme Souness took over. It maybe came back a little bit when Roy Evans came in but by then they didn't have the people with the personalities and the know-how to make the boot room work again. I think he tried to generate it by bringing in Doug Livermore, and Sammy Lee was there, but it wasn't quite the same somehow.

BRIAN HALL
No More Boots

I couldn't put a specific date on the change for you but it really began to change with Graeme. The boot room wasn't really Graeme's scene. I don't know whether it was Kenny's scene to be honest, but I certainly know it wasn't Graeme's. There were practical considerations that Graeme was thinking about in terms of training facilities and so on. I presume, though I may be wrong, that it was Graeme's decision to move everything down to Melwood. That then opened up an opportunity to build a new press room which we were desperately short of. Some space became available and the new boot room was constructed. But there is no character to it, no history to it, it's just a room where you can go and have a beer with our coaching staff, visiting staff and friends. It still happens after a game. Call it nostalgia but it isn't the same as it was. The boot room was the boot room. There's no boots in the new room, just a cupboard with a few glasses and a few bottles.

DAVID FAIRCLOUGH
All Change at Melwood

I don't really think it changes with Kenny. He had Phil Thompson and Ronnie there. He had a strong Liverpool connection. I think it probably changes with Graeme Souness. While I think Graeme was a great respecter of all of them, I think he'd seen the continental approach in Italy and thought, this needs updating; it needs to be less cliquey. Maybe Graeme thought it was too democratic and now he was the boss. I think he began to break it up then.

But it does change with Graeme. He decided to buy immediate names, Saunders, Wright, and so on. But to his credit he did recognise the talent of Geoff Twentyman. But Graeme did make a lot of impulse buying. He also got rid of too many older players, Nicol, McMahon, Whelan, they still had so much to offer.

When I was in Switzerland they had a new Yugoslavian coach and the first thing he did was to get rid of anyone who had a bit of character. And the first thing that told me was that he had a fear factor. I think that still exists in England and I've seen it on a number of occasions. I think that was a little of Graeme's thing. He didn't need to have that fear. Personally I don't like ex-players going back to their old club, particularly soon after they have finished. I don't think it works. In fact it rarely works, going back. It's usually a recipe for disaster. He was also big pals with Boersma and that didn't help in the boot room. You had that group Kenny, Ronnie, Roy who all gel together but then Graeme comes in with Phil Boersma. Thommo's at odds with Graeme and he gets the bullet. Before there had never been any threats. They'd all worked together but slowly that security is disappearing. Twentyman's been sacked by Kenny, Chris Lawler's been sacked by him as well and now Phil Thompson gets the push under Graeme. It was all a bit worrying for them.

I know Smithy had a go at him for changing everything to Melwood and so on, but it did have to change, introducing new diets, doing everything at Melwood. It was unhealthy going up and down on that bus but it was great camaraderie. The banter going down was fantastic, brilliant. Graeme took that away and we all went to Melwood in our cars but that was good; some of what Graeme did was progress but other aspects were not.

I also think the boot room fell down on the treatment side. I don't think it was that good. I remember having a long-standing injury. Fifteen years later I found out I had ligament damage which had not been identified. I was being told there was nothing wrong, are you sure it's not in your head. But with Graeme I think it was a good move to bring in a professional physio, although he also changed the pre-season training and the first day he had them doing too much and they all got Achilles injuries. The second season it wasn't so bad. But it was definitely in the Graeme period that things changed.

GRAEME SOUNESS

You Have To Have Good Players

I managed Liverpool and I found it difficult, very difficult. You're living with the past and all that glory, it's very difficult. There's no secret. In the end it's the players. Manchester United have the players now, Liverpool don't. When I was a player Bob Paisley was a wise old owl, and we mustn't forget Joe Fagan, we had the best players. People will want to impress you with science but the bottom line is that it's all down to players. You have to have good players, there's no secret, it's the players.

An extract from Radio 5, 17 May 1999

IAN HARGREAVES
Too Much, Too Quickly

You could probably date Liverpool's decline from Hillsborough. It knocked the stuffing out of the club and made a difficult job even harder. They almost won the Double that season and the season after but they were falling away all the time. Hillsborough took a hell of a lot out of Dalglish and his wife. They visited every family. Talk about counselling, I should think they needed it. They will never be forgotten in Liverpool. They did a fantastic job.

Then there was all the uncertainty. Souness arrived and he was in a hurry. You could argue that things were being broken up. He made changes, moved the boot room, changed training, it was bound to have an impact. People like Tommy Smith were writing in the paper about how things were changing and so on. There must have been niggles in the back of the mind about whether it would work or not.

Liverpool's decline also started with a failure to find high-class central defenders. The loss of Hansen and Lawrenson was crucial. There was Gillespie who wasn't bad but then they all went, and it was all at the same time. They looked at Gary Pallister but Tom Saunders came back and said he was too slow so they switched their interest to Glenn Hysen. I remember this particularly. In his first season he was splendid. He was class alongside Hansen but then he started making mistakes, just like Hansen used to do in his early days. He used to always make one major mistake each game until he learnt. Hansen was at his best when he was playing with Lawrenson but he couldn't carry a defence. Hysen was unreliable and from that point on they have never looked reliable.

When Souness came, he signed Mark Wright and for a short time he seemed to be the solution but then Wright started making mistakes, then he started getting injuries. Roy Evans tried to sort it. He signed three centre-backs and I must say that for the first

year Ruddock seemed the answer. He was not a cultured player
but he was solid, a bit like Ron Yeats, and he was a good passer
out of defence. They also got Babb who never quite lived up to
it. Then they got Scales and he was well regarded and people
assumed he would be a future captain of Liverpool. Then he
went and suddenly they didn't have any central defenders and
that's the simple answer as to why they have regressed. You
don't win anything without good defenders. Shankly's first team
had Yeats, bang in the middle. England's successful World Cup
team had Charlton who didn't take any prisoners. You tell me
any successful team that has not had a good central figure in the
middle.

I rather liked Souness. He was always willing to discuss things
with the media. He would talk about the game and what they
were doing. Shankly and Paisley never talked, certainly not
before a game. I remember Bob Paisley after they played three
in the middle, brand new then. Lawrenson, Hansen and Thompson had been fielded in a Charity Shield game which they won
quite easily. He was going into this at the press conference after
the game. Someone asked him if this was his style of *catenaccio*.
'What the hell are you talking about,' he asked, 'we don't talk
about this sort of thing 2–3–5, 4–4–2, whatever. I just picked
him and told him to get on with it, he's a footballer, he knows
what to do.'

I think Souness tried to do too much, too quickly. They tried
too hard early on in the season. He would never admit that. But
if you look at the number of players who broke down with
injuries, they had six or seven out. After the summer break the
grounds were very hard and suddenly they were training at a
much sharper rate. If you look at an Olympic athlete they are
training for an Olympic final and the timing is crucial; they are
trying to get it just right, to peak on the day, or the occasion.
The same is true with footballers. The old school Shankly and
Paisley had them training so that they didn't overdo it too much
early on in the season. You don't want players clapped out by
February.

The danger is that you introduce things too quickly. Yes, you
need diet control, strengthening exercises and all sorts of things

which are all done now and which work. You see players who are brilliantly fit. These are good things but you can't abandon the old ways too quickly. You've got to make people understand the changes, why you need them. It's no good throwing something new in and saying, it's got to work. You've got to get them to look at it, how it's worked with others. 'Let's try it. Is it helpful? Yes, good. No, then let's adapt.' That way you learn more quickly. The game is so fast now that I don't think Bill Shankly would recognise it.

PETER ROBINSON
Pulling The Boot Room Down

The official reasoning to take down the old boot room was that we felt it would be better and this was the general feeling. Graeme got the blame for it but others were involved. It was better for the players. We'd moved on. Initially a lot of players didn't have cars and we felt that it would be better for the players to report directly to Melwood each day and to train and be fed there rather than to ride up and down in an old coach as they used to. Football was moving on. We also needed to have an after-match press room and that was the ideal area for it.

But I don't think anyone within the club was opposed to that change. It suited certain journalists to label Graeme with it but it wasn't Graeme's idea. It was very much a general decision. Everybody thought it would be better if we built the extension at Melwood so that there was a lot more accommodation down there.

I think what had happened here was changing by then. I think the socialising in an afternoon had moved on. I think Kenny would have people in his office for the discussions that had taken place in the boot room. We'd moved more to these things happening in other areas.

PHIL NEAL
A Visiting Coach

I visited the boot room as an opposition coach when I was assistant to Bobby Gould at Coventry and then on my own a year later when he had left. It was nothing new to me when I went in. I just wanted to see old friends. They knew they couldn't get information out of me. I knew what the score was all about.

I tried to emulate Ronnie Moran's methods of training. Reuben Bennett was the first member of staff to keep our feet on the floor on the Monday morning. If we'd won at Arsenal on the Saturday he'd be there on the Monday to bring us right down to earth. He'd ridicule you but not in a nasty way. They would give everybody a hard time. In particular they had a go at the superstars. There was always a great camaraderie with Reuben. Meanwhile Ronnie and Roy would be in the dressing room. Reuben's role was to bring us back to earth. It's not until you walk away that you realise. He'd tear into the fellow Scots like Kenny, inspire him to train, bring him down to earth. We used to play the rest of the world versus the Scots. Reuben started it all off. Geoff Twentyman would be involved as well.

Geoff Twentyman didn't really train with us. In the early days he might jog around Melwood. Reuben might do the same and join him first thing. But once we got going into the warm-ups, it would be just Reuben. Joe and Ronnie would stand on the sidelines watching while Bob was in the clubhouse by the radiator, like a field marshal. We used to make this comment about how his legs must be burning. I remember Rushie and me hiding behind the boards at Melwood because it was so cold. It was a bitterly cold wind, and we weren't allowed bottoms, just these big heavy jumpers. When those pullovers got wet they used to hang down to your knees. Everyone remembers them. You'd leave Melwood dripping wet and get on the bus and you had to wait 20 minutes for a shower, terrible.

The boot room never really changed. They must have discussed players getting older. That must have happened all the time. They'd have worked out who the replacement would be. They were never afraid to break the teams up. They would still be there late in the afternoon talking, 4pm, 4.30pm, still debating this or that.

PHIL THOMPSON

Shivers Down The Spine

I think the boot room changed dramatically when they changed the structure downstairs when everything also moved down to Melwood. When they were knocking it down you could feel it. Shivers went down my spine. They should have done it like when London Bridge went to America. They should have taken it down brick by brick, numbered them and then transferred it to the other side. It wouldn't have been the same but it could have been pretty similar. It was a very sad day but life goes on.

RONNIE MORAN

Graeme's Changes

When Graeme came he made big changes. Melwood was transformed into a bigger place because we wanted to change down there and work down there. The boot room was finished. All that was knocked down. We weren't asked about it. It was all done through Graeme and the club. It didn't really upset us. We were always brought up never to take things for granted. Even when you were playing in the team, we always used to say you could come in tomorrow and get the sack even if we had won.

We still kept the same things going on at Melwood. People would come here and say, 'They don't do much training.' We had no elaborate training schedule. Mostly it was small-sided games but they didn't realise what was going on in those games. We'd be getting little points over in the games.

Graeme had his own ideas. He made these changes but we didn't say, 'Hey, you can't make these changes,' because he was manager. He changed the boot room, got the new place we have now. It's all carpeted but it's got no boots in. He also brought people in from the outside like Phil Boersma. Coming in on a Sunday stopped then because Phil used to do the treatment. Before that it had been Bob, Joe and myself. When Kenny took over he got a part-time physio in. That was good. He'd come in at lunchtime because he had his own practice.

There were more changes under Graeme than ever before. We came to Melwood, don't get me wrong, that was good, the players wanted it. We get changed there now, train, bathe, and have lunch there. It wasn't a case of backwards and forwards to Anfield. Sometimes in every walk of life if you try to make changes too quickly it can upset people. It didn't upset us on the staff. It was a case of, this shouldn't be done. He didn't transform the playing or training side of it. I never asked why he wanted to change the boot room. The boot room still went on, Roy, myself, Phil Thompson. We were there. Graeme didn't keep away from us. Boersma came in because he had qualifications. When he came as manager he told us he wanted to keep us on. We all got on well with Graeme. I'd had him as a player, so I knew him well.

JAN MOLBY

All Change

When Souness took over there were five games to the end of that season in 1991. So basically the season takes its course, it's just a case of playing those five games. But when we came back for the pre-season, things like going straight down to Melwood were introduced. He didn't want people to go to Anfield any longer, but it was part of the club, wasn't it? You get there in the morning, have your cup of tea, then get on the coach and drive down. After training you have your cup of tea at Melwood, get back on the coach. I think that was good for team spirit. I

remember arriving and thinking 'What's this all about?' I think
it was good, we had some good times on the coach going to and
from training. Obviously Souness changed all of that. It does
make sense to drive straight to the training ground and get yourself out of the car and get ready but I just think that when he
introduced it in 1991/92 there were some players at that time
who hadn't been at the club as long as the likes of Ian Rush,
Ronnie Whelan and myself, and I missed it. I thought it was
great crack. You get back to Anfield for a laugh.

There were more things to do at Anfield. You could go upstairs
and talk to the executive, Peter Robinson, or go and see the girls
in the ticket office or have a chat with Karen in reception or
whatever. You tended to float around a little bit longer, whereas
you didn't have those facilities down at Melwood. It was a case
of finishing training, having a bite to eat and off we go. We lost
a little bit of that togetherness. The staff at Anfield, the cleaners,
the girls in the ticket office, they missed it. All of a sudden they
never saw us, we only came on match days. I think basically
everybody missed that a little bit. I think it was in the back of
your mind, who you were actually playing for and who you put
a smile on the face of when you win games because you knew
what it meant to them, from May who's been the cleaning lady
there for 40 years. You knew what it meant to her, she'd be in
the stands somewhere and you'd see her on the Monday. All of
a sudden you just didn't have these people. It was important for
them, they'd go down to the bingo hall on a Monday night and
they'd say 'How's the players?' They'd say 'I haven't seen them
for two years.' I think that was a shame.

On the other hand, facility-wise, the way that Melwood is
developed now, it did make sense. I just think it was a shame
but I know things move on.

The boot room change just happened overnight. It was 'this
is the way we're going to do things'. I think the first time I heard
about the boot room was in the local paper. Although we went
to Melwood, we weren't aware it was going to be the end of the
boot room. These are the kind of things, like Chris Lawler being
in charge of the reserves, you think he's going to be there for
ever. We thought the same about the boot room. Whatever

happens, we thought it had played a significant role in the success of Liverpool so surely that will be there for ever. But it was obviously something that I think Souness felt very strongly about. You had to do away with some of these things to try and move on. He probably felt that the club had lived in the past for too long and it was time to move on.

If he had introduced what he introduced in 1991 possibly three or four years later, I think he would have been proved right. I think he might just have been a little bit ahead of his time. I think it's difficult to tell people that what you've been doing for many years is fine but we're not going to do it any more. I don't think he let people down gently, he just went in and did it. Maybe he felt 'Let's get it done, let's get it over with. Within a week everybody will have forgotten about it.' But when you didn't get the results to go with the changes, it just made the job twice as hard. Then everybody is going to go back and say, 'There was nothing wrong with this club when the boot room was here. There was nothing wrong with the players when they were travelling to and from training on the coach.' All that was thrown back in Souness's face.

I think it became more aggressive because of the type of character Graeme Souness is. He would fly off the handle quicker than any of the other managers I've worked with at Anfield. I think it becomes more tense because of the results. The results weren't particularly impressive during the whole of his stay there. That comfort that you've always had, Kenny was there for seven years, Joe Fagan only left because he decided to go, the same with Bob Paisley, the same with Bill Shankly. That comfort was removed with Graeme Souness with him having been there for 18 months, the papers were starting to write 'The results aren't that good. Could Liverpool sack the first manager for so many years?'

It would happen gradually that players would come in and spend six months in the reserves and whenever the time was right, someone would move on and someone would move in. All of a sudden, you had this influx of five or six players, different types of players to what we'd had. I always thought it was a great honour to play for Liverpool and when you play with the players and see them in training, you realise why it was an honour because everybody could play. Everybody was a fantastic footballer. That's why it was an honour. All of a sudden you get players who did have some qualities but they weren't of the calibre that you'd been used to. They were not the players that I played with for the first seven years at Anfield. You think this was an honour but now we're getting average footballers. This football club is not about average players. That's what happened. They did have some quality, some of those players, but it wasn't what we were looking for.

A lot of players were shown the door too quickly. When it was his time to go Hansen retired, Peter Beardsley went, Steve Staunton went to Aston Villa, Steve McMahon to Manchester City. It happened too quickly. We could see that there were potential players to take over. Kenny had bought Redknapp and Hutchison had come down from Hartlepool and these players eventually would be good enough but they weren't at the time. They weren't good enough at the time to be not only in the first team but to do their fair bit of a real man's job. They couldn't do it.

The biggest change, possibly the only change in training was the pre-season work. We went from having a reputation of never doing anything longer than six- or seven-minute runs. I remember doing pre-season training with Ajax, coming off the training ground absolutely shattered for a week, ten days. Although we trained hard at Liverpool, you never had the same feeling. We were fit if not fitter and I think it was proven over the years at Liverpool that we got stronger and fitter as the game went on. Whatever it was in the training, they'd obviously got it spot-on. It was never any longer runs than six or seven minutes. Then all of a sudden, Souness. On the second day, we started on a Thursday, and on the Friday we were up to doing 45-minute runs already. I'm not saying there's anything wrong with doing 45-minute runs but 60, maybe 70 per cent of those players had for the last five to ten years never ever done anything like this. It was such a shock to the system. It wasn't a case of the players not being able to do it. It was a shock. We're all aware of the injuries that everybody had. Everybody got these Achilles problems and there were all sorts of injuries. Whether he likes it or not, I think that's mainly down to the change in training.

Phil Boersma was brought in as a part-time physio. His main job was getting players back to fitness after injuries. Phil was good at his job. He'd certainly get you fit. He'd work you very, very hard. Phil was a great character, everybody loved him but I don't think I can say he played a significant role, negatively or positively.

STEVE HALE

His Own Man

The club has taken lots of knocks like Heysel and Hillsborough on the way and that has certainly not helped but those apart, individuals have come in and made changes, like Graeme Souness. Although I like him I think he did it too quickly. I still think had he been given another season, it might have bore the fruits. Remember it was Souness who blooded the youngsters, the Fowlers, the Harknesses, the McManamans. There were five or six young lads. He didn't go out and buy expensive players. Sure, he bought some expensive players who didn't work like Wright, but it wasn't Souness's problem that it didn't work, it was injury.

You have to give Graeme his due. Some things did need changing. He was a man's man, very much his own man. He came and he looked at the reserves, the A side, and saw the potential, brought them through. What he thought then has come true, Fowler and McManaman have become major players. He wasn't a bullshitter, he shot from the hip and perhaps that was his problem. Because I do personally like him, I think the board might have given him more time. There was more media and supporter pressure than they had imagined. After the Bristol City game the pressure was so intense. You're blooding young players and you may or may not get lucky. You get lucky and you're God, get unlucky and that's it. He got unlucky and had some bad results and became the devil. Admittedly he made some very bad buys. I think he was still on a learning curve. Dean Saunders should have worked and Paul Stewart as well. When these players were signed we all thought they were terrific buys but they never worked. Ruddock was another. For some reason it didn't happen. It mirrors life; you can be very lucky or just plain unlucky. When Souness was taken on as manager I can remember a huge number of fans in the car park awaiting him, everyone expected that he would be a superb manager. I feel that he should have been given longer. He did make errors but in time it might have worked for him. The board simply caved in to the pressure. Who knows what went on?

TOM SAUNDERS

People Resent Change

When Shanks went, it passed on. That same sort of thing repeated itself until once Joe finished, Kenny came. Then it changed a bit because Kenny came straight from playing into management and that broke the run of things a little bit. Kenny wanted to know much more about taking videos and watching the opposition and he got into that. So, that era the Shanks, Bob, Joe, Ronnie Moran era, that had run its course, and from that point on it changed a bit.

It changed after Joe. Graeme had Ronnie Moran as his assistant, and Roy Evans. Graeme had been away from Liverpool for some time, that's how it changed. The continuity was not quite the same. Graeme had been in Sampdoria and had picked up a lot of the European way of training. He came here and decided that the pre-season training would take place in a training camp in Italy. And we all went there for a fortnight and they ate pasta for their meals. There was a whole new look at their diets. That was the beginning of a whole new dawning to us that there were other ways of being successful. Now Graeme had a job to sell that as you can imagine. People resent change, they do not take to it easily. They have to see that that change is going to benefit them and it is not easy to convince people when the change is a drastic one. It has its teething problems. Sadly in the football game you do not have a lot of time. If the results are not too clever then players, being what they are, will blame the pasta or whatever, or the training, or too much running.

I think that maybe he tried to change things a little too quickly, that might be a reasonable criticism. He was an outstanding competitor as a player and couldn't possibly understand why it was that when a player put a red shirt on he did not have the same commitment as Graeme Souness had when he played. That to him was a hell of a problem. Also, we bought players at that time who did not fit in awfully well.

Once you've got a number of very good players and you have success, players want to join you. Real professionals, and there are many, want success badly and so they'll join. We lost our way somewhere in there. Whether it was as far back as Joe or what, I do not know. I suspect it was about getting good players here and we went through a period when we were possibly too self-satisfied. We thought we had the answers and the players, and suddenly the players got older but we didn't go out and attract the right fresh players in. That would seem to me to be the answer and it's over a longer period than people think.

TOMMY SMITH

Times Have Changed But People Haven't

I must admit I was shocked when it was announced that they were knocking the boot room down as they redeveloped the Main Stand. A new one was built across the corridor. It was plusher with air conditioning, but it wasn't and isn't the same.

The original boot room had no airs and graces and it seemed to sum up a club where everyone was down to earth. Anyone who came in and felt he was bigger than the club was soon knocked down to size. I recall that the staff wouldn't even let you clean the old room to any degree. They'd say, 'Don't bother sending the kids in to clean up.' I once took it upon myself to tell the young apprentices to take the old carpet out and beat it against the wall. They went mad. When I suggested that we might paint it, there was murder. This was the nearest we got to controversy in there.

On matchdays opposing managers would be invited in. Their teams had inevitably been beaten out of sight, but they were always praised and encouraged, given a beer or a scotch and sent home trying to work out the mystique of the boot room. At times you might get 20 people in there on a Saturday but no one complained about being cramped or sweaty. You were in the boot room and that was an honour in itself.

I think it is important for a club like Liverpool to hang on to the traditions like the boot room. They may not seem so important but they all contribute to the make-up of a club. Bill Shankly had lots of little habits and thoughts which were passed on from one manager to the next. Times may have changed but people haven't.

WILLIE MILLER
The Sacking Of Thompson

I think the boot room started to go wrong when Graeme Souness came in. His biggest mistake was appearing in the *Sun*, but another major mistake which he was never forgiven for, was the sacking of Phil Thompson. Souness will probably never admit that, but it was a major mistake to sack Thompson because that was when people could see the boot room going. He also physically moved the boot room, not that it was his fault in particular, although he got the blame. He also got the blame for moving the training to Melwood but the players wanted that. They wanted to go to Melwood and get changed rather than come to Anfield, get changed, get the bus, get the bus back, get changed again. Again that was not Souness's fault. They were redeveloping Melwood just to keep up with the times.

He brought in Phil Boersma and I have to worry about Boersma's qualifications. We had so many injuries. He was trying to be the doberman to Souness' rottweiler. I think that was a big mistake. That's where it started to go wrong.

I know that the boot room in the past would talk about the players they were going to bring to the club. Souness didn't. He just went out and bought, that's when the continuity started to go. It was down to one man's opinions, there was no consultation beforehand. Ronnie and Roy were still there, they knew a lot about football.

JIM GARDINER
In Defence of Souness

It wasn't a surprise Graeme Souness getting the job. It was a surprise that Ronnie Moran was never given the chance at it. I think Ronnie Moran might have been the right appointment at that time. I certainly think he had done enough in his career to be given a shot at the Liverpool manager's job at some stage. I am very disappointed that he never got that chance. Graeme Souness getting the job didn't surprise me because he was quite rightly regarded, in my opinion, as the best captain we ever had. When you had Graeme Souness on your side you were frightened of nothing and he was at the helm as Liverpool captain when we had our best teams in the late 70s and early 80s. So it didn't surprise me that he got the job. The circumstances in which he got it may have surprised me but I always saw him as a potential Liverpool manager.

Things did begin to change under Graeme Souness but again I wouldn't hold that against him. I think Graeme Souness was the right man for the job but at the wrong time. He came in and started to do things that nowadays the likes of Wenger and Houllier are being praised for: looking at players' diets; looking at the way they train; trying to change things to bring in more physical effort rather than just playing five-a-side; looking at the way they live. Souness wanted to bring Italian methods to Liverpool. Nowadays you've got Houllier and Wenger getting praised for that but when Graeme Souness tried to do it at Liverpool, there was: 'Oh you can't do that, you're messing with tradition.' I suspect, looking back, he was probably a bit frustrated by that. He wanted to do things but was being held back, possibly by people within the club who were saying 'Oh no, that's not the way we did it under Shanks.' I think he'd probably look back on it now and say 'To hell with that, I'm changing it anyway. I'm the gaffer now,' but maybe he went along with the flow at that time.

He got criticism for switching training to Melwood. But then you speak to the players and they were delighted. I know one player who said they had to go back to Anfield for lunch under the old system and so couldn't do extra training whereas now he was able to stay on in the afternoon and do extra training, practising free-kicks, doing what he wanted. The only argument there seems to be against it was 'that was the way we did it in the sixties'. I can understand why Graeme Souness was probably very frustrated in his efforts to drag Liverpool screaming into modern football.

I am not convinced that Souness did fail. Liverpool were still up there, they won the FA Cup. Graeme Souness's biggest mistake was what he did over the *Sun* newspaper and the way that came about. As he's now said, he should have resigned as soon as that happened. I know the timing of the photographs being published was outside his remit but he should never have been anywhere near that newspaper, it's as simple as that. There's nothing else to be said on that. As far as I am concerned, that's the only thing Graeme Souness did wrong at Liverpool. I am convinced that if he had stayed as manager Liverpool would have certainly continued to be very successful and be up there challenging.

CHAPTER SIX

Evans and Houllier

It was undeniably a case of back to basics as Roy Evans stepped up from his role as Graeme Souness's assistant to become the new manager of Liverpool Football Club. It came as no surprise. Anyone else would have been. Chairman David Moores, introducing him as the club's new manager, called him 'the last of the Shankly lads'. It was a fitting description. After the turbulent years of Souness everyone breathed a sigh of relief that the level-headed, amiable, experienced boot room boy Roy Evans was now in charge of Britain's best-loved club.

Souness was gone, scurrying away from Anfield in the wake of an ignominious defeat by Bristol City in January 1994. He left behind a side the shadow of the one for which he had so gloriously played. The club was also in turmoil, overburdened with average players, a spiralling wage and transfer bill and with many of its old values slipping. Where had it all gone wrong? If anyone could return the club to its former glory or at least to its traditional values, it was Roy Evans, who had been part of the boot room set-up since the glory days of Bob Paisley.

Bootle-born Evans had started supporting Liverpool as a seven year old when his brother took him to his first game in the mid-1950s. It may have been mediocre second division stuff but the young Evans was hooked. He wasn't a bad player himself either, treading the usual path, Liverpool Schoolboys and then England Schoolboys, where he came under the eye of Tom Saunders. It wasn't long before Saunders had him at Anfield and in 1964 he signed on as a young apprentice.

But his footballing career never really took off. He was a useful left-back but lacked the necessary pace for top league football.

Nevertheless, he progressed up the ladder, playing A team and reserve team football but managed only eleven appearances for the first team in ten years. He was a quiet lad and more than one contemporary was surprised that he ever made it to become manager. By 1974 he was 25 years of age, still on the fringes of the first team and at a crossroads in his career. The question seemed to be whether to quit Liverpool and drop down a division or two or stick around a bit longer and play yet more Central League football. Recurrent injuries did not help either. In the end the decision was made for him. Paisley was not going to let him go so easily and, to his surprise, offered him a coaching job. But although Evans was initially reluctant to pack in playing, others in the boot room encouraged him to give coaching a go. His playing career might have been at an end but he still had something to offer and in the wake of Shankly's resignation in the summer of 1974, Roy Evans moved into the boot room. Before long he was running the reserves, taking them to seven title wins. It was ideal training for later years.

Gradually, as each manager retired, Evans found himself promoted to take on a new role. Ronnie Moran had always been next in line for promotion to the big job but on two occasions had been overlooked in favour of Dalglish and then Graeme Souness. By all accounts Moran could probably have had the job himself if he had shown the inclination. But the feeling was that he never really wanted the top job, happy to serve rather than lead. By 1994 Moran himself was now just a few years off retirement age and again did not seem interested in taking over the reins. He'd briefly stepped in when Dalglish quit and then when Souness left and that seemed to have been enough to persuade him that it was not for him. The job was Evans's for the asking. He needed little persuasion. It was a popular appointment. The feeling was that here was a man steeped in the traditions of the boot room, who had been involved in every triumph over the previous 25 years, who had worked closely with Shankly, Paisley and Fagan, and who had helped mastermind the club's successes. If anyone could take Liverpool back to the top it had to be Roy Evans. Sadly Evans's years were to be wracked with anguish and frustration.

It began well enough. He was tough-talking, warning Julian Dicks and Mark Wright in pre-season that they needed to pull their socks up if they were to survive the distance but generally he was a calming breath of fresh air. The embattled years of Souness had taken their toll. Now at last there was a manager who could talk to the players and enjoy a beer and a joke with them.

In his first full season in charge, 1994/95, the club finished fourth in the league and won the League Cup, beating Bolton Wanderers in the final. It seemed it could only be a matter of time before the glory days were back. Just one or two more signings. The signings certainly came but they were never up to scratch. They might have been big names, and expensive, but once they arrived their failings were all obvious. The club seemed to have lost its edge in picking up bargain basement signings and although they could still attract the biggest and most expensive names such as Paul Ince, Jason McAteer and Stan Collymore, the players failed to deliver. Each season became a little more frustrating than the last. The new signings arrived but the expected trophies didn't. The side was wretchedly inconsistent. They could begin the season on a high, shooting straight to the top, but by Christmas would have lost half-a-dozen games. One week they could beat Manchester United or Arsenal, the next they would lose at home to Derby, Leicester or Coventry.

It would be churlish, and anyhow wrong, to ever suggest that Evans was a failure. There were successes. They won the League Cup and also reached the FA Cup Final in 1996, only to lose depressingly to Manchester United. But perhaps more impressively they finished no lower than fourth in each of Evans's seasons in charge. Anywhere else and that would have been a commendable record but for Liverpool Football Club that was not enough. It was always a case of so near but so far, just one or two more players.

Evans spent heavily in the transfer market in a near-desperate bid to bring back the glory days. In all he spent a staggering £40 million, but few of his signings came off. The most consistent players seemed to be the home-grown lads Steve McManaman, Robbie Fowler, Jamie Carragher and Michael Owen. Perhaps

Evans's biggest fault was never to find a solution to the problem which haunted the club for much of his time in charge – the creaky defence. For years they seemed to be scouring the globe for a central defender or two but none ever appeared. Up front they could score goals with the rampaging Fowler and sensational new find Owen but in defence they continued to leak goals like no other Liverpool defence since the fifties.

But there were other worrying signs. There seemed to be a lack of discipline among the players as too many stories filtered out of Anfield. And at times players on the field seemed only half-interested in playing for the club. Against Manchester United in the FA Cup Final their woeful performance emptied the Liverpool end of Wembley long before the players had collected their losers' medals, leaving the side to troop off overshadowed by empty terraces. It was unprecedented for Liverpool fans not to show some appreciation for their side.

What's more, the boot room was gone. It had shifted across the corridor and was used only on matchdays when it was little more than an entertaining suite. The discussions that once took place behind the closed doors of the boot room were no more. Admittedly meetings did take place at Melwood but they were more formal, more structured. There was none of the spontaneity, none of the 'let's have a drink and a natter'. The game had moved on.

As some suggest in this chapter, many of the problems may well have been generic, part of the modern game where players rake in vast salaries, have time-consuming sponsorship deals and seem to owe little allegiance to their employers. Whether it was right or wrong, the picture coming out of Anfield was one of player-power, lack of commitment, and not enough tough talking. It was not difficult to appreciate Evans's frustration. There were undoubtedly many quality players in the side, able to turn on championship performances one week against other title contenders but then the following week to give the most inept performance against relegation strugglers. The inconsistency over the years was staggering.

There was occasional talk of Evans going but nobody ever really believed it. Crucially, chairman David Moores continued to give his lifelong friend Roy Evans his full support. A couple more players and they might just turn the corner, was his view. It was a fair assessment yet when new players did arrive, they never looked the part, often played out of position and were never the central defenders the side was crying out for.

By the summer of 1998 the frustration was reaching epidemic proportions. Evans had survived one bout of sacking speculation but the unease among fans remained. Ronnie Moran had also retired after almost 50 years at the club and there was a vacancy for a new coach. The name of Gerard Houllier was suggested. Here was a foreign coach who might bring some fresh continental ideas to Anfield and who had a friendship with the club stemming back many years. But Houllier did not want simply to be a coach, he wanted more of an input, so the title joint manager was dreamt up. It might have been better if the club had fired Evans there and then. Houllier had enjoyed highly successful stints in charge of Paris St Germain and Lens, followed by a less successful term as coach of the French national squad. At the time of his appointment he was technical director of the French Football Federation, and arrived at Anfield on the back of France's 1998 World Cup triumph. What's more, he had been a Liverpool fan since the Shankly days of the sixties when he had been a student in Liverpool and supported the club from the Kop.

But in truth the arrangement of two managers was never going to work, even though everyone, including the two men themselves, pledged to work in harmony towards a common aim. That may have been their ideal but the division of responsibility could only lead to splits. The players didn't really understand who was in charge. If they felt they could get the better side of Evans they would communicate primarily with him. The arrangement lasted a mere five months before Evans decided he had had enough and in November 1998 he told David Moores he was leaving. No amount of persuasion could change his mind.

And so, as Evans made a dignified exit from Anfield, it brought to an end a long and distinguished chapter in the history of the club. In effect, the boot room was no more. True, Phil Thompson was brought back to inject some fighting spirit among the troops but with Ronnie Moran gone as well, the continuity which stretched back to when Shankly had arrived in December 1959 had now virtually gone. Shankly and Paisley had passed away, Reuben Bennett was also long dead, Joe Fagan was in retirement, Dalglish and Souness were managing elsewhere, Moran had retired, so too had Tom Saunders and John Bennison, although the latter three could still regularly be spotted around Melwood. And now Roy Evans had left. All that remained were Sammy Lee, still coaching the first team, Steve Heighway, still in charge of the youngsters, and chief scout Ron Yeats.

For the first time since Bill Shankly had swept into Anfield on that cold December morning almost 40 years ago, the club had appointed an outsider to the top job, and a Frenchman to boot. But perhaps it was time for change as the world of football had moved on from the time when a gang of like-minded, down-to-earth men could plot to take on the world from a cubbyhole.

STEVE MORGAN

The Wrong Man

Personally I thought it was a big mistake to appoint Roy and I'm not being clever with hindsight. Roy Evans is one of the world's nicest people and a great servant to the club and I think it was a tragedy the way he left the club and the way he was treated. But running businesses is like running a football club and being Mr Nice Guy is seldom the right attribute to head and lead a successful organisation, whether it's a football club, a hotel or a house building company. And to my mind Roy Evans was an absolutely perfect number two but not a number one. If you look at Roy's playing career, it was spent in Liverpool reserves, although he had a handful of first team games. To my mind a winner would never settle for that. Somebody who's ruthless and is going to win, if he couldn't get into the Liverpool first team he would have gone elsewhere. If you're going to lead, you have to be a winner. I understand the reasons behind appointing Roy, getting back to basics, getting back to the old-fashioned values which had gone by the wayside in the Souness era. Had Roy been used like an assistant manager or head coach, with somebody else doing the driving, then I think it could have been an inspired decision but I think it was a mistake to make Roy manager.

Having two bosses like Evans and Houllier is an absolute disaster. You cannot ever have two bosses, whatever business you're in. It was just a dumb stupid decision to bring two people in and say joint manager. I'm very scathing of that decision. There can only be one boss. You can work as a team, you can have two people working side by side but there has to be one person with overall responsibility. You can have split responsibilities but there has to be one man in charge, otherwise you get people playing off one against the other. It's like a kid. If parents don't agree how to bring a kid up, the kid knows how to go to one parent and play one off against the other and he knows which one to ask for this and which one to ask for that. When you have that in any household you have rows and disruption and you get an unhappy kid. I think that's what happened with that short spell with Liverpool. There were all sorts of tales of player disruption. If only half the tales that come out are true then it was proof of the pudding that it was a bad, bad decision.

JIM GARDINER

From One Extreme To Another

I suspect when the board gave Roy Evans the job it was an attempt to return a bit of stability to the club. There was no doubt, I suspect, that even player power played a big part in Graeme Souness going. I also think that if Graeme Souness had his time over again as manager, one of the first things he would do would be to look at one or two of the senior players and decide who he could let go, no matter how popular they were with the fans. One of the first things Alex Ferguson did when he came to Manchester United was to break up the little cliques that were there. I suspect there was a need within the board to say 'Listen, we've got to steady the ship. Roy Evans is a knowledgeable man, he's been here throughout all the success we've had so he must have picked up something there. He's respected by the players, let's go for it and give him the chance.'

I don't know if it was possible to re-invent the boot room. It's always difficult to go back somewhere, isn't it? I think we went from almost one extreme to another. Graeme Souness was the hard man and supposedly always at war with the players, to Roy Evans who, some would say, was too easy-going. I think Roy Evans tried to get back to the principles of the boot room, keeping things simple and treating the players as adults, but it's noticeable that he kept a lot of the things that had been introduced by Souness: the training at Melwood, looking at the players' diets, looking at the way they operated. Roy Evans was probably trying to marry the two philosophies of the old boot room and the modern attitude.

I think the boot room philosophy has gone now, to a certain extent, because of the setup at Liverpool now. The people that have come in haven't been involved. I suppose Phil Thompson has, albeit as a player, but he knew what the boot room philosophy stood for so there may be an element of it still there. It was something that was unique, that was brought in by Bill Shankly and it stood Liverpool in good stead. But it's a totally different game now. The game itself has changed and it needs a different managerial approach.

The philosophy of the boot room is an anachronism in today's game. It's not so much that there isn't room for that philosophy in today's game, it's just that the game has changed so much that it is now very much a business where you're dealing with multi-million pound players. Then you had the coaches and players very much on a similar wavelength and now you have a coach at a football team and he's dealing with seven or eight millionaires. It's a totally different ball game in motivating players and keeping control over players. How do you discipline a player? If you say we're going to fine you x thousand pounds, it's nothing to them. So we're going to drop you out of the team again, so what? They're still going to have their contracts, they're still going to pick up their money whether they're playing in the reserves or whatever. It's a totally different game now and the boot room philosophies in many ways can't be applied to the modern game.

There's no doubt that Alex Ferguson is successful. I suspect in many ways he is more of a Graeme Souness character. Alex Ferguson makes his decisions there and he has his lieutenants but he is in total charge and makes all the decisions. The boot room was an amalgamation of different people's thoughts, whereas Alex Ferguson, I suspect, has more of an autocratic style. You can't knock the man's success or Manchester United's success but I don't think it's down to the same sort of philosophy the boot room had here.

The boot room was just a phrase. It was important to the fans on the Kop because everybody saw it as being part of Bill Shankly's philosophy and how he wanted it to be played. Bill Shankly was and still is worshipped by Liverpool fans. It was seen as part of Bill Shankly and therefore something to be revered. You felt the Kop was in good hands because decisions were being taken and it was known that they were being taken in the boot room.

JAN MOLBY
Roy Takes Over

Roy took over in January '94. He had been there for that many years already, I think he was aware of what needed to be done in terms of the team. He let that season run its own course. That summer of '94 was going to be very important to try and bring in some new players. That was going to be when he was going to stamp his authority on things. He came back for pre-season training, he brought in Dougie Livermore as his assistant. Souness had brought in Sammy Lee and got rid of Phil Thompson. Chris Lawler going was a shock, but Phil Thompson going was an even bigger shock. I think we were all surprised because although Sammy had been away from Liverpool for a number of years and played in Spain, he was an old Liverpool boy. Everybody knew Sammy, he was a bubbly character. We all knew who Dougie Livermore was by name but it was 'Who's this guy?' Maybe Roy identified then that there might be a need for new, fresh ideas from the outside. Doug had worked with Terry Venables at Tottenham and maybe Roy thought 'This guy might just be right to bring us some new ideas that we can use.' Dougie Livermore is not the type who would go around ranting and raving, he's a very quiet man. We get the first full-time 24-hour physio with Mark Leather, full-time goalkeeping coach with Joe Corrigan and they were basically the changes that Roy made. They were the right changes, it's only right for a club of the stature of Liverpool to have these people.

I think Roy got it back to basics and comfortably had us as a top six team but it's not what Liverpool Football Club or the fans are looking for. They want more, they want to win things and Roy couldn't get them back up there. It's that final step, that final hurdle and he couldn't do it. When he went and spent big money, he was umming and ahhing a little bit. I think he got it wrong with a lot of the signings that he made. He was great working with the players that were there. He got the maximum out of the players that were there. But when he had to go and buy two players to maybe make us champions, that's when he failed.

I go back to that first summer of '94. Babb and Scales were his first two signings. He spent £8 million on two centre-backs, not particularly good business. The Collymore signing, Leon-hardsen, people like that, when you were looking for him to be spot-on. The failure to get two central defenders goes back to Souness taking over in '91 and making Mark Wright his first or second signing, shortly followed by Piechnik because he didn't fancy Ablett. There was Ablett, Gary Gillespie and Glen Hysen, he didn't fancy those, he wanted his own people in. Mark Wright proved to be okay but they were always playing catch up. Gil-lespie had gone before we knew he had been properly replaced. They'd all gone and it was a case of 'what we're stuck with is what we've got'. It wasn't a case of 'all right, Mark Wright needs another three months or Piechnik needs six months to settle down and we can play Gillespie while that is happening'. These people had gone and I think that was the biggest problem that they had. There was nothing to revert to. Those boys that won't let us down weren't there. The same thing happened when Nigel Clough was brought in. Peter Beardsley had gone. It wasn't a case of 'Nigel might need a bit of time, let's play Peter'. People went far too quickly for my liking.

I think next season for the first time people realise that what we need to do won't happen over a season. It will take two or three years.

MIKE BERRY
Back To Basics

Roy's first comment when appointed to the job apart from being very proud was that we are getting 'back to basics'. I think that had been one of John Major's phrases. We're going to get back to doing things the Shankly way, the boot room way. I don't know whether he did go back to those ways as I was not privileged to be part of that or be involved, to be honest. But during those years you can't argue he had fourth, third, fourth, fourth. Today we would be happy with that and we would be in Europe. Next season we are out of Europe for the first time since, I think, 1964. I can't believe we haven't qualified. It's the only time since I've been supporting them that we haven't qualified, apart from the ban, of course.

I do think that the boot room is an anachronism in today's game. I think the boot room mentality is a manager with a good team around him working together as a unit. There are boot rooms at many, many clubs. Look at Man United over the last five years, it's been Alex Ferguson, Brian Kidd and the rest of the back room staff. I think it has been very, very similar. Shankly started it all here. He was so strong in his personality. In my lifetime there have been only two people I have known as people whose mammoth personalities had an effect on my life, they were Bill Shankly and Muhammad Ali. It's amazing the effect Shankly has had on Liverpool Football Club. I went past Shankly's statue last week and it says on the bottom: 'He made the

People happy'. That sums it up. He did. People are not happy at the moment. There's something not quite right but we do have to give the new manager time.

The Anfield boot room as we used to know it is definitely gone but hopefully some day a manager and his assistant will get some success. I don't think a boot room is a place, it is a team of people. There could be five stood on a field and it would be the field room. As a Liverpool fan since 1959 I can't get my head around the last five years at all. The person I feel most sorry for is my son Stephen. He's a Liverpool fanatic and he thinks I'm a cynical old man talking about the glory days. All he's seen is the Cup in '92 and the Coca-Cola in '95. He's getting Man United rammed down his throat as we rammed Liverpool down other throats for 26 years. It was very enjoyable for those 26 years! We were lucky because we were the best in Europe.

JOEY JONES

Roy Evans – No Fancy Dan

The boot room could have been any room, the kit room, the medical room. I don't know what the secret was. All I can say is that at Liverpool they never complicated things. They'd discuss things in there but it was always the same training, year in year out. There wasn't really a secret. We'd have a team talk at Melwood on a Friday, the boss, Joe and Ronnie. He'd go through it briefly, for 20 minutes or so. But again they never complicated things, no boards or diagrams. They just kept it simple. Once they had finished talking about the opposition a bit, it was then about us and we were told who we had to pick up or what.

Roy was the younger one. He was great for Liverpool. He gave me a lot. I enjoyed playing for Roy. You get some players who dropped down into the reserves and thought it was beneath them and didn't want to perform. But Roy had the knack and knew how to handle them and get the best out of them. Getting the best out of them is good because that has an effect on the youngsters. He might have had a reputation as manager of being soft but in my experience he was not soft. I've been on the receiving end of his tongue and I've seen more senior players than me get a good bollocking off him. But he was only trying to get the best out of them. I think he learned a lot from Ronnie Moran.

I think the boot room is also about characters and I think it would be difficult to find that again, even at Liverpool. I don't know if the characters are there any more. I don't know what Gerard Houllier is like but Phil Thompson and Sammy Lee are like that. But it would be very difficult to have a boot room like they had at Liverpool. I've said it before but it was about simplicity. They have executive lounges nowadays at Liverpool. But in my time it was simple, the old beer crate, a few skips and the chat about the game. No fancy Dan stuff.

ALAN BROWN

Not The Same Anymore

I think Roy was stupid in leaving. I think he has too much to offer Liverpool Football Club. I tried to persuade him to stay but he had it in his mind that he wanted to go, he'd had enough. It wasn't working between the two of them.

The club used to be more jolly. Now they just get in their cars and go home, there's no banter like there used to be. They used to sit in the little restaurant at the end which is now the lounge and they'd have a sandwich. Kenny would always eat beans and pies, Souey would always have pasta. Then they moved to Melwood and everything changed, maybe for the good, I don't know, maybe it's better for the training system but maybe not for morale. They used to go on the bus and come back on the bus; you had them all there then and they all used to fool around. Now they've all got cars and they're away. In the old days everybody stuck together in a little clique. By the time Roy came, it had all changed, they had moved to Melwood. It had all been planned.

Even as a manager Roy would come into the boot room after

the game, right to the very last. He'd go and see his wife who would be in his office, say hello, but then he'd come down to us. He'd stay with us for an hour or so. Joe Fagan used to stay when he was manager. The chairman comes in now every game. Joe was a lovely man, destroyed by Heysel. I think we were all destroyed by Heysel. That and Hillsborough knocked the stuffing out of this club. I was with Kenny's lad at Hillsborough. Kenny was searching for us, he was so worried. Awful. It all affected us so much. Heysel was dreadful. The ground was appalling, we saw all those bodies. The club has not been the same since.

Gerard comes in and says hello after the game. Ronnie Moran still comes in, Stevie Heighway, Phil Thompson brings his dad in and a few friends. We have a few drinks, the chairman likes his gin and tonic. We've still only got a little fridge. We had no fridge or anything like that in the old boot room. Candy gave us a fridge when they were sponsors; they gave us a fridge and a crushed ice thing, it was lovely, but before then it was bottles and cans.

The bald eagle Jim Smith still comes in and he's still the comedian he always was. Big Ron Atkinson used to love coming in. He had a brandy. Ferguson still comes in. Never ever fails, that man, always comes in. Cloughie used to come in and then once Joe Fagan said something, so he didn't come in after that. But the managers always come in. Keegan never misses and says hello, Alan Hansen still comes down. All the old players, if they are around, come. The young players are never allowed in, but if Cally, Willie Stevenson, Roger Hunt, Mark Lawrenson or Clemmy ever come to a game, they pop in. All the managers, Joe Royle, Bryan Robson, Walter Smith come in and have a chat about the game. No arguments, they just relax. That's what it was about, you could relax and have a chat.

Shanks had a charisma, a power over players. But Bob to me was a tactician, knew exactly what he wanted, he was a brainy man on the football side. Shanks had the power and started it but Bob was always guiding him. And when Bob took over it proved how good he was. He bought all good players and usually cheaply, moulding them into great players. You could count his bad buys on one hand. Okay, Shanks started it, he was the man of the people, but Bob has never had the full recognition although they are now going to have the Paisley Gates, so at least he's getting something. Bob was the quiet one, a bit like Roy. Broke my heart when Roy wasn't successful. He nearly was. He wasn't far off, one or two more players, a good central defender.

I think if Souey hadn't have chopped and changed so much and got rid of the older players we would have won the league that year and we would probably still be up there. It was his downfall. He brought the younger players on much quicker, Fowler, McManaman, Redknapp and so on, a year earlier than might have happened. He deserves credit for that but if he had kept the old players we would have won the league. He admits that now. He got rid of too many quality players too quick and they were still playing at the top level four, five years on. He wanted to change things too quickly.

The boot room was about coming in, relaxing and having a drink after the game. That's what it was about, really relaxing, after being wound up for a week, just coming back to earth. It was a place to come in and chat, that's what it was about, chatting to all the managers, chewing things over. It was a generation that has now gone. It's not the same anymore. It can't be. Things have changed so much.

BARRIE HOLMES

A Business

There was a faith, a belief that you were part of the club, helping the club as a fan. I think that part of it is not the same now. I think the club is now a business whereas in those days that was not the prime mover. In those days as well the fans all came from Merseyside. I think it was interesting listening to the half-time presentation this week and last week and there have been no winners from Liverpool. There's no problem with that, it's good for the club to have fans all over the world, but in some ways it is a little sad because that homeliness that the boot room personified has now gone.

BARRIE HOLMES
Like New Labour

I think there is a good analogy with the Labour Party. A lot of
it is about presentation and business. It has changed its constitu-
ency. The Labour party is no longer about the working class and
heavy industry. Similarly football has changed, it's more about
social mobility, the middle class. When I first started going, it
was four old shillings to get in the Kop. But these days the
emphasis is on the corporate side. Certainly, from my dealings
with the Supporters' Club there is a lot of bitterness, a feeling
from the fans that they have been let down. Examples of that
are the way the dates are changed to accommodate television
and the shirts which change with regularity. But as the club will
point out, you don't have to buy the shirts. But football has
moved into a different era and I don't think we can ever go back.

I often look back and wonder why there was never a major
disaster on the Kop. One season they discovered all those cracks
under the Kop and had to have major repairs done. When I think
back on particular games, particularly the Ajax match when I
went in the Kop, there was a tremendous amount of steam. I
started off somewhere three quarters up towards the back and
ended up at the front. There was more movement on the Kop
that night than I have ever known. When you look back, you
just wonder why there was not a major accident prior to Hillsborough. I wouldn't go back to it. I went in the Kop for the last
game against Norwich. I came out thinking, yes, that was fun,
but no, I wouldn't go back to it on a regular basis. But that's
probably me getting older.

It's about being part of a huge social club. I sometimes wonder
if we are looking back through rose-tinted spectacles. I used to
get there pretty early, about 1pm and queue up, go in and the
whole run-up to the kick-off was an experience in itself. There
was a unison about the place. People would pick up a song from
nowhere and suddenly the whole Kop was singing. I think it may

have been part of a sixties thing. It was part of being in Liverpool at that time. The population was much higher. There was still the docklands, the manufacturing and of course the humour was more obvious in those days than it is now. Individually I think Liverpool people are still very humorous but collectively I don't think it is there in the same degree. It happens in fits and starts now but in the sixties it seemed to be there with every game. I don't think it will ever be the same atmosphere. There was a uniqueness, it all came together at the same time, the Beatles, Bill Shankly, the sixties, it was one of those fatal combinations that just seemed to work perfectly. I don't think the crowds are the same although that may be because of the constitution. They are not all working class, they do not all come from Liverpool, you've got people from all parts of the world. That's fine but it means you don't get that collective wit. Sitting down is also a bit more alienating. People feel more inhibited. There is a more studied approach to spectating these days. Part of the experience of going to games was just being in the Kop.

After a few lean years I am encouraged, I feel that we are on the right track again. Although Gerard Houllier is a very different manager, he is probably nearer Bill Shankly than many of the others, in the way that he talks, approaches the game, and the confidence that he gives. It's the first time for a long time that the fans I have spoken to feel confident about the future. I think this year is very much a transition but the confidence for next year is tremendous. So we are moving forward in the right direction. I don't think we will be consigned to the museum just yet.

I think for a long time this city has struggled to compete with Manchester. But I think there is a realism now that we cannot compete on a city basis. Manchester has different attractions and is in a different league from a city point of view. Having come to terms with that we can begin to build on our strengths. I think this has been reflected in the football team.

BRIAN HALL
The Modern Game

The boot room is not an anachronism. Those conversations and those discussions which once took place in the boot room, they still take place, though now it's down at Melwood. The same talking about players, team performances and so on, that takes place now in a more structured format, all the time with our management team. It's just a different environment.

But the game has changed radically from my days. I was going to say it's more professional but that's the wrong word. It's more scientific. The way that we trained and were managed was almost instinctive. The management team knew how it worked. If you asked them what made a player fit, a team work, they probably could never have expressed it in any clear way whereas now with all the modern systems you could plug into a computer and measure it. That's progress. The football and sporting world is now more scientific. Everyone is more scientific. That's the difference to me. It's a more scientific approach though what they are physically doing is not that much different. In our days it was a case of, 'he's not fit/ he is fit', it was an opinion. Now they measure it.

There's something else as well. Football is a team game and is littered with mistakes, even the best teams in the world give the ball away. That for me is one of its appeals. Forty-five thousand people can watch a game here and all have different opinions on a player's performance, it's very subjective. You can quantify injuries and so that's not subjective, it's objective so we've taken an element of the modern game away from that subjective view. I remember some days I've gone out feeling absolutely awful, got a cold or whatever, and yet it just happens for you. Then you go out other days and you feel, yes, this will be good, and in fact it doesn't happen. Whether that is physiological or what, we don't know. But it is more possible now to analyse games more thoroughly. We can identify how many passes you made, or failed to make, etc. But you can make ten passes, give nine away, then with the tenth someone scores. How do you quantify that? So in a way it's still subjective. Professional people in the game want to quantify that and make it less subjective. Wimbledon did this. They quantified how goals were scored and decided to go for the long-ball game. I think that is the biggest change in the game for me, it's more scientific.

DAVID FAIRCLOUGH
Need For Change

Souness didn't have people under him like Shanks and Bob did. Roy was more a pal to the lads. I think he found it a difficult role to suddenly become the disciplinarian. I don't think Roy Evans fulfilled that role when Graeme Souness was manager. Now, when he comes to take over, maybe he doesn't have the respect that he deserved. Maybe that's where they lost it. Ronnie was well respected and there should be no underestimation of his role. In all this success he was the one constant, particularly in the later period. Ronnie did all the bawling and shouting.

Personally I felt that the boot room had run its course. It might sound controversial but having seen and done things abroad in Switzerland and Belgium, and seen how the game was changing, I thought when I was in Switzerland that Liverpool, even though they were still European champions, were falling behind. I could see the game changing. I thought ultimately Liverpool would have caught up by the time I had got back by broadening their vision a little bit. I don't think Liverpool or English clubs for a while were aware of what was going on on the continent. I've heard a number of managers say they don't know who so-and-so is. I'm a fan of the European scene and English managers don't know players, don't know systems or what is going on.

The game has changed dramatically. The Bosman ruling for one thing has altered things. You now have to be far more aware of talent and need to broaden your methods. It is a European game now. Liverpool have this attitude that we are Liverpool, we are the best, why should we change things, we've won trophies. We were always tempting fate. It went on for so long, it was always going to end some day. We should have been more aware. When I came back from the continent I could see this. The attitude of only promoting from within, that you could only be a Liverpool manager if you had played for the club, had run its course. I think Liverpool were a bit blinkered.

I came back after six months in Switzerland and was telling people that we did this and we did that, and someone turned around to me and said 'That's bollocks, all that.' But I hope I didn't look at things like that. When I went to Switzerland I thought, this is great; they were so professional, I was so well looked after. But it's a blinkered approach in Britain. The players at Lausaunne were better treated than ever the players at Liverpool were: how we prepared for training, massage, and so on. The boot room had this British bulldog attitude: when it rained you still went out there in your little shorts. That didn't worry me because I don't like tracksuit bottoms but I know some of the players would have preferred to put them on. But there's an 'it's namby-pamby to wear them' attitude. The first winter in Switzerland, the kit man had all the kit laid out and there was a pair of tights automatically put out. I thought, I'm not wearing them, I've been brought up in Liverpool, I'm tough. But the next game I wore them like the others. Now that would never have happened at Liverpool. Admittedly it changed after John Barnes came on in his. But I came through the Shankly, Joe Fagan, Bob Paisley era and they would never have had any of that. John Barnes, being from Jamaica, preferred to play in gloves or tights. I think that's a big part of how the game has changed, not all players are the same.

It was very basic training stuff we did at Liverpool. It worked for us but when you go to the continent and see what they are doing, it's much different. For instance, we had massages throughout the week. There was much more thought put into things like that. All these things made me think Liverpool needed to change. I think it's very interesting that Gerard Houllier was brought in. The pre-match warm-up that he has introduced is very continental, you see it all the time on the continent. I remember playing for the England B team in Germany in 1978 and we didn't even go out practising on an icy pitch. We went out five minutes beforehand and that was it. The Germans prepared better, wore tights and so on and went out to get used to the conditions beforehand. These little things are good. It doesn't always work to your advantage, but more often than not, it does. The preparations are better. That is a European approach. Warm-ups do help. Some of these players, particularly the younger and continental players, do it far more now than the older ones.

JOHN BENNETT
A Young Roy Evans

Roy Evans was two years behind me. I just remember him as a very quiet lad but always very keen with a good left foot. I didn't have an awful lot to do with him, I didn't socialise with him. When you're 17 or 18, two years is a big difference and he was two years younger, so you didn't socialise. That's the way it was then. You socialised with those of your own age. As for the first team, you only spoke to them if they spoke to you. I think Roy was groomed, I think Bob saw something in him. I don't think he would have made the grade as a player but obviously Bob saw something in him.

JOHN BENNISON
Still Training

I kept working up until 1994, I was 66 then. A new rule had come in that anybody who was 65 would have to retire. That first year I was 66 there was a mass exodus: the stadium manager had to go, Eli who was the groundsman here and was 77, had to go. We all went. We got some consolation. The Queen was coming because it was our centenary. We all met the Queen and had our photograph taken with her. Souey was the manager, and he said we'd have to go but he said what you can do, you can come here whenever you want. You've been a decent bloke, you come to the dressing room for first team games and can help tidy up and so on. But once the manager changes, that changes because you just can't go bashing into dressing rooms. So I come in a couple of days like this, keep out of the way, respect everybody who's here. I bumped into Gerard the first day and introduced myself, told him who I was, told him I was on the staff for 20-odd years but now come here and do a bit of training. 'You just enjoy yourself, John,' he said. They respect that. We keep out of the way.

PETER ROBINSON

Right For Its Time

I think the boot room was right for its time. That was the way football was. You have a much bigger staff these days. You're much more into football science than if you look back 30 years ago but I think it was right. It had the spirit amongst the management and staff that was necessary for the time. Now things have changed and there are different ways.

I think it was a lead that others followed, though not perhaps in the same way. I think the Anfield boot room was very much a Liverpool creation. You couldn't ever imagine Bill having a load of people having a few beers after a game in his office because Bill, although he tolerated alcohol, would never have encouraged alcohol.

PHIL NEAL

A Fire In The Corner ... Slippers Warming

When I went back with Coventry it had been moved to the opposite corridor. When the boots were taken away and moved across, it wasn't palatial, but it was more of an entertaining room. It wasn't the boot room any more, the boots had long gone. There was more lavish food coming in after the game, it was a hospitality box.

All those meetings went astray. Where do those meetings take place now? That's where I think the less successful times started to appear. I'm not saying it's down to the boot room, that's just one case. But those meetings that they had were important. Those discussions about training, players, and so on. It was like a war room. Churchill had his war room and that's how I regard the boot room, everybody knew their role. He had his commanders and they would give him the right information and decisions would be taken. People also knew they could comment. Maybe those on the periphery thought it would be better to throw in a comment in the boot room, rather than in an office or the board-room. They were on home territory. It was done in a relaxed way. It was homely, simple. I suppose it was inevitable that it would disappear but I think the people were happy in that environment. Those decisions may have later been discussed in the board room but they began in the boot room. They were working-class guys, happy in their environment.

I remember Bob bringing in Alan Kennedy to take over from Joey Jones. Every year a new face would appear, someone to replace an older player. Those kind of decisions would have been discussed openly in the boot room. The door would always be open. Life has to move on but I still think there is a place for the boot room. I created a place at Coventry where the staff could meet. It was a kit room where we sat on stools and talked over things with a cup of tea. There was a canteen but it was too public to talk. Sometimes meetings need to be secret. Talk was always kept in house, there was trust, people privy to those discussions didn't go jabbering to the press or anyone.

I don't know whether it's all gone. During the 13 years I've been in management I have tried to create that pocket. Even at Man City we used to have our little boot room and in the afternoon when all the training was over we'd have our chat: who did well in training, about what do you think about Saturday, what about the reserve team? It was a togetherness with people I could trust. As a manager you need to have people you can trust. I don't know but it may well be with M. Houllier that it's his decision and his alone. I don't know whether they discuss things like that any more. But they did in the past. In the old days that boot room might be open until 7pm, until the right decision had been made and they would be there on a Sunday morning as well. It was seven days a week.

I think there is still a place for that kind of meeting place. It needs to be in a bunker, it needs to be small. As far as I was concerned, that boot room made all the right decisions. The boot room ought to have had a fire in the corner, slippers warming, pull up a chair, pour yourself a drink, Guinness over there in that crate, bottle of whisky here. It was that kind of a place. They would feel at home and free enough to make an adverse comment. Take them upstairs and put a few boardroom members around them and they wouldn't say anything, they wouldn't feel comfortable and free to speak. The adverse comments could be just as good and important. As a manager you need the staff to be loyal to you and able to speak their minds in a trusting way. That's what the boot room was about.

PHIL THOMPSON

The New Boot Room

I don't think there can be a boot room as it was. We go to clubs now and go to their boot rooms and some of them are quite plush with nice food laid on. But those rooms which we see now have all evolved from the Liverpool boot room. Nottingham

Forest still have a traditional homely boot room. Ours here is still small, a place where people want to go but not of the same character.

It's difficult to get the same consultation because we are not there on a day-to-day basis. We obviously discuss things here at Melwood every morning from about quarter past nine to about quarter to ten. We have discussions about training, the players, so in a similar way that is happening. But I couldn't for one minute say that that is the same as the boot room. There is a mystique about the boot room that will never be rivalled. Although you knew it was special, you often wondered why. I think the thing that did make it special was that you picked up trophies at the end of the day and that's what it is all about. The boot room would not be legendary if there weren't the trophies to go along with it. I think when the boot room was dismantled, that's when it all changed. But I don't think you can put the two together and say that the demise of the team was due to the pulling down of the boot room. In the end it comes down to the players.

RONNIE MORAN
Loyalty

I don't think the boot room as we know it is possible in today's game. We can still have the boot room but it's more like an office now. It started off with Bob and Joe having a natter. I was lucky in being involved with such great people. And we all spoke the same language of football. We had our little different views but nothing out of the ordinary. What's the secret? Well, we all spoke the truth. We were fortunate in having loads of good players. We knew that with some players we wouldn't get a full match out of them. You don't know a player until you've bought him and worked with him. It doesn't matter what walk of life, you don't get to know someone until you've worked with them.

If you weren't loyal you didn't have a chance. You have to be loyal to your manager. I've seen it at other clubs where if we had won at some place, someone from the opposition staff would come in and say, 'Oh, he picked the wrong team today, our manager, we should have done this, we should have done that.' We'd look at each other and think, cor, we wouldn't have that at our place. If that ever existed you would have no success. Once players see a little bit of difference between the coaching staff, even when you're out training, you have a bit of a battle with them. In the Anfield boot room we all had our little ideas but more or less we all had the same ideas on the game. And that's why we had so much success because we had harmony there. There were no arguments of any sort. I can't remember an argument between coaches. Sometimes, you'd suggest doing it this way, but if the manager said no, then fine. Even in the boot room itself, in private, among the staff there were no arguments. You backed everyone up to the hilt. We'd knock the ideas together in the boot room and then try them out in training.

People would come down and didn't understand. Shanks would say, play the simple ball. But what is the simple ball? Bill would say, get them fit, keep them fit. We wouldn't go mad in pre-season training. Bill would say it's not a sprint, it's a nine-month race. No good killing your players off in pre-season or having them good for just the first month. If you work the pre-season right then about the late September they start to come good. Then you just keep them at that level. If you have hard games, then cut back a bit on the training. Sometimes you'd have it in your mind, we'll do that today, you'd have it worked out. But then when you were having the warm-ups you'd try and weigh up the players. You think, there's two or three won't be able to do it; players going through the motions. So you just changed straight away to do something else.

I think things have changed now. Some clubs have their system worked out for the whole week. I don't say that's wrong. Graeme had learnt the continental way. He'd had some success at Rangers so he changed the training a bit, more eleven-a-side games.

It's the same with players misbehaving. It goes on at every club. You have to train but sometimes players don't turn up. If you let it spread, it causes a problem. It's happened here in the last five or six years. Certain players have done this or that and haven't turned up for training. You might not be worried about them turning up but it's how it affects the other players. You know, 'Well he's not bothered turning up today, so why should I bother?' Even in my day players didn't turn in. I still went out and did my training because I always enjoyed it. You can't make people train but you can change things to help them enjoy it. So if some of them are just going through the motions then you change it a bit. It took a man like Bill Shankly to transform the club, make the decisions, recognise the need to change training so that more of them enjoyed it.

I never used to talk about the past. Sometimes players would ask me about past players. I'd just say they were good players but I would never say they were better players. You mustn't do that. In my playing days I'd hear staff say, you're not as good as so-and-so. I'd tell players they were as good as such-and-such a player of the past.

STEVE HALE
A Bit Of Steel?

It was reckoned that in the Roy Evans period a bit of steel was needed. Roy has gone down as a lovely man but it was said he needed a bit of steel. But they had that steel with Graeme Souness. But was it too much that they couldn't take it? So what do you do? If Houllier works out, great, but if it doesn't, where do we go from here? Since they last won the league championship they've only won the Cup and the League Cup and they've failed in Europe.

TOM SAUNDERS
Honesty, Decency And Continuity

There are many myths about the boot room, I feel. But the people who were there were special in that their feeling for the game and their knowledge of the game at that time was unsurpassed.

I think we, as a club, had that continuity about us. The Peter Robinsons of this world did a magnificent job in a very quiet way, picking up vast experience over the years which proved to be inestimable in terms of running a successful football club. Now people ask the question: why is it we've fallen by the way-side? Well, it's a very ruthless, competitive industry and other people have competed and caught up and surpassed us and it now behoves us to get back in amongst them again and I'm sure they will do, given time.

I think the boot room was about honesty and decency. I think the honesty has always been there, ever since I came here. Wherever I travel abroad to vet the opposition, Liverpool always has a very good reputation for dealing with football in the right manner. I suspect that that is about the people who have worked for Liverpool, many of them long since gone, who built up this reputation for fair play and honest dealings, doing the right things for the right reasons. And it's lived with us and long may it remain. And no matter how important winning the prizes are, I think the football game is about people. You've only got to walk to the ground on matchday and watch people. Their fanaticism is tremendous. I never cease to marvel at that side of it. It's all about those people, the spectators. But it's always been brought about by those people who work here. I don't just mean the present people or even the Bob Paisleys but the Tom Bushes of this world as well. There are many of them who did excellent work here.

TOM SAUNDERS
The People Were Special

It is an anachronism now, I think. The boot room was about the people. Because Liverpool was successful people wanted to find out why. I was there coaching in those days and even in the coaching world people used to ask: how did they do this, how did they do that? And I would say you can come and have a look at the training. And they would come and they would look and see how things were done. And there were a lot of things they felt that they hadn't seen. They used to say to me, 'Tom, is that the end of the training session?' And I'd say 'Yes.' I don't think they believed me because the team was so successful on a Saturday that they couldn't relate that to what they'd seen at training.

In those days, they don't do it now of course, the main focal point of the training was the small five-a-side game. And that was about playing. The philosophy was that small sided team game It threw up all the problems that you get in an eleven a side game. But in a smaller place you get much more of it. It's more condensed and this was the best way to train with the competitive element as well. That was the main training. They did some formal work such as restarts, free kicks, but nothing like as much as they do today. Less scientific, but I think your problem is that you are looking for something about this boot-room that really isn't there. You're looking for the same thing that people as coaches came here to see on the training pitch and went away disappointed. Now somewhere in between that you've got to unravel it. And good luck to you ! All I can tell you is that the people were special in my view and that's about it.

WILLIE MILLER

A Multi-Million Pound Business

I think it starts to go wrong with Heysel. I think that knocked the stuffing out of the club. You talk about Joe Fagan. He was devastated after Heysel. You have this image of him coming down the steps of the plane, this picture of him crying as he came down the steps. Things did go wrong there and you would have thought we would have learned from it.

Then it came to Hillsborough. I don't think the club has ever got over Hillsborough. I went to the tenth anniversary the other week and I was standing on the Kop crying my eyes out. I was at Hillsborough, I was there in the stand above. I could have

saved people. I used to be a fireman. If I could have got to people
I could have resuscitated them, I could maybe have saved some
people. But I couldn't physically get to them. That will never
ever go away. But Hillsborough certainly knocked the stuffing
out of the club. And that is not an excuse. That was when so
many people looked at Shankly's famous saying about football
is more important than life and looked at that and thought, hang
on. It broke the spirit of the club, snapped it.

I remember John Aldridge after Hillsborough. The FA wanted
to get the game against Forest played and Aldridge, who absolutely loves football, was saying that he didn't want to play
football. You never thought you'd hear him ever saying he didn't
want to play football again. And the rest of the team, they were
not interested in playing football. The whole of Liverpool was
totally devastated. The atmosphere around the city was horrible.
During the eighties Liverpool and Everton Football Clubs stood
for a lot more than just football. This was the time of
Thatcherism and the Tories would knock us at any opportunity.
Jobs were going here and there but the football kept the people
of the city proud. There's that natural pride with Liverpudlians
but that was a time when the football clubs kept us sane. Then of
course the atmosphere after Heysel. We got the blame, scousers
rioting, fighting. Then just as people were coming to terms with
that, there was Hillsborough and in my opinion the club has
never recovered from that.

When Sir John Smith was chairman of the club, we didn't
really have any problems. What problems we did have were
sorted out inside the club. Today the media go after them. But
who was more high profile in the seventies than Kevin Keegan,
when incidents which were kept in house? They never got out
into the papers. The team that won three titles on the run, to
say that some of them liked a drink would be an understatement.
But nobody bothered them because they were winning things. It
was all kept in house. The leadership of the club under Sir John
Smith was magnificent.

It used to be the Liverpool way to buy players and then stick
them in the reserves. Now, if you stick them in the reserves they
want a move because it's in their contract that they have to play

for the first team. It's a mess, player power is much bigger. The boot room was part of the jigsaw but it will only make sense if the rest of the pieces fit in. And at the moment the rest of the pieces don't.

Roy was a great believer in the boot room. That's why he brought Joe Corrigan in as a specialist keeper trainer. But Roy knew that things were changing. At the same time he was not getting the commitment from the players. They were getting their ten grand a week or whatever. I think it was brought up at the shareholders' meeting where someone asked, 'We're paying the top wages in the whole of the Premiership and this is where we are. What's wrong?' The chairman couldn't answer. Yes, it is a difficult question to answer. It's player power. But United have a wage structure and Arsenal have a wage structure so why don't we say, right, there's the basic and we'll give you so much for points, and if you perform you will end up being the top wage earners in the country. That's the way it used to be. And that's how United do it. Give them some hunger, some incentive. Okay, but where's the pride. United go out and run their cotton socks off. It's got to be the motivation and where does the motivation come from? The top, the manager and above him.

I think it will be a very, very sad road to go down if they decide to go public.

The contracts aren't worth the paper they're written on. It's become a multi, multi-million pound business and with the extra money comes greed. You won't get the people now who used to play for Liverpool for 10, 12, 15 years. You will never get another like Ian Callaghan, who wanted to play his whole career for the club. They don't need any more money, they can't spend any more money.

I look and see what the boot room set-up is at Anfield, compared to what it was. I think it's still possible if you've got the right people around you. Alex Ferguson has the right people around him at Man United. Okay, he's the one who's been firing the bullets but he's loaded himself with a very good team around him. It's different now because of the managers now. Look at Bill Shankly, he used to do his own typing. Now they don't even reply to letters. There are so many demands placed on them. If you look back at the total staff at Liverpool, it used to be Harry the painter, Joe the electrician, Sammy the groundsman. The amount of actual full-time staff was small. It would be interesting to compare how many they have today.

If we talk about the boot room we have to talk about everything else, the whole structure at Anfield. It's gone tits up, for want of a better expression. It's gone. The structure is not in place. The team will not start gelling together until the club itself, the club as an institution, gets its act together. Football is an industry now. They need to get marketing people on and they need to sell Liverpool FC. In the past they've had people come to us, queuing up, wanting to see Liverpool FC. I wonder how easy it will be to sell Liverpool Football Club next year, after thirteen defeats this year, including appalling performances at home. How easy will that be to sell? I think the club is in a terrible mess. There are people close to retirement, is their heart still there?

The people who worked in the boot room were the heart of the club. Joe Fagan was the heart and soul of Liverpool FC, he knew football inside out. He was very astute. Bob Paisley was obviously the man who took what Bill Shankly had started. He'd built a good team around him. It was not luck rather than judgement. I think he knew what he wanted to do. He had this vision. But don't forget we went from '67 to '73 without winning anything. There's a lot of people who have obliterated that period totally. It was the development of that second team, so there was a lot that people have conveniently forgotten. But they stuck with it, they stuck with the continuity and said, okay, things will change. The boot room was also backed up at board level. Their decisions were always backed up because Bill Shankly would have no messing about from the board. He said who he wanted and who he didn't went. There was the famous incident when he threatened to resign over John Morrissey going to Everton. After that they never bothered him again. The board backed him 100 per cent. The boot room was only part of the jigsaw, they knew that their job was to look after the football side. Then they had the other people there on the board whose job was to provide the money for the boot room to look after the football side. I would say you had the manager, the boot room, the board of directors, and then the other people, the ancillary staff from the cleaners to the groundsmen. They were part of a jigsaw. The boot room was not the be all and end all, they were a part of it, a part of the jigsaw.

It was a smaller jigsaw. There were not even any manufactured scarves. People had them knitted with the names of the players on: Hunt, St John. I don't remember the first souvenir shop. But they still had the support all over the world. The world is smaller now. You come here to the Moat House at a weekend and it's packed with Norwegians, Irish, people from all over the world coming to the city. Liverpool FC has done so much for the image of this city, so much good.

You know, there's a lad who comes to do our decorating. Great lad. He's been a rank-and-file Liverpool supporter for years. He has the routine where they go to the pub before the game, the same four or five of them. One of them will go and pick up the tickets for the away game and they'll all pile into the car and go together. And he says to me the other week, 'They don't deserve me.' And that is so true, they don't deserve him. He's so right.

WILLIE STEVENSON
Could Shanks Cope Today?

I would like to think there is still a place for the boot room. Even managers, trainers, and all these people, they all need somewhere where they can talk to each other honestly. I think they like to feel free to talk. They all love the game of football and they love talking about it. They can't always do it with the players around, and sometimes they like to swap stories with opposition managers and trainers. Most of them go back a long time together. There should be a place for it. But Shanks would never be able to cope with today's game, but then not many managers today can cope with it. Bill Shankly was not known for his patience. Things would not move quick enough for him. Transfers these days can take months. There was a time when nobody knew, it happened almost overnight. I asked for just 24 hours so that I could speak to the family. It was all done and dusted inside a day. Now it takes six months of negotiating every eventuality.

STEVE MORGAN

The Future

Whether we like it or not, Premiership football is big business and needs to be approached with a very businesslike and commercial attitude. I think the club has been a bit slow getting into the commercial world. If you look at Chelsea's website you can order whatever you want, replica kits and all sorts of souvenirs, and it will be there within 48 hours and credited to your credit card. We haven't even got a website and we've given our own merchandising rights over to a third party. I am just astounded by some of these decisions.

I am someone who believes in evolution, not revolution, and I do believe in the boot room, not as in the Bob Paisley/Bill Shankly era but in the boot room mentality. Football clubs are big businesses today. They have to be commercial and Manchester United have led the way in this. But at the same time it's all about playing football and those lads going out on the park and winning the matches, that's what it's all about and let's not lose sight of that.

The boot room is a philosophy to me and it's the philosophy of the club, it's the way the players think. One of the things about Liverpool of the seventies and eighties in particular and the mid-sixties is that, generally speaking, there has been evolution, not revolution. There was no revolution until Souness came. We all remember Kevin Keegan's last game for the club. He announced months before that he was going at the end of the season. Nobody did that in those days, nobody left Liverpool but what did Liverpool do? They went out at the end of that season and bought Kenny Dalglish: the King is dead, long live the King. If you look at the way Liverpool brought their players on, they used to buy young players, play them in the reserves for a season or two and gently ease them into the Liverpool way. There has always been a Liverpool way, a Liverpool culture and to me the boot room is at the heart of the culture of the club, the pride, the passion. Personalities have changed, Bill Shankly went, Bob Paisley took over, but the emphasis and the consistency and the culture was still the same. Things always change and you have to move with the times, you can't stay back in a time warp, but it's evolution, not revolution. There is a place for a modern-day boot room culture that is a modern day version of what we have known in the sixties, seventies, eighties. Yes, of course there is a place for it, absolutely.

JAN MOLBY
A Family Club

I think that kind of set-up can still exist in the modern game. If anyone was to have a boot room again, it would never have the same significance and it would never create the same interest as Liverpool did but I think it could have a place. I don't think people have got the time but in those days the Liverpool back room boys had the time to spend in the boot room. They probably spent many a day, many an hour in there talking a load of rubbish but every now and again something would come out, whether it was a new player, or it was a new way of playing. I don't think that every day in there was a day that they would remember, maybe only very few moments, but they took their time. It goes with what Liverpool stands for, being a family club. There was a time and a place for everybody.

I don't know Gerard Houllier well enough to pass a comment but I don't think they have these kind of get-togethers where everybody has a say. I would like to think that Gerard knows what he's doing, he probably confides a lot in his man Patrice and Phil Thompson. In many ways it's a shame because whatever you say about the boot room, I think a lot of good has come out of it. There will be people who will say what a load of

rubbish, it's got no place in football today. I have heard that
there's a similar thing at United where they all have to report
back to Alex Ferguson and they all sit and talk. I don't think
that happens at Anfield any more. It is a shame.

ROY EVANS

From Apprentice to Manager

My first memory of the boot room was that it was a scruffy little
room where the boots of all the first team and reserve team
players in the club were made ready. As an apprentice I spent
most of my time in a little ante-room cleaning these boots to be
hung up for the next match.

The room became symbolic, but it wasn't to do with the actual
physical place itself. It was to do with the amount of talented
people who were in there to talk about football. It was about
the wealth of information, the wealth of knowledge that was
contained within those four walls.

Later on when I joined the staff, we used to go to the boot
room on Sunday mornings and sit there for an hour or two
discussing the previous game or what was going to go on the
next week. Sometimes Bill Shankly would be there. He didn't
use it an awful lot, he was usually in his office on Sundays and
even after a game he wouldn't turn up often. Bob Paisley, Joe
Fagan and Ronnie Moran – they would be in the boot room
more often than not, exchanging their little ideas.

It was actually a small room with a separate outside area where
the boots were on benches. As an apprentice you'd knock on
the door to take the boots back and hang them up, on the pegs
labelled one to eleven, and if you wanted to speak to the coaches
you'd knock on the inner door. That's where they were based;
they didn't have offices in those days. Nowadays, they have better
facilities beneath the stands. If you wanted to talk to them or
they wanted to talk to you, they'd take you inside and give you
words of wisdom, advice or criticism or whatever was called
for.

There were old basket skips which we used to sit on, and a table and a couple of chairs. I recall there was always a couple of cases of lager stored there and a case of Guinness which the club used to get off the local brewery. You chose your seat and the coaches would speak to you. When I later joined the coaching staff, I remember we would discuss things most of the time over a mug of tea. Apart from the Sunday, that is. By the time we'd finished our work on a Sunday, treating the players and getting all the kit sorted out, we'd then have a beer and maybe three-quarters of an hour conversation about the game the previous day.

Bob Paisley was responsible for initiating my move to join the coaching staff. Shanks had retired and Bob came to me one day and said, 'Roy, we want you to come on the staff'. I was about 25-years old at the time. There was no way at that age I'd even contemplated being a coach, so I said, 'No, I want to carry on being a player'. But then Joe had a quiet word as did Ronnie, then finally Tommy Smith. In the end I asked, 'Why do you want me to come onto the staff? What could I bring to the role at such a young age that was going to be beneficial?' Tommy replied, 'You can always try it, son, then go back to football later', although privately I'm sure they didn't think I'd end up being in Liverpool's first team for any great length of time. They said, 'Your enthusiasm for the game is the most important thing.' They thought that was a really vital aspect of being a coach. And eventually, after weeks, maybe even a month or so, they persuaded me to have a go. As it turned out, it was probably the best move of my footballing career.

So I became part of the boot room. You couldn't appreciate the depth of conversation and the thought and planning that went into a game until you were actually part of it. As a player you had the coach's meeting before the game. You didn't realise throughout the week the little things that had to be considered from the injury point of view, or from a player's fitness point of view. At that time I don't think Liverpool picked too many 'tactical' teams because of the quality of players we had. We thought more about the way *we* played, rather than the way the opposition played. We very rarely changed the way we played to suit the opposition. Of course, there'd be one or two minor adjustments if we thought we could gain advantage from them. Certainly in one or two European games we deployed man-to-man marking with the likes of Ian Ross and Sammy Lee, and that proved successful. But it was very rare that we changed our own strategy; we thought that if we were at our best, we could beat most teams.

There weren't so many transfers in those days but the Liverpool management team wouldn't hesitate to ask your opinion of a player. We all used to go and watch games, but not to the extent that the scouts employed by the club do now across the world. If there was a player that was really fancied, we'd all have a little look and our individual opinions were assessed. That was the nice thing about it from my point of view. When you were only in your twenties, it was great that they'd listen to your opinion and encourage you to give it. That was the first thing they said to me when I became part of the boot room fraternity – 'Whatever you've got to say, don't hold back. Okay, we've been in the game a long time. Yes, we are experienced and, yes, we have the knowledge, but sometimes a young man like yourself might see something different. Sometimes you might say something stupid, but that doesn't matter because one of these days you'll come up with a gem and it will help us all, so don't be frightened to open your mouth.'

They made me feel right at home. I think the nicest thing was that we became great friends, even though Bob, Joe and Ronnie were much older than me.

They all had a part to play. Bob would sometimes instigate a conversation with a remark while Joe was the out-and-out down-to-earth, sensible one; if it needed saying, he would say it. Ronnie was the antagonist in many ways. Don't take that the wrong way, because he was a very valuable antagonist! He could be very constructive in saying, 'How do we sort the problem out?' There was a nice mix of conversation and nobody was really in awe of anybody else. In a relationship with four or five coaches, if you're not in fear of people that you work with, then you will express yourself and you will come out with better ideas.

Shanks was different. You didn't really discuss too many things with Shanks, but I think he was clever enough to listen to people when they were talking to each other and pick up points. Most of the time, Shanks would ask something but it wasn't a question, it was more a statement of fact. I think he instilled confidence in people by the way he spoke confidently himself and all his words were really factual, like 'What a great player you are, son'. But if he wanted to knock you down, he could be just as cutting. He wasn't a great conversationalist. He liked to get his bit over very quickly and leave the rest for the others to sort out. But he would listen to Bob and Joe, and to Ronnie, for sure. They said he was very much his own man but he realized what a good backroom staff he had. Reuben Bennett was his right-hand man and Reuben stayed on with Bob once Shanks retired. He was a man with a great deal of knowledge, one of the first to be a one-to-one coach with the players. If there was a player dropped from the team, Reuben was the man to go and put his arm around him and say, 'Look, you've got to get yourself together. You're out of the team, but you've got to pull your socks up, work a bit harder and see where it goes from there.' By the same token, if you were the opposite and showed any signs of being slightly big-headed, Reuben could kick you up the backside and tear you to shreds.

It's often said that Bill Shankly had the charisma and Bob Paisley had the brains. I wouldn't argue with that statement, but in saying that it shouldn't take anything away from Shanks because at the end of the day they were his ideas. The way to come and play the game, the simple passing routine, the simplicity of the game – all were principles from Shanks that Bob took on board. Bob was probably a better judge of players and tactically he was probably better than Shanks. Shanks gave you self-belief, while Bob and Joe would then fill in the finer points about how the other team would play and who they thought would be dangerous. So it was a great mix of personalities, not only on the pitch but on the coaching staff; if you could strike a good balance, it brought results.

I'd say there were no great changes when Joe Fagan became manager, he kept things going after Bob. Bob had been so successful that he was a very difficult act to follow. I don't think Joe really wanted to be a manager; I think he took it basically to make sure that we all stayed in a job. That was the kind of man he was. He always thought of other people first. But he was very refreshing in his short spell because he was so open, straightforward and honest with everybody. With the players, if you were playing well, he'd praise you, and if you were playing poorly, he'd tell you. If there was a lack of effort he would crucify you, but you knew where you stood with Joe. I don't think he sat comfortably in the manager's chair, and he didn't like his office. He spent a lot more time in the boot room, even as a manager, while on the Friday nights before games we used to go to my room or Ronnie's room or Joe's office, and sit and have a couple of drinks. We formed a great think-tank and this would happen every away game when you would spend two or three hours talking about football but in a light-hearted way.

Joe didn't like the paperwork side to the job – in fact, none of us did – so he would spend a fair amount of time in the boot room. His decision to step down came very much as a surprise from our point of view. It was the time of the Liverpool v Juventus Heysel match, and we'd been over at Adidas doing a presentation before returning to the ground to have some lunch. Looking back now, we thought that Joe might have told us then.

It was the day before we travelled over to Belgium. It was only on the morning of the game, when we heard rumours circulating about Joe. We gave him his boots for the training session and I asked cryptically, 'Is this a testimonial?' Joe sort of looked at me and walked away. He wasn't going to say. I think he was criticised for that later by some of the staff who felt we should have been told then, but I know Joe, I think he promised the board that he wouldn't tell us. If Joe Fagan promises anybody, then he keeps his promise and you can't criticise a man for doing that. I think he had had enough. He's a great family man, Joe, and I don't think he really enjoyed football management and all the problems that came with the job. He was very good with the media, he was open and honest and just spoke his mind. People liked him for that, but there were so many other things to deal with on a daily basis. As a manager, you're not just dealing with a football team, you're dealing with everything outside of that, and I don't think Joe enjoyed that side of it. You've got to realise how many years he had been associated with football – forty-five to fifty, I think – and with different clubs. Sometimes you come to a point where you say 'That's my lot'.

I was just devastated for Joe that his time as manager ended on a very sad note with the Heysel stadium tragedy. The man broke down on the plane coming home. I'll never forget that. In football, he was like a father to me. To see him so unhappy tore me apart at the time.

We found out officially that he was stepping down the next day. John Smith came up to me and Ronnie and said, 'Joe's stepping down and we're going to appoint Kenny Dalglish as manager, but we'd like you two to stay on and do the job you've been doing and be helpful'. I wouldn't say the appointment of Kenny was a surprise, we all knew Kenny and the talent he had, and it was quite an innovative move for Liverpool, to be fair to them. It was just that the timing wasn't quite what we'd expected. We'd assumed there would not be an announcement until maybe a week after Heysel, but the news was out and he was appointed straight away. He came direct to the boot room from off the plane and said to us, 'We want you lads to stay on and to give me all the help you can', which we were only too pleased to do.

There was quite a funny story during the run up to Heysel. We were playing a game without Kenny, who had been injured and was on the bench. Kenny's always an enthusiastic onlooker and when one of the players missed a pass, Kenny made the remark, 'Why the hell did he do that?' Ronnie Moran quipped, 'Hey, you're not the manager yet, enjoy the rest' , without realising that in the weeks to come he would become manager!

Kenny was a boot room man, definitely. He was still playing at the time, so we tried to make sure we could take as much pressure off him as possible. Tom Saunders was a great help. He's one we haven't mentioned really and over the years, with John Bennison, he's been a constant at the club, then Steve Heighway and Sammy Lee in the later years. Kenny would always come in and have a little chat, he liked that boot room mentality. Sometimes he would bring a video in. Kenny got to the stage where he would like to watch the games of the team we'd be playing against. We'd watch a video and have a beer.

In the early years, if you got invited to the boot room as an outsider, it was fantastic. If you had any sense, you went in and listened. It wasn't always serious football chat, but there would be some great things said. You'd get Cloughie in occasionally, and there would be some great banter going around. Win or lose, the opposition were always invited in for a drink after the game. Okay, we didn't lose too many in those days so it was quite easy to be the great hosts, but that was the style we set. We used to play great teams away from home and not get invited for a drink, go to Europe and not get invited for a drink and we'd say we'll do the same to them on our patch. But Joe Fagan would say, 'No, we won't do the same to them, we'll kill them with our kindness and show them what they should have done and then they'll feel twice as bad'. I think that was a great philosophy and we kept it going for a long period.

In those days we probably wouldn't have got to meet the other coaches anyway unless you invited them into the boot room. Occasionally you'd ask them what they did in training, or if it was Norwich, say, how did you travel up here, did you come on a train, and you could learn little things. You're just trying to pick people's brains all the time for a crumb of information which might help your team and they would do the same to us, which was fair enough. If you were speaking to someone from, say, Ipswich they had different ideas, on whom they could buy, to us, so they would just give us the information on players. They probably couldn't afford to buy the people we were looking for. The coaches in there, they all knew the score.

We were one of the first teams in to be really successful in Europe on a regular basis and lots of managers or coaches would ring us up and ask, 'What do you do before a European game? How do you travel over there, etc?' Our policy was not to arrive in these places too early, not to spend a lot of time there before games, because in those days if you went to the Eastern bloc, the hotels and general facilities were far from good. Nowadays it's different of course although there are still places where you'd have to take your own food.

When Kenny Dalglish became manager I think things changed. We still kept the diaries of the daily training routines, which were especially useful for identifying injuries and recovery periods. I remember one time Ian Callaghan had a cartilage problem and so we went back to these books to see what players with a similar injury had been doing that was different, in order to try and get the problem solved quickly.

Kenny became his own man but he still kept to the Liverpool traditions. He let us get on with most of the training sessions. When it came to picking teams, he certainly was in charge. If he had a hunch, he'd go for it. If he had a hunch with a young player, he'd play him. Once he'd picked him, we'd back him to the hilt. That was always another thing about the boot room. You were allowed to say anything in the process of picking the team, giving your point and why you don't agree, and that's fine. Once the manager picked the team, then you backed him all the way.

Kenny's got great talent; in fact, he's got everything and he's lucky with it and that is a great thing to have. If you go back to Alex Ferguson's early days at United, I suppose you could say that for five years or more he didn't have the luck. Now he can't do anything wrong, he's great, he has the experience to carry him through. Slowly, everything started to go right for Kenny as well – we used to call him 'golden bollocks' in the nicest possible sense. As a manager he had a great style about him. He put a lot of hours into the job, but he did make some time for himself, to play golf, and to be at home with his family. He put the time in when it mattered. He'd go to three games in a day, Kenny. He wouldn't sit in the office all afternoon if there was nothing to be done.

Graeme Souness's arrival as manager wasn't a watershed. Graeme takes a lot of criticism that things changed dramatically when he came back to Liverpool. Some of the training routines became slightly different, but you can't live in the past forever, harping on about how successful we were thirty years ago. Graeme came to us after a very successful period at Glasgow Rangers. On taking on the Liverpool manager's job, he changed one or two things. We started to move the whole training complex to Melwood, as Anfield itself was getting a facelift and the boot room was demolished, or rather, it became a press room. Of all the things it had to become ... a press room! I suppose it's down to progress again. For an eight-foot square room to stop a whole major development being built, you'd would probably say no, that's crazy. You probably would have liked them to move it somewhere else. We still had the room across the corridor and, to be fair, that's still a boot room of sorts if you're talking about the concept of sitting in there and having a chat, although even that changed somewhere down the line. I'm not sure if it was with Kenny or with Graeme. We ended up all going to Melwood for training, which was the more sensible thing to do. The meetings still carried on with Graeme, and we kept the diaries. Graeme came up with great ideas in his time as manager. Unfortunately, he got criticized at the end as things started to go wrong.

Out of all the people I've worked with at Liverpool, there's nobody who tried harder than Graeme Souness to bring further trophies to the club, but it just didn't happen for him. He was impetuous, I have to say that, in his early days, but only because he wanted to be successful. There were two or three players that he didn't fancy in our squad, so he wanted them out immediately. Sometimes you can't just do that. He'd want other players in immediately even though they had yet to be signed up. And I'd say, 'Great players, but we've not signed them yet.' He'd say, 'Well, we'll try and get them.' He tried to change things too quickly, player-wise and personnel-wise, instead of looking at the situation and saying, yes we'll change it, gradually, and maybe get a better quality of player in. But he tried his hardest and I've never seen a man so distraught at not being successful.

Sometimes I used to drive away from the games and I used to feel for Graeme. I used to worry about him leaving the club. He looked so very sad, he had nowhere to go and that was a worry. Of course, he had problems with his heart – again he was the bravest man in the world to carry on through that – and you have to remember that we did actually win the FA Cup with Graeme in charge.

On the playing side, we always used to say to players to look at themselves and ask, 'What type of player am I, and what are my assets?' If you could understand your assets and your failings, and play to your assets then you'd be a better player. There are a lot of footballers at the top level of the game who I would say were average players who became great players because of the team they played in. That's not a criticism, that's actually praise because they learnt.

Balance and variety in your team is all-important. Kevin Macdonald was a great balanced player who would play alongside Jan Molby, and say, quite honestly: 'I'm not as great a passer of the ball as Jan, but I'm more mobile and I'm quite prepared to run my legs off to make sure that this guy gets enough of the ball'. Kevin would cover for Jan's defensive deficiencies, but that was balanced by the fact that they were prepared to work for each other. The ability to do that is a great example of how Kevin became a great player in my book. Terry McDermott became an outstanding player because not only did he score fine goals, but he learned to work in the team and to provide balance.

Terry Mac was a great character in the dressing room as was Joey Jones. But you find that most of the lads – Steve Nicol was another – were great value for money. There's always been one great personality and you like to have that spirit. Graeme made a good comment once about players and dressing room discipline. In his playing days at Liverpool, when the team was really doing well, the players disciplined themselves. You could do what you liked – you could fine them or whatever and, yes, we did all that. We fined players and we tried to keep it quiet and do it in a dignified manner, but at the same time we expected the likes of Graeme and Kenny to pull team-mates up and say, 'Look, this is the way we do things here at Liverpool.' It wasn't that often, just occasionally. They were strong enough and successful enough to do that. It was great to know that most of the time we could let the lads shape their own discipline and it was self-monitored. But they still had a good time, they didn't live like monks. It's different today because of the media hype; you only have to look the wrong way, and you're in trouble.

When I became manager in 1994 I made a conscious effort to try and change things, that's for sure. I'm a great one for talking to players and hearing their point of view, how the game should be played, how they want to play, because they have to go out there and do it. I used to talk to three or four of the players and if there were discipline problems we had a little committee to try and sort it out. But again we stuck to the basics.

We didn't try to change much. We had a back three at one stage which, considering the defenders we had at the time, I thought would work. It did for a couple of seasons, but when it went wrong we got highly criticised and we were almost forced to go back to four at the back. You change things on a weekly basis if it's not going right, but we didn't alter anything major. We still had the regular meetings with the staff, once a week or once a fortnight. There's so many things going on outside football nowadays, so that much of your time is taken up. We always ended up talking about things off the pitch – health, diet, and so on. Graeme started all that. He'd been to Italy and introduced better diets for the players. We took it on from there and brought in a dietician. We also introduced a goalkeeping coach. We improved Melwood, which is fantastic now and has what is probably the second best gym in the world to Juventus. We had a trainer who could do one-to-one sessions. We tried to modernise the whole setup, making it more professional. The game in this country was screaming out for it. But even now I can recall Ian Rush saying, 'I eat pasta now, but when I was scoring 50 goals a season I used to have a steak pre-match!' One player said he had steak and kidney pie and chips for his pre-match meal. Well, I wondered how could you play on that, but he did and was very successful.

Now the emphasis is on eating pasta, carbohydrates and drinking plenty of fluid. We've had a few players on the books who could go and have a good night out and then train heavily the next morning and get it all out of their system. But they did it at the right time – on a Wednesday or before. You don't necessarily like it as a manager, but you can accept it so long as it doesn't create a problem on the pitch.

If you think of the boot room as a physical place where people sit and talk and pass on information and are not dictated to by one person in the group, then possibly it has gone now. My thoughts of the boot room were that we all sat down and had an equal say, but the manager would always make the final decision. But in the meeting as a whole, the manager would have no more say than me as a kid. So the meetings where we sat around and talked about things off the cuff, yes, I think they're gone now. It's more of a teach-in, there's more of a dominant figure in charge. I don't think it's as open. I always wanted my staff to be open. The last thing in the world I wanted was for people to agree with me all the time as there's no benefit from that. If it is right, then agree, yes. But you want the likes of Ronnie Moran to say no; that's why Ronnie was a vital part. He didn't just do it to be antagonistic. He'd always throw a spanner in the works to cover all angles. I think that's important.

We were successful as a club, probably second only to Fergie's United. I think there was certainly one year, 1995/96, when we should have won the Championship, We were good enough but lost some valuable points at home. You can't explain why. There were games we controlled and should have won, but we failed to put our chances away. I honestly thought we were good enough that one season. We might have gone on from there. A bit of success breeds more confidence. In terms of talent, we were as good as anyone.

People sometimes criticise the club over its discipline. I think the discipline was reasonable when I was manager. When we signed Stan Collymore, it became a problem because he wouldn't move up to Liverpool and he didn't turn up for training on numerous occasions. Then the rest of the lads would say, well he's not here, what are we doing? It set the club back a good 12–18 months. I wouldn't want to blame Stan for all our problems, because on the pitch he was excellent for us. He and Robbie as a partnership were good. Had there not been problems off the pitch, they would have been as good as anything around. I still thought Stan was going to be a great player and feel he still could be. If only we could have taken him on from there. If only Michael Owen had started pushing Robbie and Stan for a place back then. If only some of the younger lads had not lost a bit in terms of team spirit.

Buying good central defenders at that time was a problem. We tried to get Laurent Blanc, as well as Matt Elliott and Juergen Kohler. We knew that if we could defend the aerial stuff, we could win games because we were scoring freely at the other end. But we just couldn't buy anyone. They either weren't available or wanted a lot of money, and with Liverpool being out of Europe, we couldn't tempt them with that any more. Players want to join the likes of Manchester United and Chelsea now, and for less money, because there is the chance of being successful.

GERARD HOULLIER
The View From Abroad

I came to Liverpool because I was a teacher in France and I wanted to improve my English. So I came here as *un assistant*, working at a school in 1969/70. The main part of my work consisted of teaching in Alsop comprehensive school. The other reason for coming to Merseyside was that I was in the middle of my university studies and I needed to write a thesis on the social aspects of Liverpool. Its title was 'Growing Up in Deprivation in a Deprived Area'. So my time was shared between the teaching and the research. I had to spend a lot of time in the difficult areas of Liverpool, Liverpool 8 mainly. I was here for one year.

My first experiences as a fan date back to that time. I think the first European game I went to see was when Liverpool won 10–0 against Dundalk in a UEFA Cup tie. It's funny because my friend Patrice [Patrice Bergues, now Liverpool coach] was there with me, having come over to visit me, and we went to the game together. I went to see as many other games as I could when I was not playing myself for the Alsop old boys' team which I enjoyed very much. I watched the matches mainly as part of the Kop. At that time, the Kop was a swaying mass of colour and sound, and a truly memorable experience.

I was a fan of Liverpool before coming here. In my university you could choose where you went to do the research for your course, and I was fortunate to be able to choose Liverpool. I deliberately chose to come here because of the football. It's very strange when you look back and consider the reputations of the two Merseyside clubs. I think Everton were an even better club at that time. Despite this, and for reasons I don't know, Liverpool FC, certainly in France, were more popular back then.

The boot room would be mentioned sometimes in the press, but the perception you have of something you don't know about but hear people talking about is a bit mysterious. It is an enigma. As a football player you imagined what it could be like. It was a sanctuary room where the coaches would gather and talk about the game that had just been played. It was just one of these rooms where you had a cup of tea and solved the problems of the world! On the continent there was no perception of the Anfield boot room. You would talk about the club, the managers, the technical staff but not the boot room.

Has the boot room changed? It all depends on what you call the boot room. It has changed *physically* from the old days when the players used to change at Anfield and travel on the coach to the training ground at Melwood. The boot room was at Anfield then. It was where they would meet before and after the training. Now the players have the facilities at Melwood, they can change there and then go home after training. We don't gather at Anfield any more.

But the tradition and the spirit of the boot room has been perpetuated because even when Roy Evans was manager we used to have boot room meetings. I can imagine, in the old days, Bill Shankly having meetings with Bob Paisley, Joe Fagan and Ronnie Moran. That sort of meeting we still have. For instance, every morning all the technical staff gather for about half an hour, no phone calls and no interruptions, just to talk about training, the team, the players and so on. That's day in, day out. Even if there is no training, there is always three or four of us here. So the boot room tradition still exists. I am very keen and insistent on keeping that. We know that we will arrive at Melwood some time between 8.15am and 8.30am. We know that we will be having a meeting for the next three-quarters of an hour, having tea and coffee, sometimes having a good laugh, and a discussion about the various technical problems we face.

But we do not meet after a game. The scenario has changed. Nowadays you have post-match interviews on television, radio and with the press for half an hour or more. To be honest I do not like to talk after a game. What you say can be either hyper-positive or maybe sometimes too negative. The emotion can be too great and the memory too partial. I prefer to talk the next day.

We still keep a club diary. Patrice, my French colleague, could tell you that this time last year we did that session, those players were there, and so forth. We keep a record of what we are doing. It is important if you want to improve, because sometimes you try things that don't work and at some stage you are confronted with poor results or difficult situations. It is important to find out what happened before and having a record does help.

Has the boot room been a burden to me? Definitely not. You learn from the past. It would be crazy not to. I like the idea of the culture of the club, both the traditional and the modern aspects. The only burden we have here is the tradition of success. This club has achieved so much that it creates a feeling of expectation that is incomparable to other clubs. I even have Bill Shankly's photo in my office. He was a key figure at the club and we have to bear that in mind.

I would tend to imagine – and I'm sorry if this removes some of the mystique of the Liverpool boot room – that in every club, at some level, you have a boot room tradition. Maybe it is only 20 per cent of what we have here, but you have a similar exchange of dialogue between the staff. I imagine now that after training at many clubs they have a meeting and talk about technical aspects of the game, the team or training. I know that my friend Arsene Wenger at Arsenal usually has meetings in the morning with his staff. Sometimes after training, if a couple of things have not gone well, we call a boot room emergency meeting. I imagine it's the same at any club.

You win together, you lose if you're alone. You get a better chance to win if you work as a team. And now the professional level of football has reached such heights that you need a team behind the team. The boot room is the team behind the team. And if that team is strong, competent and hard working, if the individuals are complimentary and get on well, and if everybody does their job then the team on the pitch sees that and they respond by being more effective.

As a manager you always have to manage many teams, including the team which is a bit off the circle of players and staff. The boot room here is a daily meeting of five 'technicians', as I call them: the manager, the assistant manager, the two coaches and the goalkeeping coach. The important thing is to ask questions. The more you ask in the boot room, the better for the manager. Then just listen. Feedback is so important.

Even as a manager you have to be careful; you don't necessarily hear what you want to hear. It's better sometimes to raise a question and listen to different points of view. You will be the one with the final say. Sometimes we disagree. For instance, in a previous week's meeting everybody was in favour of playing a certain player, but I said 'No, I am going to play another player' and I gave my reasons. At the end of the day, I did what I wanted to do. When we discussed it the following morning, they said, 'Yes boss, you were right'. I think it's good to talk but also to test your ideas against each other. Then comes the final decision, which the manager makes.

Management is a huge word. I believe that good management is centered around three principles. The first one is competence. You have the initial credibility, the main authority. The first influential power you can have over people is competence as a technician, to know football. That is very important. The higher you go, the more skill you must have in your job and be able to refresh your notions all the time.

The second principle is your personality, which is made up of so many points. It is very difficult to say in a few words. Sometimes you are a leader, sometimes an animator, sometimes a disciplinarian. Sometimes you have to be soft, other times you have to be harsh. Your personality means that sometimes you have to be strong, and at other times nice. You cannot be a dictator anymore because now you have to handle people of multi-nationality, and multi-millionaires, so you have to explain why you are doing things. A strong personality is important, especially with enthusiasm and a very positive outlook. A good sense of humour is very important. I think you also have to be generous and to like people.

When you are a young manager you are not very prone to listening to people, but then you have a couple of experiences where you learn and then you think, 'My God, I should have done that'. I think experience also counts when setting objectives and deciding to run with them.

The third principle is to always have a perspective and a philosophy of the future. This is my team, this is my target, how am I to go about it? As a manager you have to decide the way you get to that target. Are we going to take some risks, or are we going to be prudent? In management you need to have what I would call a strategy. You can't be just emotional.

Only the manager can decide how to reach a target. It is also a human thing. Whatever the physical preparation, I think the mental side, especially the handling of people, is so important. This is why the boot room existed because it is a human thing.

List of contributors

JOHN ALDRIDGE Signed from Oxford United by Kenny Dalglish in January 1987 for £750,000 as a replacement for Juventus-bound Ian Rush. Liverpool-born Aldridge went on to score 50 goals in 83 league games before leaving in September 1989 to join Real Sociedad. Capped more than 60 times by the Republic of Ireland. Now manager at Tranmere Rovers.

JOHN BENNET Joined Liverpool as a schoolboy during the 1961/62 season. Played A team and reserve team football but never made it to the first team. Released by Liverpool in the summer of 1966, he joined Chester where he played for three years before playing non-league football with Macclesfield and Stalybridge Celtic.

JOHN BENNISON Former coach and boot room boy. Worked particularly with the young players. Now retired but can still be spotted putting in the laps around Melwood most Friday mornings with his old pals Ronnie and Tom.

MIKE BERRY Runs a marketing, publicity and promotions company in Liverpool and has organised the testimonials of a number of former Liverpool players. Liverpool fan since the 1950s.

ALAN BROWN Lifelong Liverpool fan. One of his first games was the 1950 FA Cup Final. Now semi-retired, he has been a regular visitor to the boot room since the days of Bob Paisley and counts many of its inhabitants among his friends.

GORDON BURNS Well-known television presenter and producer who used to produce Granada Television's football coverage. Later became presenter of the *Krypton Factor* and is now presenter of BBC Television's *Look North West*.

IAN CALLAGHAN Liverpool midfielder of the 1960s. Played a record 800 plus games for the club in all competitions with 69 goals. England international who played in the 1966 World Cup finals. Won European, league and cup honours with Liverpool.

PHIL CHISNALL The only player to have been transferred directly between Manchester United and Liverpool since the 1930s. Has the rare distinction of having played under both Shankly and Busby. Joined Liverpool in 1964 from United but played only a handful of games before joining Southend. Now lives back in Manchester.

KENNY DALGLISH Generally regarded as Liverpool's finest post-war player. Joined the club from Celtic in August 1977 for a record £440,000. Went on to win every honour in the game as well as 102 caps for Scotland. Became player/manager of Liverpool in May 1985 following the Heysel disaster but shocked the football world when he quit in February 1991, claiming that the pressures had become too great.

ROY EVANS If anyone ever deserved the title 'boot room boy' it is Roy Evans. An apprentice with Liverpool he played just a handful of games before Bob Paisley persuaded him to join the coaching staff. Went into the boot room to help mastermind domestic and European successes. Appointed manager after Graeme Souness left the club but quit in November 1998.

DAVID FAIRCLOUGH Supersub, the man who will always be remembered for the dramatic impact he made when he came on against St Etienne in the European Cup quarter-final of 1977. Played 88 times for Liverpool plus 62 appearances as a sub, scoring 52 goals before leaving to play his football in Switzerland and Belgium. Now a media pundit.

JIM GARDINER One of Liverpool's most dedicated fans. Edinburgh-born Kopite who has seen virtually every Liverpool game home and away throughout the world since the mid-1970s. Affectionately known on the Kop as Jimmy the Jock.

BOB GREAVES Was for more than 30 years a presenter with Granada Television. He was also a regular match reporter with the *Mail on Sunday*, a job which took him to Anfield on numerous occasions.

STEVE HALE Well-known freelance Liverpool photographer who has been covering games at Anfield and Melwood since the 1970s. Also the author of a number of illustrated books on Liverpool.

BRIAN HALL University-educated midfielder with the successful Shankly team of the 1970s. Won FA Cup, league and UEFA honours before leaving in 1976. Later went into teaching but is now back at Anfield as Community Development Officer.

ALAN HANSEN Joined Liverpool from Partick Thistle for £100,000 in 1977 and went on to win just about every honour in the game. Scottish international, despite the dodgy knee. Now a media pundit with BBC Television's *Match of the Day*.

IAN HARGREAVES Former sports editor of the *Liverpool Daily Post and Echo*. Covered Liverpool as a sports journalist for most of the years of the club's great success and befriended a host of Liverpool managers. Now retired, but still writes a regular rugby column for the *Post*.

BARRIE HOLMES Liverpool supporter since the 1960s who has witnessed most great Anfield occasions. Helped set up the International Supporters' club and was secretary of the Merseyside branch for some years.

GERARD HOULLIER Liverpool manager. Former manager of Lens, Paris St Germain and France. Was technical director of French football when they won the World Cup in 1998. Joined Liverpool as joint manager with Roy Evans that summer but became manager in November 1998 when Evans left.

EMLYN HUGHES Liverpool and England captain of the 1970s. Signed from Blackpool for £60,000 by Bill Shankly. Won European, league and Cup honours with Liverpool. Nicknamed 'Crazy Horse' by the Kop.

ROGER HUNT The greatest goalscorer in Liverpool's history with a total of 245 league goals between 1959 and 1969. Also scored a record 41 league goals in the 1961/62 season. Won league and cup honours with Liverpool plus 34 England caps and a World Cup winner's medal.

JOEY JONES Much loved full-back with a never-say-die attitude. Born and bred in Llandudno in North Wales but with strong Liverpool roots. Joined Liverpool from Wrexham in July 1975 and played just three seasons, winning European Cup and league honours before returning to Wrexham. Later played for Chelsea. Won 72 caps for Wales. Now on the coaching staff at Wrexham.

ALAN KENNEDY The man who scored the winning penalty in the European Cup Final against Roma and the winning goal against Real Madrid. Bob Paisley paid a record fee for a full-back when he signed Kennedy from Newcastle in 1978. Affectionately nicknamed Barney by the Kop.

CHRIS LAWLER Liverpool-born full-back who joined Liverpool as a schoolboy back in 1960. Played under Bill Shankly, winning cup and league honours as well as four England caps. An attacking full-back, he scored an astonishing 61 goals. Rejoined the club in 1983 as reserve team coach but was surprisingly sacked three years later by Kenny Dalglish.

TOMMY LAWRENCE Liverpool goalkeeper of the 1960s, commonly known as the 'flying pig'. Won league and FA Cup honours with Liverpool as well as three Scottish caps. Now lives in retirement.

MARK LAWRENSON One of the finest central defenders in Liverpool's history. A £900,000 signing from Brighton in 1981 who went on to win European and domestic honours. An Achilles tendon injury brought his career to a premature end in 1988. Capped 31 times by the Republic of Ireland. Had a brief spell as manager of Oxford United. Now a media pundit on *Match of the Day*.

SAMMY LEE Joined Liverpool as an apprentice in 1975 and made his debut in 1978. Won European, league and cup honours before leaving to join QPR in August 1986. Capped 14 times by England. Found his way back to Liverpool as a coach under Graeme Souness. Now first team coach.

ALEC LINDSAY Classy Liverpool full-back of the 1970s who joined the club from Bury. Won FA Cup, league and UEFA honours with Liverpool as well as four England caps. Left Liverpool in 1977 to join Stoke but quit after a few months to go to the United States. Now runs a pub in Leigh.

LAWRIE McMENEMY Former Sunderland and Southampton manager. Now manager of Northern Ireland. Great admirer of all things Liverpool and a regular visitor to the boot room during his days with Southampton.

WILLIE MILLER Lifelong Liverpool fan who helped set up and now runs the Liverpool FC Former Players' Association. He also organises dinner speakers for various functions.

JAN MOLBY Danish international midfielder signed from Dutch club Ajax in August 1984. Superb passer of the ball. Played more than 200 games, picking up league championship and Cup honours. Had a brief spell as manager of Swansea. Still lives on Merseyside.

RONNIE MORAN Joined Liverpool in 1949 as a schoolboy amateur, turning professional in 1952. Played 379 games, mainly as a full-back until 1965 when he joined the coaching staff. Had a brief stint as acting manager, retired in 1998 after 49 years' service.

STEVE MORGAN Liverpool born multi-millionaire chairman of Redrow Homes. Also life-long Liverpool supporter who still remembers seeing Liverpool win the second division championship.

PHIL NEAL One of the most honoured players in the game with four European Cup winner's medals, countless league championships and four league cup winner's medals, plus 50 England caps. Bob Paisley's first signing in October 1974, went on to play more than 600 games for the club. Had subsequent spells as manager of Bolton Wanderers, Coventry City and Manchester City and also worked with the England squad under Graham Taylor.

BOB PAISLEY The most successful manager in the history of British football. Liverpool player 1939–54 before taking up a coaching position at the club. Became manager following the resignation of Bill Shankly in 1974. Retired 1983 and became a club director. Died 1996.

RICK PARRY Chief Executive of Liverpool Football Club. Formerly Chief Executive of the Premier League and before that an accountant. Lifelong Liverpool fan.

PETER ROBINSON Long-serving secretary of Liverpool since 1965. Now a director of the club and executive vice-chairman. Over the years one of the most important and influential people in the history of the club.

IAN ROSS Boyhood friend of Kenny Dalglish. Joined Liverpool in 1966 and went on to play just over 50 games for the club before joining Aston Villa. Had stints as a manager with a variety of clubs including Huddersfield Town. Now a publican at Timperley near Manchester.

IAN RUSH The greatest overall goalscorer in Liverpool's history. Signed from Chester, he went on to score 339 goals in all competitions, helping Liverpool to European and domestic triumphs. Left Liverpool in June 1987 to join Juventus but returned a year later.

IAN ST JOHN Scottish international striker signed from Motherwell in May 1961 for a club record fee of £37,500. His recruitment was to change the fortunes of the club. Scored the winning goal in the 1965 FA Cup final. Now a media pundit.

TOM SAUNDERS Former head teacher in Liverpool who joined the coaching staff in 1970. Since then he has coached and trained Liverpool sides at most levels but especially the youth sides. Said by Peter Robinson to have given more to Liverpool over the years than any man alive. Now a director of the club.

BILL SHANKLY Legendary Liverpool manager and without a doubt the most important single figure in the club's history. Became manager in December 1959, leading Liverpool out of the second division and into Europe. Inspired Liverpool to league, FA Cup and the UEFA Cup. Sensationally quit the club in the summer of 1974 after winning the FA Cup and went into retirement. Died September 1981.

TOMMY SMITH Legendary Liverpool captain who scored in the 1977 European Cup Final, to help Liverpool win the trophy. Had a brief spell on the coaching staff. Now a pundit with a regular column in the *Liverpool Football Echo*.

GRAEME SOUNESS Tough tackling midfielder, nicknamed 'Champagne Charlie'. Signed from Middlesbrough in January 1978 and spent six years at Anfield, inspiring Liverpool to their greatest triumphs. Left the club to join Sampdoria. After a highly successful spell as manager of Glasgow Rangers he returned to Liverpool, taking over as manager following the resignation of Kenny Dalglish. Sadly, it did not work out and in January 1993 he left. During his time as manager the boot room was torn down.

WILLIE STEVENSON Tall, cultured left-half who joined Liverpool in 1962 from Glasgow Rangers. Won FA Cup and league honours with Liverpool before leaving in 1967 to join Stoke City.

PHIL THOMPSON Once said that if you cut his legs in half they would have 'Liverpool' written through them. Supported the club as a boy from the Kop before becoming player and coach. Appointed assistant manager in November 1998. Played more than 450 games for club, winning every honour in the game, including 42 England caps.